Please re...

Maurice J deVigny

The
Academic
Dean

The
Academic
Dean

Dove, Dragon, and Diplomat

Second Edition

Allan Tucker
Robert A. Bryan

AMERICAN COUNCIL ON EDUCATION M MACMILLAN PUBLISHING COMPANY
NEW YORK
Collier Macmillan Canada
TORONTO
Maxwell Macmillan International
NEW YORK   OXFORD   SINGAPORE   SYDNEY

American Council on Education/Macmillan Series on Higher Education

Macmillan Publishing Company
866 Third Avenue, New York, N.Y. 10022

Collier Macmillan Canada, Inc.
1200 Eglinton Avenue East, Suite 200
Don Mills, Ontario M3C 3N1

Library of Congress Catalog Card Number: 91-221

Printed in the United States of America

printing number
1 2 3 4 5 6 7 8 9 10

Library of Congress Cataloging in Publication Data

Tucker, Allan.
    The academic dean : dove, dragon, and diplomat / Allan Tucker, Robert A. Bryan.—2nd ed.
        p. cm.—(American Council on Education/Macmillan series on higher education)
    Includes bibliographical references and index.
    ISBN 0-02-932695-8
    1. Deans (in schools)—United States. 2. Universities and colleges—United States—Administration. I. Bryan, Robert A. II. Title. III. Series: American Council on Education/Macmillan series on higher education.
LB2341.T778 1991
378.1'12—dc20   91-221
                                                                        CIP

*Dedicated to the academic deans of
colleges and universities
in America*

Contents

Preface

Dove, dragon, and diplomat: all three are roles that academic deans must at various times assume in fulfilling the leadership responsibilities entrusted to them by their respective colleges, schools, or divisions. There are times when the dean must be the dove of peace, intervening among warring factions that are causing an unacceptable level of turbulence in the college. Academicians can fight among themselves with an almost religious zeal, and almost always these conflicts leave everyone involved impoverished in one way or another. It is the duty of deans to see that departments and programs under their jurisdiction are enriched, not impoverished—hence the necessity to act on occasion as peacekeeper or peacemaker. Sometimes deans must be dragons and drive away internal or external forces that threaten the value system, the financial health, or the very integrity of their academic units. These forces of destruction, while varied and sometimes very subtle in form, are nonetheless real, and sometimes only a dragon can conquer them. But the role the dean most often assumes is the role of diplomat. Academic life is a meritocratic life, and each member of the academic community strives for excellence; the competition for meritorious recognition is fierce and unrelenting. External criticisms of the academic community are often just as fierce and unrelenting as those internal ones. Only a diplomat can guide, inspire, and encourage the people who live and work in such an environment. This book, then, is a handbook on how to be a dove, a dragon, and a diplomat.

Most academic deans in institutions of higher education preside over colleges, schools, or divisions, such as arts and sciences, business, education, engineering, music, fine arts, home economics, and health sciences. Each of these colleges, schools, or divisions consists of a specific group of academic departments or programs that have a rationale for being placed together, although the rationale may vary from one institution to another. In most instances, they are grouped together if their academic disciplines are directly or indirectly related. A department or program, however, that seems to have no disciplinary relationship with any other may be included in a group consising of related departments rather than allowed to be independent and deanless. The dean of a group that includes such a department has the problem of maintaining the morale of its faculty members by not treating them as second-class citizens. Occasionally, for administrative expediency, all of the unrelated departments in an institution are grouped together under one dean, who must preside over them carefully in much the same way as the head of the United Nations presides over his constituency.

Not all deans in colleges or universities have the same types of responsibilities. Some have institutionwide functions, such as the coordination of faculty affairs, student affairs, graduate studies, undergraduate studies, continuing education, and admissions. These individuals are usually considered part of the institution's central administration. Most of them report to one of the vice presidents, but in some cases, one or two of them may themselves hold the dual title of dean and vice president. Deans of this type generally have no direct jurisdiction over faculty members.

In this book, the authors are primarily concerned with those deans who have jurisdiction over academic departments and programs that include faculty members, budget, and curricula. It is an attempt to provide advice about how to solve the problems—or maybe only how to recognize the problems—that confront these individuals, whether their title be dean or director. We will treat the following topics: the allocation of funds to departments, personnel management as it relates to departmental chairpersons and faculty, means of interaction with the central administration, relationships with students and the external public of the college (alumni, parents, trustees or regents, and legislators), and methods of dealing with the support agencies of the college (the offices of purchasing, finance and accounting, alumni affairs, and fund-raising).

We believe that this book will be useful to seasoned deans, new deans, decanal aspirants, and department chairpersons. Seasoned deans will find opportunities to compare their experiences and leadership styles with those herein described. Such comparisons will at least confirm their (and our) belief that there are no easy solutions to the complex problems every dean faces. This book will also give seasoned deans some idea of the current state of the art of decanal leadership and thus help them to judge how close or far away they are from that state. For new deans, the book will serve as a guide to help them avoid many of the errors that the authors have observed deans commit. It may also provide new deans with a sense of direction as they begin what is unarguably a challenging and exciting job. Decanal aspirants will find the book useful because it will give them a sobering view of the tasks that must be performed. Viewed from afar by aspirants, the dean's job may appear to be glamorous and easy, but our microscope (the authors are aware of the very detailed nature of the book) will reveal more than glamour and happy times. Department chairpersons will find the book useful for several reasons. First, it describes how deans select, manage and evaluate chairpersons, and second, it gives insight into how deans administer departments in the context of other departments, schools, and colleges. Appreciating the environment within which deans face constrained choices should help department chairs make better decisions and recommendations.

The principles of academic management as discussed in this book are common to all sizes and types of postsecondary educational institutions. The examples described are drawn from small, medium, and large colleges and universities, and many of the situations depicted are likely to occur in any institution, regardless of size, especially situations concerning difficult relationships between deans and department chairpersons and between chairpersons and faculty members. Readers who serve as academic deans or department chairpersons at public or private institutions, whether community colleges, baccalaureate-granting colleges or universities, or large comprehensive research universities, will be able to identify with most of the problem situations discussed. Following each chapter are questions designed to help the reader relate these problem situations to his or her own experiences. In many cases, reasons are given as to why certain courses of action should be selected or rejected in making workable decisions and setting priorities. Obviously, there are no maxims that will apply universally to every decanal problem, but we believe that there are useful guidelines that can be set forth in a manner that will help make a dean's professional life, if not euphoric, at least tolerable.

This second edition was written in response to the many readers who made suggestions for additions and changes to accommodate needs that were not addressed in the first edition. A chapter has been added on the transition from faculty member to administrator entitled "To Be or Not to Be a Dean." In that chapter, we describe the various types of opportunities available to faculty members with administrative aspirations and we give advice about the different kinds of choices they will have to make if they pursue an administrative career. We have also added a chapter on the do's and dont's of making decisions and managing change and have expanded the final chapter of the first edition to include a description of some of the career paths followed by those who have left the deanship. In summary, this second edition includes two new chapters, new material in the last chapter, revisions in several other places, and an updated bibliography.

ALLAN TUCKER
ROBERT A. BRYAN

Acknowledgments

Together we represent sixty years of experience over a thirty-year span in various positions as academic administrators in institutions of higher education. This book is based on our combined experiences and observations during those years. We express our appreciation to the universities that provided us with opportunities to practice the art of leadership and the science of management and planning, for without these opportunities we would not have been able to gain the experiences, make the observations, and suggest possible strategies for dealing with the wide array of problems discussed in the book. We are grateful to the mentors who gave us advice and guidance during our early years as academic administrators. They helped us understand, and be sensitive to, the human nature of academics, an understanding and sensitivity necessary for effective leadership. We are also grateful to the many deans from the state universities of Florida as well as deans from other public and private universities and colleges in other parts of the country who read and critiqued various chapters of the manuscript. Their suggestions for modifications and revisions have been incorporated in the first and second editions of the book. And last but not least we wish to acknowledge the assistance of Mrs. Barbara Allen and Mrs. Linda Black, who patiently typed and retyped the many different drafts of the manuscripts as they were being written, revised, and re-revised.

1

The Perfect Dean

Anyone who has ever been an academic dean has surely engaged in a fantasy of what the perfect environment for the perfect dean must be like. Amid the daily swirl of unpleasant personnel problems, shortfalls in equipment budgets, inability to offer a competitive salary to a prized recruit, wars over space allocation, lengthy and inane requests from the central administration for seemingly irrelevant data—amid all these problems that drive deans into rage or despondency or both, fantasy sometimes takes over. What would the perfect life be like for an academic dean?

The budget given the dean would not be adequate; it would be generous. It would provide enough salary dollars to reward the deserving, to recruit a Nobel Prize winner, and to hire the brightest young Ph.D.s from the best schools in the land, and it would have enough reserve dollars in it to meet any personnel emergency. The equipment dollars would allow the purchase of all the latest and most fantastic scientific instruments known to man; it would provide enough money to put the most high-powered personal computer on the desk of every faculty member and every graduate student; it would provide enough money to equip a computer laboratory for every ten students; and every computer and terminal would be networked to every other computer and terminal. The expense budget would provide all the dollars required to fund the maintenance contracts on all equipment; it would provide enough dollars to send

1

every faculty member to three national meetings per year, two
regional meetings, and one international meeting. There would
be enough money to buy all of the supplies requested by every
department chairperson, to fund an elaborate touchtone telephone system for each faculty member, and to pay all utilities
bills, no matter how fast the faculty ran up those bills. Enough
dollars would be provided to allow the departments to pay
graduate student stipends that rival the stipends of the wealth-
iest schools in the land. Not only that, but the budget would
allow each department chairperson and the dean to pay consultant fees and honoraria to the best people in the country to
come to campus whenever necessary to perform their services.

The department chairpersons would all be unfailingly courageous in their personnel decisions, and no tenure or promotion decision would ever be flawed. Assignments to faculty
members would always be made so rationally and fairly that
no disputes over work loads would ever reach the dean's desk.
Both the central administration and the department chairpersons would always agree with the dean's personnel appointments because they would always be the right appointments.
The central administration would be completely supportive of
the college's goals and missions; such dreadful things as funding priorities or program priorities would be unnecessary because there would be enough money to fund handsomely all
of the university's programs. This would mean that the central
administration would leave the college deans alone and would
spend its time polishing the university's image and raising
even more money. Furthermore, the central administration
would be made up of benevolent, kind, and brilliant people,
polymaths whose knowledge of every discipline on campus
would be exquisitely detailed; and, as we all know, with
knowledge comes tolerance and understanding.

In such an environment, deans would live wonderful lives.
Loved by everyone, our deans' judgments and decisions about
faculty members and programs would be made without stress,
since no faculty members or programs would be hurt by any
of the decisions. Deans would be looked up to as they were in
the so-called good old days and treated with the respect they
deserve. They would have time to devote to scholarly pursuits
and not be stereotyped as mere bureaucrats following orders

from higher-level bureaucrats. In other words, they could live like monarchs in a constitutional monarchy with a perfect constitution, perfect citizens, and unlimited resources.

Such is a dean's fantasy. But such fantasies are, by their very nature, Edenic. We do not live in a perfect world. Generosity, benevolence, intelligence, insight, courage, diligence, and even knowledge are not found evenly distributed across a university campus. And even if there were enough money to do the job right, deans are only mere mortals and suffer from the same imperfections and shortcomings as do their colleagues in the central administration. In the real world, deans must struggle in an imperfect environment almost every day and night of their professional lives to keep the college going in the right direction. They must do their best to improve programs and faculties bit by bit and to make sure that students are well and properly educated. For this, after all, is the whole reason for a college's existence.

If, then, it is the dean's responsibility to make sure that the students in his or her college are properly educated and if this task must be accomplished with an inadequate budget, a faculty burdened with all the imperfections of mortality, and an administration that is neither benevolent nor omniscient, the dean must learn the art of management. But in academic circles *management* is an unpleasant term. It implies activities generally associated with industry, commerce, and the Harvard Business School. Only in the 1980s did the term gain any currency in academia. Before World War II there was not that much to manage on a university campus, and after that war, up until the late sixties, there was too much to manage, and so the American higher-educational establishment expanded largely without focus or direction. Now, the growth has stopped, but the students, faculty, and facilities are in place without adequate funds to keep the whole enterprise going at the pace of the fifties and sixties. Now, for the first time, the call seems to be for academic managers; the notion that colleges and universities can be run only by committees seems a little quaint. Deans, department chairpersons, vice presidents, and, yes, even presidents have to learn how to be managers.

Colleges or universities are very unlike standard corporations or businesses, and we believe that principles of management cannot be applied to both in the same way. General Motors, for example, makes cars; McDonalds makes hamburgers. The making of cars or hamburgers can be turned into a science, and managers of such enterprises must become social scientists. But what is the product of a college or a university? Knowledgeable people. And who "manufactures" this product? Faculty. In terms of knowledge, the configuration of General Motors or McDonalds is a regular pyramid with the most knowledgeable people at the top. In those same terms, the configuration of a college or university is an upside-down pyramid with the faculty at the top and the managers at the bottom. Yet the managers must allocate the money to the faculty who educate the students. Thus, academic managers cannot view their job as only a science; it is also an art. While one could argue endlessly about whether being a dean is an art or a science, whether a dean is a leader or a manager, we hold that a dean is a leader and a manager who uses science in the performance of an art, an art that finally defies precise analysis.

Questions

Review in your mind the departments and/or programs under your supervision and contemplate answers to the questions below:

1. What problems or circumstances prevent your deanship from approaching the perfection described in chapter 1? For example, how would you complete the following thoughts?
   a. Not enough budget to do _____
   b. Not enough personnel to do _____
   c. Enough personnel, but none qualified to do _____

   d. Lack of equipment to do _____
   e. Inability to satisfy faculty needs or wants, which are

   f. Poor relationship with academic vice president in areas such as _____

   g. Not enough good students, thus affecting the depart-

ments in ways such as _____

    h. Some faculty members don't get along with each other, resulting in consequences such as _____

2. List other problems that prevent you from achieving your goals as a successful dean.

3. What steps can be taken to improve some of the situations?

4. What situations can never be improved?

2

To Be or Not to Be a Dean

The majority of faculty members never have to face the painful prospect of changing their careers. Most of them decided long ago in their graduate school days that they would eventually struggle through their dissertations, receive their doctoral degrees, pass through the initiation rites of being an assistant professor, and proceed up life's ladder through associate professor to professor, and perhaps even beyond to that most enviable state of being in academe, the distinguished (or named) professor. They came to believe that their destiny is to teach; to write; to serve as consultants, editors, and advisers of various sorts; and to lead to its fullest the *vita contemplativa*. Yet for a minority of faculty, there comes a time when they are faced with a choice: give up the goal of the distinguished professor and try academic administration or stay in the library, the laboratory, the classroom, and the seminar room for the better part of their lives. This is not an easy choice, for leaving the professorship to enter the ranks of academic administration is to forgo the *vita contemplativa* for the *vita activa*; it is to fly in the face of the training they have received in graduate school and to set aside the value systems they were taught by their graduate professors. And let no one believe that academic administration is, because of its environment and its ambience, a quiet, rational, totally orderly life. It can become, by the time one reaches the

6

decanal level, a life full of conflicting priorities and personalities, an almost always desperate search for money, and a life led more in public than in private.

Yet, this choice will be presented to many who in graduate school, learning their profession, never even dreamed of confronting such a dilemma. How and why does this happen? Generally, the candidate for administration has inside his or her genes an irrepressible trait: a rage for order. Early indications of this trait are easy to spot: grade sheets are turned in on time; course syllabi are models of clarity; student examinations are unambiguous (unless there is a need to be otherwise); work schedules (class time, research time, preparation time) are carefully structured and easily adhered to; and the candidate's mind suffers a restlessness over the way, for example, multisection courses are being administered or the content of these courses. This restlessness usually drives the candidate to volunteer to serve on the departmental curriculum committee or to help in some other way that ultimately addresses itself to the operation of the department or program he or she is attached to. Thus is born the potential dean. The progression is generally very predictable: committee work at the department or program level, then chairman of the department or program, or assistant dean. Some faculty decide after a few years as a chairman or an assistant dean that academic administration is a slough of despond and return, happy and relieved, to their professorships. Some, however, never lose that rage for order and, having seen just enough of administrative life to know that they can do all those things a dean does better than those they have observed, finally wheel and confront the central question: Is becoming a dean worth giving up all they have trained for since they were first admitted to graduate school?

Typically a flood of emotions greets the person who finally faces this question. First to come are the feelings of guilt; how can the candidate essentially forsake the preparation he or she has undergone to be able finally to study a certain virus, track down a particular fossil, classify a special set of larvae, unlock the mystery of Spenser's *Faerie Queene*, pursue the formulation of yet another alloy, find the real causes of the Crimean War, or study whatever one was trained to study? And what about one's students, both graduate and undergraduate? Who can be trusted to teach and train them the way they ought to be taught and trained? On the other hand, the prospect of changing, building, restructuring, and making better an entire college is at the very least challenging and at the very most undeniably exciting. The frustration with the way one's particular college or school is being run, the missed opportunities, the great adventure of it all is often overwhelming. Yet, there is almost always a temptation to believe that one can have his or her cake and eat it too; to believe that one can teach and be a dean or conduct research and be a dean; or, worse yet, to believe that one can teach, do research, and be an effective and successful dean. The authors assert that only a genius can do all three, and there are, alas, not enough geniuses in academic life, and those that are there can seldom, if ever, be made to believe that their talents are worthy of academic administration. Consequently, we are left with ordinary mortals, persons who are of course well above the national average in intelligence and insight, but far from being able to do two mutually exclusive tasks with vigor and success in both of them.

The Self-Questioning Process

The candidate for academic administration needs to ask and answer truthfully several questions. It is vitally important to the candidate—and to the candidate's colleagues, present and future—that he or she be painfully truthful in formulating answers to these questions, for self deception is a terrible way to begin a decanal career.

First, what experience has the candidate had in academic administration? It might have been lots of fun to have been chairman of the curriculum committee, but was it as much fun as being department chairman or assistant dean? Did the candidate really enjoy most of his or her work as department chairman? Does the candidate realize that the woes of the dean are the woes of the department chairman writ large—and in only one language? Being an assistant dean is fun because the buck can always be passed to the associate dean and the dean. But did the candidate, while he or she was an assistant dean, observe closely the work load and life-style of the dean? During these observations, was the candidate appalled, excited, contemptuous, impatient, bored, anxious, eager?

These questions must be answered carefully and, if possible, reasons for those answers must be generated. If, for example, the candidate is an assistant dean and is excited every time he or she watches the dean at work, what is the reason for the sense of excitement? Does the candidate think that he or she can do as well, can generate in others as much of a sense of excitement? The fundamental question that must be answered truthfully is starkly simple: Did the candidate enjoy his or her work as department or program chairman or as assistant dean?

In large universities and sometimes, although rarely, in small universities and colleges, the candidate's knowledge of college and university organization may be extremely limited. Department chairmen and, particularly, assistant deans, often have limited experience with the large organization of which they are a part. Life can be quite cozy and insulated for some assistant deans, and chairmen of small departments can sometimes lead busy and blissful lives, remaining generally unaware of the stresses and strains of the larger bodies of their institutions. All this is by way of stating that the prospective dean must learn something about college and university organization before he or she can make a really informed decision about what kind of life and work load a college dean must sustain.

Once the candidate has a fairly firm grip on the way college and university organizations work, it will be possible to ask another important question: Does the candidate have the patience to work through hierarchies in order to achieve his or her goals? While there are some fundamental differences between educational institutions and corporate or government entities, one thing all of them share is a sense of hierarchy and a stratified bureaucracy that, despite all protestations to the contrary, spends a good deal of energy and time protecting itself and the body it serves from free-lancers, free spirits, end-runners, and all manner of anarchists.

The sense of hierarchy and the consequent bureaucratic stratification flourish as easily and readily in the groves of academe as they do anywhere else. The prospective dean thus needs to determine whether he or she has the patience to seek a solution to a problem through several layers of potential resistance, including the faculty, the department chairpersons, one's own decanal colleagues, vice presidents and/or provosts, and possibly even presidents (although most college and university presidents have little time to resist almost any decanal solution to almost any problem). The point is that there are no instant solutions to the problems most deans face most of the time. Problem solving at the decanal level is almost always a slow tedious process and thus requires a patient temperament. Without either this temperament or at least an acceptance of these points of view as a necessary evil, the candidate's life as a dean is likely to be short and unhappy.

Unhappiness can come in many ways to a dean, but its most traveled route is through criticism, raw and unfiltered, occasionally even mean-spirited and vicious. Receiving criticism is as much a part of a dean's life as it is of a football coach's life. The difference is that the coach has to accept his through those helpful media, newspapers and television, while the dean receives his or hers through letters, polite and impolite, and through private meetings with small groups of people or even individuals who are variously angry, frustrated, baffled, ignorant, avaricious, idealistic, or childish. (There are, now and then, children to be found among the faculties of colleges and universities.) No one likes to receive criticism; everyone—or almost everyone—likes to think that he or she does a good job in fulfilling his or her tasks. Yet no one is infallible; therefore, mistakes will be made and criticism will flow. The candidate must be able to face this reality, not shrink from it, and be able to function effectively in the face of criticism. In short, the candidate must be able to enjoy administration, despite the criticism that will inevitably be produced by doing it.

Clearly, the candidate must have more going for him or her than just the wish to be a dean, patience, and the ability to endure criticism. The candidate must also have either good leadership and management skills or the ability and willingness to develop them. These skills are rooted in the ability to make decisions about people, programs, and money. The most important kinds of decisions are those that establish priorities, those that, quite bluntly, favor one person over another, one program over another, and find expression in the allocation of funds to the favored person or program. To be able to make these decisions, a dean must be able to listen—to listen and to separate rhetoric from substance, chaff from grain, special pleading from real need. The dean must therefore be able to enter conflicts, mediate and manage them, and, in taking sides, find reasonable solutions to those conflicts.

The overriding criterion the dean must always—not frequently, but literally always—bear in mind is that the good of the organization is far more important than a particular point of view argued by a persuasive and powerful group of people. This means that seldom, but inevitably, there will come times when the dean will have to remove people from their administrative jobs; the dean absolutely has to have the ability, the courage, to fire people. A lucky dean may never have to fire anyone, but any good dean will do so if necessary, and his or her colleagues must be convinced of the dean's ability to perform that painful act if necessary. All of these personal prerequisites for the job of dean lead to one obvious question: Can the candidate truthfully state that he or she likes people, likes to deal with people, likes to spend most of his or her working day with people? If the answer is an unqualified yes, then the candidate is ready to consider yet another set of questions.

What does one give up and what does one gain by becoming a dean? The losses are substantial as they are applied to one's personal life. Upon becoming a dean, one immediately gives up freedom of action; the dean's calendar is ruled by the college's or university's calendar, the president's calendar, the regents' calendar, the state legislature's calendar, individual legislators' calendars, individual trustees' calendars, and, if the dean is involved in fund-raising (almost all deans are), potential donors' calendars. In short, the dean's life is no longer his or her own; the dean must schedule his or her life around other people and around events that pertain to the operation of the university or the college.

The dean must understand that in any and all public utterances, he or she will be viewed as speaking for the college and/or the university. While this may not be fair, this is the way life is led in a society that is driven by instant communication, the technology of which in turn is driven by reporters and commentators, who are often ignorant about the subjects they treat in their jobs. Indeed, if they are not themselves ignorant, they often assume their audiences are, and thus fashion their reportage and commentary to fit the lowest common denominator, which, at least in the case of television, is embarrassingly low.

Now, the dean can be a free spirit and speak in a totally uninhibited manner about any and all subjects. While often fascinating and sometimes amusing, this free-spirited approach usually forces the dean into spending almost all of his or her time either explaining or defending previous flights of fancy delivered at the public rostrum or before the all-seeing television camera. Becoming a dean does not entail surrendering one's First Amendment rights, but it does mean that a dean is a public figure and must always exercise a degree of prudence that is somewhat above the level of the average citizen of academe. A college dean is a public figure, and like it or not, deans belong to the public and are often held accountable to the public not only for their actions but for their words.

Accepting the Challenge

In view of these great disadvantages, why would one even consider becoming a dean? The answer lies in the challenge of the job. A dean is a person who can, with help and with luck, make things generally better for the college's faculty and its students. In short, a dean's job is to help other people. This is generally what is meant by ''building'' a college; it all comes down to the dean's ability to recruit good faculty, to retain them, and to reward them so that they feel good about themselves and their students. If the faculty are happy, then it follows that the students will flourish. But making faculty happy is not an exercise in group dynamics; it means fighting for larger budgets for better salaries, more equipment, and better and more facilities. The sense of achievement in realizing any of these goals is high, but the potential dean must measure it against the satisfaction of a purely intellectual achievement, such as those mentioned earlier in this chapter. This, for many potential deans, will be a difficult choice, but only the first of many if the candidate decides to become a dean.

Before considering the next step in the process of becoming

a dean, it is necessary to consider one further advantage of the position. Clearly, that advantage is a financial one. Deans generally make higher salaries than professors, although seldom are deans the highest-paid persons in their colleges. That distinction usually belongs to the research stars of the college, a natural reflection of the value system currently in place in most American universities and colleges. Nonetheless, becoming a dean generally means a substantial salary increase.

The reasons for the increase are not always obvious to either the general faculty or the general public, but they are real and compelling. First, the dean works longer than most faculty; he or she is employed year round, while most faculty are employed for nine or ten months with opportunities, usually on a restricted basis, for summer employment. Second, and more important, the dean has chosen to put himself or herself at a competitive disadvantage with colleagues in his or her discipline. Five years in administration takes its toll on the dean's knowledge of, and achievements in, his or her discipline. Journals go unread, research languishes, the honing presence of students is forsaken, and when and if the dean returns to his or her professorship, he or she is almost always at a competitive disadvantage. As noted earlier, it is very, very difficult to teach, conduct research, and be a successful dean. Small wonder, then, that those who choose academic administration can, and should, demand substantial salaries for their services.

The candidate has to bear in mind yet another paradox in weighing the advantages and disadvantages of becoming a dean. Usually decanal appointments are limited-term appointments; generally a dean is appointed for five years (with, of course, annual evaluations) and is eligible for a renewed appointment of another five years, although sometimes the renewed term is less than five years. Some colleges and universities allow a dean to be reappointed for an unlimited number of terms, and in some few places, the old practice of dean-for-life still exists. But clearly the national trend is for term appointments for all academic administrators, including presidents. (The term appointment for a president is superfluous; few presidents are willing to serve beyond one term, no matter how successful that term has been.) Thus, after his or her first or second term, the dean has yet another choice to make: whether to return to the faculty at a competitive disadvantage with one's colleagues in the field or to push on to become a vice president, provost, or president. The great majority of deans appear to have made the second choice and pursued a lengthy career in academic administration. The dean who wishes to become a vice president, provost, or president has of course a significant advantage over those aspirants for such positions who have not served as deans. Thus, while becoming a dean often means bidding farewell to working in one's chosen discipline, by the same token it often means receiving new opportunities for serving in new academic positions. The candidate is thus warned: in many cases, there is a certain inevitability to one's life when one becomes a dean.

Let us assume that the candidate has passed through the dark night of the soul, that emotional tug-of-war about whether to try academic administration, and has decided that maybe the life of an administrator has in it enough challenges and rewards to make it worthwhile. Since a decanal position is in some respects a political position, it follows that politics are involved in seeking and securing such a position. The candidate needs, then, to find answers to the following set of problems: Are there people who will be willing—preferably enthusiastically willing—to nominate the candidate? Are these people willing to write letters of reference to support such a nomination? And, regrettably, but most important, are these people influential in their fields, their jobs, or with others who have influence? The authors do not suggest that a successful campaign for a dean's position has to be politically wired, but the advocates for a candidate have to be people who possess the kinds of credentials that will make selection committees attentive in reading letters of recommendation or listening to advocates of the candidate.

Furthermore, any careful search conducted for a dean will involve, on the part of the search committee and ultimately the president and/or the provost of the institution searching for a dean, a good deal of telephone conversation with the candidate's references and with his or her supervisors. This, then, is the first real checklist of the candidate's viability as a potential dean. If the candidate believes that he or she can garner support, can find important advocates, and can secure positive endorsements from his or her supervisors, the next step is to start hunting for the job as dean.

The Job Quest

A generation ago, a person started looking for a position in academic administration by studiously avoiding any appearance of looking for the position. It was considered bad form to seek out a job; the job, it was thought, should seek the man. (Not many women were considered for jobs at the decanal level or above.) One wonders how all the deanships, vice presidencies, provostships, and presidencies ever got filled if all those positions had to seek the right person to fill them. It was important for someone who wanted to be a dean to deny interest in such a job, to mumble amiable insults about "paper shufflers," and to express tireless dedication to the important issues in one's own academic field of endeavor. Then, having established a high degree of purity in the eyes of one's colleagues, the candidate could go about the business of arranging to be talked into the job. Somehow, this charade generally produced good leadership, although it is doubtful that it produced the best leadership that was available. Since search committees as we know them today did not exist, since positions were seldom commercially advertised, and since formally designated applicants were seldom sought and hardly ever received, the competition for jobs in academic administration were localized or, at best, regionalized, and the idea of national searches must have seemed quaint to all but the very best institutions in America, such as Harvard or Stanford. (Of course, in those days there really were only ten institutions in the nation's "top ten" universities, whereas today there are likely to be twenty-five to thirty in that increasingly crowded double handful.) Now, of course, almost every search is a national search, and formal applicants are eagerly sought and enthusiastically received.

Some of the old "let the job seek the person" attitude still lingers among some faculty, but generally speaking, it is no longer considered bad form for the candidate to express openly an interest in a decanal position. Open, aggressive campaign-

ing for the job is still frowned on, but it is now clearly acceptable for a candidate to announce an interest in academic administration and to pass word of his or her interest through all
available informal networks. And in virtually all academic institutions, the only way to get into position for active consideration for such a position is to become a formal applicant. And
one becomes an applicant by using the informal network available to the candidate and by reading and responding to various
job announcements found in *The Chronicle of Higher Education*
(the most compendious and thus most-used source in American higher education) and the specialized journals of various
academic disciplines.

Great care must be taken in responding to job announcements in these publications. Candidates should apply for those
positions that fit not only their professional and personal qualifications but also their location priorities. Consequently, geog-
raphy will play a large role in deciding what jobs to consider.
The candidate has to make an early decision about where he or
she wants to live, not as a faculty member, but as a dean.

The dean's work is much more influenced by the environment than is the typical faculty member's, for the dean must
spend a larger portion of his or her professional life interacting
with the city, state, and region in which his or her new institution is located. In both public and private institutions the dean
has to spend a lot more time with the concerns and aspirations
of the college's alumni than does the faculty. In public universities and colleges, the dean also has to worry about local and
state officials. All of these concerns get back to geographical
location and to the local customs, mores, and value systems.

Next, the candidate should decide what size institution he
or she wishes to work in. Large institutions generally have better support systems for their academic deans than small institutions; yet, deans of large colleges often have to act more like
corporate officers than deans of small colleges. These differences must be weighed carefully by the candidate as he or she
takes into account his or her personal styles of management,
and decanal preferences. In other words, just how far down in
the trenches does the decanal candidate want to get?

Then, too, there is the question of the kind of institution
the candidate wants to work in. Public, private, and special

institutions (Georgia Tech and MIT, for example) all have special characteristics that the candidate must analyze. The emphases and value systems of special schools speak for themselves, but the candidate should realize that one of the major differences between public and private institutions is that there is generally a much heavier emphasis upon private fund-raising in private schools. Almost always the dean of a college in a private school must be prepared to spend a significant fraction of his or her time in private fund-raising activities. More and more, however, public institutions are turning to the private sector to raise funds for programs, professors, and facilities. It is critical that the candidate try to make sure that a decanal position for which he or she wishes to apply will make a good fit between the candidate and the school.

Once the candidate has reviewed the decanal job vacancies available throughout the region or nation, he or she should narrow them down to a select few (no more than three or four), for nothing can hurt a candidate's credibility more than to have it known that one is being considered by a dozen or more institutions at once—and known it will be through the academic grapevine, an almost miraculous thing to behold when it begins to function. Certain precautionary steps are now in order. It is almost a truism to observe that some searches for persons to fill academic administrative positions are not really searches at all, but mere window dressing. In such searches, an inside or outside person—almost always, wired searches involve inside candidates—has been chosen by the hiring authorities before the first public advertisement for the position has even been written. Then ensues a solemn and often expensive ritual wherein candidates are brought to campus, wined, dined, interviewed at length, and sent home. After a decent interval, the hiring authorities announce their selection of the person who had been picked before the search process began.

Generally speaking, this kind of melodrama is carried out for what the actors believe are good reasons: a perfectly fine person, known to all parties involved in the search process is the person they believe can do the best job in the vacant position. The problem, of course, is the ubiquitous requirement that a search must take place in order to fulfill affirmative-action regulations and to meet the undeniable logic that the campus does not contain all the great intellects of the world; there might be a few located at other universities. Never is the search used to circumvent an affirmative-action hiring; indeed, virtually every institution of higher education in the nation is only too willing to hire minorities into academic administrative positions. The problem is that there are far too few minority candidates for these positions, and sometimes the next best thing to hiring a minority member is to hire the local person or someone from outside the campus who is well known to the hiring authorities and will do the kind of job that is critical to the success of that particular enterprise.

Somehow, the decanal candidate must find out if the search for the position he or she is interested in is wired. Usually, but not always, this can be discovered by a direct and frank conversation with the chairman of the search committee. If the decanal candidate has a friend (or a friend of a friend) on the campus where the vacancy exists, it is usually easy to discover if there is a favorite candidate and, if so, why. The authors strongly recommend that decanal candidates stay far away from wired searches; the candidate can gain virtually nothing except some experience in being interviewed, and the chances of winning against preselected candidates are close to zero.

The candidate's introduction to the search committee responsible for the candidate's fate is his or her biographical resume. It typically will be but one of scores (occasionally even hundreds) of resumes that the search committee has to review. The candidate is totally depersonalized at this stage of the search, an abstraction stretched out on four or five pieces of paper. Thus, the candidate's summary of his or her life achievements and qualifications must be formulated in such a way as to create quickly a positive impression on a harried member of a search committee assigned to make an initial review of between forty and sixty resumes, which review is essentially a culling operation.

A resume must be easy to read and fairly short—six double-spaced pages are quite enough—and the categories of achievements (publications, courses taught, university service, honors, etc.) should be clearly marked and separated from each other. The candidate should analyze carefully every entry in the resume in order to make certain that it cannot be misunderstood or misinterpreted as padding or redundancy. Nothing more quickly and surely turns off a resume reviewer than a hint of puffery. If the candidate's list of publications runs on for many pages, then a summary of the more important publications should be provided in two or three pages, with a notification to the reader that the full bibliography is contained in an appendix or is "available on request." The question arises of whether to list references in the first submission of the candidate's credentials to the search committee. The authors believe that no references should be supplied at the first submission; the simple notation "references available upon request" is sufficient to convince the reviewer that he or she can find plenty of people to attest to the candidate's integrity, courage, intelligence, and all-around worthiness. Upon subsequent submissions of material to a search committee, the candidate must be certain that each person named as a reference has been submitted with the full knowledge and approval of that person. The candidate should discuss this personally with each referee. It does no one any good to assume that an old friend, professor, or supervisor would have no hesitation in having his or her name used as a referee; such an assumption can sometimes have embarrassing, even painful, consequences.

The Job Interview

Let us assume that the candidate has made the search committee's short list. References have been cross-checked, and the people searching for a dean are now down to three or four candidates, each of whom will be invited individually to visit the campus where the vacancy exists and meet all the players. Once on the campus, the candidate should ask as many questions as he or she is asked; no candidate should visit a campus and spend all his or her time answering questions. Some of these questions must be asked over and over again of different people, and each answer to the same question needs to be weighed carefully. Obviously, the decanal candidate needs to find out from everyone he or she meets what expectations for the college are held by the university. Do the people on campus want the college to assume a new role? Expand into new departments or get rid of some old ones? Take on more students or reduce enrollment? Increase research activity? Clearly, whomever the decanal candidate talks with will argue that the college must be made better, but the candidate should be totally attentive when he or she is told how the college should be made better. The candidate should also remember that sometimes silence speaks louder than words: if the candidate encounters a lack of answers to his or her questions, it is a warning that no one has thought a lot about the college, and if no one has thought about it, no one cares about it.

The candidate will, of course, be interested in the resources available to the college. No matter how clever, courageous, and insightful a dean may be, there generally can be little or no improvement in a college without additional resources. The candidate should ask for both budget and planning documents because nothing cuts through the rhetoric of recruiters quite so clearly and so easily as the financial capabilities and the financial plans a university has targeted for each of its colleges. Most decanal candidates can learn a great deal from an examination of financial plans, but it is always important for the candidate to obtain from the institution's president and/or provost the priorities of the institution's five- or ten-year plan. (If an institution does not have such a plan, then the candidate really needs to begin to worry.)

Program priorities in colleges and universities, particularly those in the public sector, are seldom fixed in concrete. Priorities change for four reasons: a change in the leadership of the program, a change in the faculty who conduct the program, a change in the availability of funds to support the program, and a change in society's needs for the program. Hence, the decanal candidate need not be immediately discouraged if he or she learns that the college in question has been assigned a low priority at the time of the candidate's first visit to the campus. The candidate can use his or her candidacy as a lever to change the priorities for the college if they are excessively low; indeed, frequently a change in the decanal leadership of the college is a signal that the priority ranking of the college is about to be changed and to be improved. The candidate is, oddly enough, in the strongest position to negotiate for better funding, better faculty, better space allocations for the college *before* he or she is actually appointed as dean—assuming, of course, that the candidate is the first choice of the president and provost. In other words, the honeymoon occurs before the honeymoon; the period of warm and good feelings that occurs immediately after the appointment is just that—a period of warm and good feelings. The period of real generosity occurs before the appointment and is generally measured by how highly sought-after is the candidate. Thus, it is critically important for the future of the candidate's college that he or she learn as much as possible about priorities for, and funding of, the college during that first visit to campus.

The dean's best professional friends on campus are always going to be the president of the institution and its provost or vice president for academic affairs. These are the persons who will be his or her supervisors, who will conduct the candidate's annual evaluation, determine his or her salary compensation, and be the main figures in the institution's support (or lack of it) of the candidate's college. To be sure, the dean will work more frequently and often more closely with the college's department chairmen, its faculty, and the dean's personal staff of assistant and associate deans. But unless the dean has a good working relationship with at least the provost or vice president (some presidents make only cameo appearances on campus), it will be difficult to build and improve the college. Consequently, the candidate must learn as much about the president and the provost or vice president for academic affairs as possible during the first visit.

Most people who become academic administrators are intelligent, insightful people who want to excel in their jobs as leaders. But their styles and temperaments are vastly different from one another. Some are gamblers; some are inordinately cautious. Some are relaxed; some are exceedingly intense. Some are cheerful and optimistic; others are dour and pessimistic. Some are warm and friendly; others are cold and distant. But most of them care deeply about their jobs and their institutions. (Beware the administrator who truly does not care.) The candidate has to be able to juxtapose his or her style and temperament with those of the future supervisor and figure out if coming to work every day is going to be fun. It is not the degree of difficulty the job poses for the candidate that really matters, but whether the attitudes of one's supervisors are congenial.

Now, it should be noted that congeniality comes in many different sizes and shapes. Not every supervisor is going to be warm, friendly, and a barrelful of laughs. The authors have worked for cold, distant, humorless people, but what counts is the degree of respect, even admiration, a supervisor generates. It can be just as much fun to work for someone who is respected and admired as it is to work for someone who is warm, friendly, and funny. In the final analysis, only the candidate can decide what it is going to be like working with a particular president, provost, or vice president for academic affairs. But it is a decision that has to be made, and gathering evidence for the decision should be started during the candidate's first visit.

How does the candidate respond to that first and often critical session with the search committee? The cliché answer: honestly, fully, and candidly. Who would think of doing less? Yet each of these adverbs deserves at least a little explanation. To be honest is easy; to be honest yet diplomatic is sometimes a little different. The candidate will have formed at least some general impressions of his or her possible future home long before arriving on campus for the first round of interviews. It is necessary that the candidate, when faced with providing his or her analysis of these problems, flaws, or disadvantages, address them honestly. To do otherwise serves no good purpose for either the interviewer or the person being interviewed. Acknowledgment of problems is one thing; castigation of them or the causes that created them is quite another. Institutions often get into difficulties in spite of themselves, and concentrating on fixing blame for their problems rather than suggesting remedies is useless and, worse still, detrimental to the candidate's advancement. Every candidate should remember that suggesting remedies for problems is really a form of analysis of the causes of those problems. This is the best form of criticism, one that can be both acceptable and successful.

While the candidate should attempt to answer all questions as fully as possible, it is good to remember yet another cliché: when asked the time of day, do not respond with a lecture on how to build a watch. Too little detail in response to a question can arouse suspicion and doubt; too much detail can be simply boring. The candidate should remember that he or she is already well thought of by the search committee, or otherwise he or she would not be on the short list being enthusiastically interviewed and courted. Thus, there is no need to show off one's detailed knowledge of each and every issue that arises during the interview process.

The true test of candor finally comes down to this: if a candidate does not know the answer to a question, the only possible answer is, "I don't know." For example, generally those candidates who have made the short list are sent large amounts of material about the university or college interested in recruiting them. These materials must be read, but not memorized. After all, the candidate is not being examined by a doctoral qualifying committee; the candidate is being interviewed to determine his or her levels of intelligence, general knowledge about academic life, courage, and common sense. Not only is a detailed knowledge of the institution that the candidate is visiting not necessary, but the flaunting of such details can arouse suspicion.

That is not to assert that detailed knowledge of the institution is unimportant to the candidate; clearly, the more the candidate knows about the institution, the easier the decision will be when the candidate is extended an offer to become the new dean. Usually, however, the details provided by the official publication of the university or college are the product of a public relations office determined to put the highest gloss on every aspect of the institution. Better sources of detailed information are those grim, forbidding columns of figures in the institution's annual operating budget and similar figures in the request budget (prepared for either trustees or state legislators) for the coming year. Also very revealing are the annual operating budgets of the institution for the preceding five years; these figures, when compared with the request budgets for those same five years, will tell the candidate a very great deal about the institution's general priorities and how successful it has been in convincing its trustees or the state to fund those priorities.

Other sources of information available for the candidate are, of course, those ubiquitous networks that spread through the groves of academe: the professional societies, both academic and administrative (academic administrators have many professional associations, as do their faculty colleagues), such as the Modern Language Association (MLA) and the American Society of Mechanical Engineers (ASME). Nor should the candidate overlook those deep wells of academic gossip, the national associations at One DuPont Circle in Washington, D.C., the Association of American Universities (AAU), the National Association of State Universities and Land-Grant Colleges (NASULGC), and the American Council on Education (ACE), to name a few. Finally, the candidate may have friends or friends of friends on the faculty of the college that is interviewing him or her. These are, of course, good sources of information, but they should never become the candidate's sole source of information about either the college or the institution at large.

Obviously, the candidate has to get a very clear understanding of the term of his or her employment. The equally obvious source for this information is the president and the provost or vice president for academic affairs. (Such matters, understandably, should never be broached by the candidate with the search committee. Only the candidate's supervisor will have the authority to make commitments on these matters.) The candidate for a decanal position must insist on a tenured faculty position as a condition of employment. Tenure in a decanal position is, of course, unavailable anywhere in American higher education, but no one should leave a tenured position in one college or university to accept an administrative position at another institution without a tenured faculty position in that new institution. Accepting a decanal position is, as noted earlier, something of a gamble; there is no need to increase the level of risk by making one's entire academic career dependent upon the success of an administrative job that is subject to the ebb and flow of human caprice and economic cycles over which one does not have control. The candidate should know if the decanal position is a term appointment and, if so, the exact nature of those terms. Nationwide, there are a dwindling number of dean-for-life appointments. The standard appointment now for a dean is between five and seven years, with a renewal option of from three to five years. Few deans serve more than ten years; they either move up or out to the faculty after a decade. Thus, a term appointment is natural, and the candidate should not feel constrained about accepting such an appointment.

Every once in a while, a potential candidate may find that he or she can be considered for a decanal position within the institution in which the candidate is currently employed. While becoming an internal candidate for a decanal position is often gratifying, there are probably more disadvantages than advantages in assuming such a status. The authors know of no national studies that analyze the success or failure rate of internal candidates, but it is their impression that the success rate—that is, the chances for being appointed dean—is not anywhere near as high as the success rate for external candidates. Clearly, internal candidates do not have a lock on the jobs they seek within their own colleges or universities.

Two forces operate against the appointment of an internal candidate: first, most institutions prefer to hire persons from outside in order to bring new ideas, new perspectives, and unfettered leadership into the institution; second, any internal candidate worth his or her salt will have generated some opposition from some sector of the institution. Leaders seldom please everyone, and often the rage for order that characterizes the strong leader can also generate uneasiness and, in some cases, even fear in the minds of what is generally termed in most institutions as the "old guard." It is a curious fact in academic life that the old cliché that "a known evil is better than an unknown evil" is often completely reversed, with decanal search committees choosing the relatively unknown over the clearly known. Once again, if one decides to become an internal candidate, it is essential to have already been promoted to professor. A good way to be a lifetime associate professor is to stand for dean as an internal candidate and then be selected as the new dean.

Sometimes decanal aspirants are asked to become acting deans while the search for a new dean spins out over a long period of time. Aspirants for the deanship should be very cautious about such opportunities; they are usually far from golden. It is often very difficult for an inside candidate functioning as acting dean to be appointed permanently. Not only are the usual prejudices against the inside candidate operative, but the additional handicap of being an acting dean greatly reduces the chances that such an aspirant in such a position can win. An acting dean who is an aspirant for the deanship can attract criticism from all sides: if the acting dean assumes a caretaker role, he or she will be criticized for not being aggressive enough to provide the leadership that the college is perceived to need; but if the acting dean charges ahead, making decisions right and left, he or she will surely be criticized for being presumptuous or for having made the wrong decisions. If the inside candidate is more or less forced by fate and circumstance to take the job as acting dean, the only honorable course of action is to forge ahead, making decisions at every opportunity, letting the chips—and the critics—fall where they may.

If at all possible the aspirant should shun the job of acting dean unless he or she can reach an agreement with the central administration that as acting dean, the aspirant will not be considered for the deanship. This allows everyone breathing room: the aspirant can make his or her decisions in an unconstrained manner; also, the aspirant can get a taste (or maybe even a large dose) of what being a dean is all about. The central administration is relieved of a potentially awkward position, and the college is free to judge the acting dean without prejudice. At the very least, the aspirant has a nice entry in his or her resume, and at the very most, the aspirant may perform so brilliantly that, against all odds, both the central administration and the faculty of the college will ignore the caveat that the acting dean cannot be a candidate and select him or her as dean.

Let us assume that all of the pitfalls and hurdles have been overcome, all of the advantages and disadvantages of decanal life have been duly considered and the decision has been made to seek a deanship, and that finally the candidate has been successful and has been appointed dean of a college in an institution of the candidate's choice. What then? What should the new dean do first? How should he or she do it? Answers to these questions will of course be shaped by the circumstances surrounding the new deanship to which the candidate has been appointed. These local conditions aside, it is important for the new dean to decide as quickly as possible what goals he or she wishes to achieve during his or her tenure. Obviously, every new dean wants to make his or her college better. But better in what way? Should the quantity and quality of the research done by the faculty be improved? If so, this means the new dean has to emphasize a particular kind of person in all new faculty hires. This may mean the reallocation of current resources, in terms of both people and dollars. Does making the college better mean the addition of new programs? Is the college committed to excellence in teaching? If so, how is that commitment being met? In other words, very quickly in the new dean's new life, a whole host of issues will come swarming into the dean's office, and sooner or later they will have to be dealt with. How fast or how slowly the new dean should move; what changes, if any, the new dean should make; how he or she should go about making those changes; how to organize or reorganize for those changes; how to make tough decisions in the categories of program, personnel, budget, and development and planning—all of these matters will be dealt with in this book.

3

Making Decisions and Managing Change

As we shall see, every dean, at some time or another, has to make decisions on large issues, such as priority allocation of resources (budget, personnel, and space), and on smaller issues, including the allocation of travel funds and even the color and design of the college's stationery. The list is endless and includes decisions about personnel problems, interpersonal problems, organizational problems, and even, on some campuses, parking problems. How does the dean deal with all these decisions?

A study of the decision-making process reveals that most decisions are based on the use of a simple problem-solving model. Ordinarily, when a person becomes aware that a problem exists, the first step is to identify and clarify the nature of the problem. Then a list of possible solutions can be formulated. (The possibility of doing nothing is frequently the first item on the list.) Thinking about solutions always has to lead to a consideration of the possible consequences of each alternative. Then, obviously, the decision maker decides which solution seems most likely to produce the desired results and tries to implement that option. But life, of course, is never that sim-

Some elements of this chapter are drawn from the book *Chairing the Academic Department: Leadership Among Peers,* by Allan Tucker.

ple. In all colleges or schools, there are times when several decisions must be made simultaneously. Within this context, some deans come to think of themselves as firemen, rushing about trying to extinguish small fires before they become large conflagrations. Others fail to see the first signs of impending difficulties and react only after a crisis has occurred. Even though the dean's personality greatly influences his or her approach to decision making, there are methods that he or she can consciously adopt that will help make the decision-making process easier.

The dean must take the lead in deciding if things are to change or stay the same in the face of the exigencies of academic life. The questions of how to decide and who is to be involved in the decision-making process are difficult and challenging. Most administrators recognize the desirability of involving faculty members and sometimes students in the problem-solving and decision-making processes. Nevertheless, many problems do not permit a great deal of faculty or student participation, simply because they must be dealt with swiftly. In any event, the question of the degree of faculty and student involvement in decision making is one that most deans must address. The degree of faculty and student involvement is always related to the dean's attitude and style. The dean's style of leadership can range across a broad continuum, from extremely authoritarian or autocratic to extremely democratic.

The variety of styles within these extremes has been described by Robert Tannenbaum and Warren H. Schmidt in their article "How to Choose a Leadership Pattern." Summarized below is their list of leadership styles. Notice that as the styles become more democratic and less autocratic, more relationship-oriented and less task- or directive-oriented, they become more complicated and difficult to implement, yet more likely to succeed in an academic environment.

1. *The dean makes the decision and announces it.* The dean identifies the problem, evaluates alternative solutions, chooses one of them, and announces to the faculty and/ or department chairs which solution will be implemented. The level of faculty participation in this kind of process approaches zero.

2. *The dean makes the decision and tries to sell it.* The dean recognizes that his or her decision may not be accepted outright by all concerned. He or she seeks to reduce any resistance by indicating what the faculty will gain. What is critical in this process, however, is that the dean provides the rationale for his or her decision *after* it has been made.

3. *The dean makes the decision and invites questions.* The dean seeks acceptance of his or her decision by helping the faculty understand it by means of a question-and-answer session. This could be called the Socratic gambit. It may simply be a subset of style number 2, for it shares with that style the critical element that the faculty is not consulted formally (or informally) until after the decision has been made.

4. *The dean presents a tentative decision subject to change.* This style permits the faculty and/or department chairs to exert some influence on the decision, but of course it may jeopardize the decision that the dean privately likes.

5. *The dean presents the problem, receives suggestions, and makes the decision.* The dean comes to the faculty with a problem that he or she has identified and analyzed, but has not solved. He or she asks the faculty for suggestions; however, all understand that the final decision is the dean's. In short, the dean asks for help and, in so doing, is likely to engender the trust and respect of the faculty.

6. *The dean defines the limits and asks the faculty to make the decision within these limits.* The dean delegates to the faculty (including himself or herself) the freedom to make the final decision. Before doing so, however, the dean states the problem as he or she sees it and sets the boundaries, or areas of freedom, within which the decision can be made.

7. *The dean permits the faculty to make the decision within broadly defined limits.* This situation occurs when problems are vague and require a high degree of freedom of exploration if creative solutions are to be found. Only broad limits are imposed, and the dean, if he or she participates at all, participates as an equal. In this model, the

dean can be accused of abrogating his or her responsibility to formulate and make decisions.

Criteria for Degree of Faculty Involvement

These different kinds of leadership styles suggest that deans can perform their functions in a variety of ways. Many believe, as a matter of principle, that faculty involvement in decision making should be maximized, and to complicate matters even further, there are those who believe that students should also be consulted in all or most decision making that occurs in the dean's office. The truth of the matter is that not all faculty members or any students can be, should be, or should even wish to be involved in every decision a dean makes. There are instances when faculty members and/or students should be asked to participate in the decision-making process. Those instances are best defined by answers to several essential questions based on three relevant criteria:

- *Expertise:* Who knows how to solve the problem? The dean alone? A particular faculty member or group within the college or school? The whole college or school? Do students know how to solve it?
- *Acceptance:* Is faculty acceptance of the decision crucial for effective implementation? Will implementation fail if the faculty refuses to go along with the decision?
- *Time:* Is there enough time to get the faculty involved in the process of decision making? Is the issue so crucial that an immediate decision is necessary?

While these criteria are logically independent of one another, they should all be considered when an important problem or issue arises. Each needs to be considered separately.

EXPERTISE. Some decisions require expertise in specific areas. If the dean possesses such expertise, he or she is perfectly capable of making a decision alone. Lacking that expertise, the dean may seek it from department chairs and/or faculty members and should not hesitate to call on those who have experience and interests in areas connected with the problems to be addressed. Sometimes the expertise needed for successful decision making may be found outside the college but within the institution, and is available for the asking. The dean should not let simple pride or fear of asking for help prevent him or her from using institutional resources wisely and advantageously. Sometimes even a provost may have the requisite expertise to help the dean. While this may be a revolutionary thought, it is nonetheless a useful one.

ACCEPTANCE. Some decisions, important or not, require that the faculty accept them if they are to be carried out, and all important decisions affecting the well-being or survival of the college or school will require the faculty's acceptance if they are to be implemented. Some decisions that are seen as unimportant are readily accepted by the faculty, who are grateful not to have been bothered with them. On the other hand, some seemingly unimportant decisions may require faculty involvement in order to gain acceptance. The dean must rely on his or her judgment to evaluate the faculty members' level of tolerance for accepting decisions about which they have not been consulted.

People willingly participate in an activity when they can see the benefits that accrue from that endeavor, when they see the college's success as synonymous with their own. On the other hand, the most benign and rational decision can be resisted, subverted, or rejected by a group if it feels that it had no share in making the decision. What better way is there to encourage faculty members to accept and implement decisions than to have them participate in the process of making decisions?

TIME. Occasionally problems arise and decisions must be made with great speed. Although most of the time, the typical academic bureaucracy moves with majestic slowness, infrequently opportunities arise that must be seized without hesitation or they will be lost. In such cases, the dean has to judge whether an immediate decision is better than no decision at all.

Implementing Change

These three criteria—expertise, acceptance, and time—obviously vary in importance according to circumstance. Considering these criteria when the question of faculty involvement arises will generally help a dean decide whether, in those particular circumstances, the faculty ought to be involved. A related problem is *how* faculty members can be encouraged to participate in the decision-making process. Some are ready and eager to be involved in problem solving (perhaps too eager), while others show little interest in sharing in the hard work that is a part of intelligent decision making. Clearly, no single method of involving faculty members in the decision-making process is best. Each dean's decisions about the methods and techniques of faculty involvement must take into account the special, often idiosyncratic characteristics of the college and department involved. Nevertheless, each dean must determine whether a matter should be brought to a meeting of department chairs or the full faculty, referred to a committee, discussed informally with faculty members, or acted upon according to his or her own best judgment. These determinations depend partly on how the dean views his or her role and partly on his or her experience in working with each option.

Many deans, on the basis of their past experience, choose to share the decision-making process with their faculty members for several reasons. First, faculty members will have to implement most of the decisions the dean makes and are therefore more likely to be cooperative if they are involved in making the decision. Second, as mentioned earlier, individual faculty members often have expertise or experience to contribute to the decision-making process. Third, when conflicts do occur, resolving them in the context of open discussion is less disruptive than neglecting them altogether and possibly causing them to multiply unnecessarily. Finally, college decisions take place within the broader contexts of academe and a democratic society. The university has a long tradition of collegiality; the idea of a community of scholars is compatible with processes of shared decision making by equals. Nonetheless, after all the consultation is over and done with, the dean must take responsibility for making the decision and implementing it. Committees, as the authors repeatedly insist, cannot make decisions.

Some decisions can be implemented only by first changing a specific policy or procedure. Change, it has been said, is society's only constant. Certainly a significant number of changes have taken place in colleges and universities in recent years, and these changes reflect changes in society as a whole. In most social groups, a creative tension exists between forces that operate to bring about change and forces that operate to resist change. Although the American education system in general and institutions of higher education in particular are conservative and resist change, the continuous pressures of political and social events demand responses, and these responses generally result in a good deal of change. During the turbulent sixties, it seemed as if the pressures for a radical democratization of educational curriculum and governance would revolutionize the structure of higher education. Yet, the seventies showed a great decline in student unrest, and many predictions of the preceding decade failed to materialize. Nevertheless, there is now a good deal more student participation in academic affairs than occurred in the fifties and sixties; for example, students now sit on boards of regents and on many academic committees.

Colleges and departments have been, and are, subjected to many pressures for change from within and without the institution. Hence, one of the chief stimuli for decision making is related to the kinds of change that colleges and departments are required to make. The dean's role in bringing about needed change is central in determining whether change is indeed desirable, in planning for change, and in providing leadership in the process of implementing change.

Amitai Etzioni, the famous sociologist who has investigated problems of change, argues that attempts to effect behavioral change in humans through educational and advertising methods may not be successful unless there are accompanying changes in the environment. In his article "Human Beings Are Not Very Easy to Change, After All," he cites failures in anti-smoking campaigns, alcohol and drug abuse programs, and traffic safety programs that depended primarily on didactic efforts. He contrasts these failures with efforts that succeeded in altering behavior when persons were removed from situations or environments that contributed to the problem in the first place. In discussing the dismal failures of the first intensive educational efforts to help disadvantaged children, Etzioni con-

cludes that educational programs will continue to fail as long
as the children's total environments are unchanged. Change
has been implemented successfully when persons *willingly* enter a new social community. Etzioni suggests that the total-
change approach, exemplified by people who join a kibbutz or
an organization like Alcoholics Anonymous, is often successful. While total change appeals to a radical perspective, it obviously works only with volunteers, and many persons will simply not volunteer for a radical revision of their social
environment.

Although Etzioni's research is not primarily concerned with
change in academic organizations, some of his findings are applicable to this problem. For example, a college dean, as the
sole representative of her institution, participates in a national
workshop for academic administrators. She returns with enthusiasm and a few excellent ideas for implementing change,
only to encounter an intransigent environment that rejects her
efforts. In this case, motivating the dean to desire change was
in itself not sufficient to bring it about.

Etzioni's research also suggests that finding new persons to
implement decisions for change may be easier than obtaining
cooperation from those whose ways are set. Unless positions
are available for new faculty members, deans of some colleges
must wait for recalcitrants to retire before attempting any
change. In those instances when the chairperson is the obstruc-
tion to changes necessary for a department's survival, the dean
must seek ways of changing the chairperson's behavior or, if
that fails, of changing the chairperson.

In his article "Hauling Academic Trunks," J. B. Lon Hefferlin notes that few institutions change spontaneously and suggests that the most important factor influencing change is the
market conditions under which educational institutions operate. Colleges and universities and their departments must attract resources or fail in their mission. Departments compete
for scarce resources within and without the institution. If they
fail to compete, they are likely to wither away. A department's
curricular offerings must attract students, and the working conditions must attract faculty members, or mediocrity and stagnation will result. Many, if not most, departments closely watch
what departments at other institutions are doing and try to do

the same sorts of things; that is, they sail with the wind rather than trying to go against it.

The second most powerful factor influencing academic change, according to Hefferlin, is the institution's ethos toward change. Each college, university, or department has its own historic orientation toward change. This orientation, whatever it is, tends to be self-perpetuating, since those in power usually choose persons like themselves to succeed them. Yet choosing innovative successors often results in meaningful change. It is easier to replace persons than to change their attitudes. The result, therefore, is that frequently curricular or structural changes in universities or colleges take place at the time when old professors retire or leave and new ones replace them.

A third factor that influences change in higher education is the institutional structure, which can be an aid or a barrier to change. The same is true of college and department structure as well. The dean's decision-making process may be facilitated by clear procedures, by the nature of committees within the college, and by the rules that govern curricular issues and personnel policies. Some colleges have written bylaws that outline the structure, while others have a structure based on higher authority. Colleges and/or departments that have no formal rules or procedures often have informal rules based on precedent or tradition. A problem in most large institutions is the rigidity of the bureaucracy. Strict, bureaucratic rules and procedures certainly operate against policies that are flexible, adaptive, and responsive.

Hefferlin, in the article cited earlier, lists five techniques for implementing academic change: the administrator must determine the obstacles, provide reassurance, build on existing concerns, avoid rejection, and respect the past. Although Hefferlin is speaking of change at the institutional level, his techniques may be applied at the college or department level. If changes are contemplated, the dean should anticipate possible obstacles to implementing these changes. These obstacles may be internal or external. They may be due to apathy or lack of information.

Change is sometimes threatening, and the threats can be real or imagined. The dean should think of ways to assuage fears and consider techniques of conciliation, compromise, and confrontation in the attempt to implement changes. When discussing change, the dean must at all costs avoid distortion and misrepresentation. The dean can avoid opposition by clarifying the ideas and activities being considered. The more information the faculty members receive, the more likely they are to feel reassured. Change that builds on the existing concerns of the faculty is more likely to gain acceptance than change that does not. Changes should address problems that the faculty sees as urgent. The task force approach to change, which allows interested faculty members to participate, is recommended as a way of channeling the concerns of faculty members.

One way to avoid rejection is to propose change for a specific experimental period, a "pilot program." If such a proposal is rejected, an optional parallel program can be suggested. Then, if the proposed change works well, the rest of the faculty will be more likely to accept it. Optional parallel programs work well in the area of curriculum.

Finally, change in academia may be garbed in tradition. Hefferlin cites President A. Lawrence Lowell of Harvard, who in 1938 said of the college president:

> If he desires to innovate he will be greatly helped by having the reputation of being conservative, because the radicals who want a change are little offended by the fact of change, while the conservatives will be likely to follow him because they look on him as sharing their temperament and point of view.*

This canny political advice can be applied to the governance of a college as well. Tradition should be respected while change is fostered.

Dealing with Change and Resistance to Change

Clark Kerr, a former president of the University of California, once said that changing a university curriculum is like trying to move a cemetery. His statement aptly characterizes faculty

---

*J. B. Lon Hefferlin, "Hauling Academic Trunks," *Elements Involved in Academic Change* (Washington, D.C.: Association of American Colleges, 1972), p. 10.

resistance to change. Because faculty members perceive change as threatening and manipulative, deans tend to shy away from talking about it directly in order to avoid provoking anxiety and resistance. Faculty members feel less anxious, however, when discussing such subjects as self-renewal, organizational development, or faculty and staff development, all of which are actually efforts for planned change. For deans to act as leaders or facilitators in these efforts, they should know and understand the process of change.

When faculty members resist change, what are they really resisting? Will a plan be automatically accepted if it is logical and educationally well conceived? Not necessarily. As we noted earlier, plans for change that rely exclusively on rationality are not always successful. A faculty member's first reaction to a proposed change is to ask how it will affect him or her personally in terms of opportunity for professional development, promotion, salary increases, and work assignments. Faculty members will also be concerned about how the change will affect their future relationships with coworkers, students, administrators, colleagues, and so forth. To ensure the greatest likelihood of acceptance, therefore, a proposed plan for change should not only be logical and well conceived but should take into consideration the personal concerns of those involved. The dean should seek out those who feel that they will lose status if the change occurs. If their fears are unfounded, they should be given the necessary assurances. If indeed the change may cause them to lose status, the dean should think about what, if anything, could be done to make up for this loss or to improve their present status. When the dean shows proper concern and interest, resistance may be converted to support.

As the authors will repeatedly point out, proper and frequent communication with faculty members before, during, and after a change will help alleviate many of their personal concerns. Those who will be affected by a proposed change should be provided with as much information as possible about the situation. Lack of knowledge about what is going on causes insecurity, and insecurity increases resistance, regardless of the merits of the proposed change. Information that presents the rationale for suggested changes may be sufficiently persuasive to reduce resistance or gain support for a proposed plan. Changing a person's knowledge base is frequently a prerequisite for changing attitude and behavior.

Another impediment to change often results from the requirement that plans for proposed changes must be reviewed and approved by many persons and groups in the institution's governance hierarchy. Any faculty committee or administrator may veto an idea as it travels the hierarchy from department to dean's office, to faculty senate, to president's office. Whenever a new idea for change is presented to a faculty committee for the first time, the reaction is generally negative, and after the initial rejection, committee support for the idea is difficult to obtain. Almost always the dean must be a lobbyist for the change he or she is trying to effect; he or she should discuss the idea individually with several members of the committee before making the presentation to the committee as a whole. If individual members are persuaded that the idea has merit, they will help obtain support from the rest of the committee. Proper and frequent communication with committee members and administrators during the development of the plan can reduce resistance.

Change involves considerable risk because it will not necessarily solve a problem. Not every new approach will prove effective, and when a change fails, the innovator may be criticized and sometimes even removed from his or her administrative position. A wrong change could stir up conflict, upset sensitive balances and relations, and waste faculty members' energy. Therefore, before the dean decides to implement a plan for a change, he or she should collect data that will help determine the probability of the plan's success without demoralizing the faculty. It is well to keep in mind also that the smaller the change, the less resistance it will generate. If a change is necessary, it is best to select one that will solve the problem in the simplest and least noticeable way. Do not amputate a leg to cure a toe infection.

What motivates faculty members to change? First, many are motivated by the desire for competence and the need to achieve. These persons are primarily interested in job mastery and professional growth and are constantly thinking of better ways of doing things. They are willing to participate in planning and implementing change for the sake of their own professional improvement and the department's improvement. Second, some faculty members are motivated to change only if they can anticipate a more tangible reward. Third, some faculty members are motivated to change only when they consider the consequences of not changing—if, for example, they thought that unwillingness to change could cause them to lose privileges or face possible termination. A department with decreasing enrollments generally can be motivated to modify its recruitment policies, its curriculum, and its goals and activities if decreasing enrollment would lead to a reduced department budget and a reduced number of faculty positions. Faculty members' response to the need for change is generally based on a combination of all three factors, each of which may be weighted differently for different persons. But there are some faculty members who just will not endorse change under any circumstances. Generally, about all the dean and his chairman can do is to put the intransigent faculty member on the shelf (or in a corner) and work around him or her.

When considering the feasibility of implementing a plan for change, the dean should try to anticipate who will support the plan and who will resist it. The dean should make a list of potential supporters and the reasons for their support and another list of those who are expected to resist the plan and the reasons for their resistance. The supporting faculty members and their rationale can be thought of as "driving forces" and the resisters and their rationale as "restraining forces." Because the faculty members on each list will vary in the degree to which they support or resist the plan, the dean can rate the strength of each person's support or resistance on a scale of 1 to 5. When all the driving and restraining forces have been listed and the strength of each force has been rated, totals of the driving forces and the restraining forces can be calculated and then compared. Now, human nature can never be reduced to mathematical equations—it is too quirky—but this kind of human calculus can at least give the dean a general idea of what kind of of task he or she faces in trying to effect change. Then the dean can be better prepared to know whom to lobby and what kinds of lobbying efforts to use on each target or groups of targets.

In summary, the following points should be kept in mind in selecting and implementing plans for change:

- Select changes that are most timely and appropriate for the college's current situation.
- Select plans for change that have a reasonable chance of success, such as sufficient faculty support, sufficient resources, and sufficient administrative support.
- If possible, select plans that require the least drastic change to solve a problem; there will be times, however, when only drastic action will work, and it is during these times that the dean's leadership skills will be most severely tested.
- Develop plans for responding to the personal needs of those who will be affected by the changes.
- Develop strategies for communicating appropriately with those who will be affected by the change as well as those who must approve it.
- Develop strategies for obtaining faculty members' commitment to supporting and participating in the implementation of the plan.

In bringing about needed change, the dean should have the ability to perform the following functions:

- provide guidance to the faculty in developing and updating goals and objectives, or, in other words, help the faculty to recognize not only the need for change but to define the nature of that change
- develop action plans for the needed changes
- bite the bullet and implement those plans

Specifically, in dealing with change, the dean must be able to design and implement strategies for changing curricula and programs (always very difficult and apt to be very controversial). The dean must have the ability to develop long-range plans and strategies for timely appointments, promotion, tenure, and retirement of faculty members that will enable a department to remain responsive to new and changing needs.

Not only must the dean worry about these kinds of basic changes, but he or she must also think about the impact of these changes on the faculty and thus have the ability to identify and develop programs to meet the professional-development needs of faculty members if the changes result in retrenchment.

Intervention Plans

Of all the strategies that are available to the dean to help him or her in effecting change, perhaps none is more effective than what ought be called the strategy of intervention. For our purposes, an *intervention* is defined as a person's action or series of actions that causes a change in the behavior of another person or group. A dean can devise an intervention plan that will move a department in the desired direction and at the same time improve faculty motivation and morale. A well-planned intervention may further the goals of collegiality and shared governance. Intervention can take many forms, but its general characteristics include presentation of alternative courses of action, relevant information generally based on research, and reliance on academic tradition, and academic mores. Some interventions seem especially appropriate to the university setting, with its horizontal structure and its traditional framework of collegiality. There are all kinds of ways for the dean to use intervention as a force for change. Listed below are nine interventions and how they might be useful to deans.

1. Sometimes a dean simply has to call attention to a contradiction in action or attitudes. Recently a chemistry department had the opportunity to fill a vacant position at the associate professor level. In establishing the criteria for the application, the faculty members stipulated at least five years' teaching experience, significant publications in major journals, national visibility, demonstrated service in the profession, and the ability to direct graduate students. Some months later, an assistant professor in the department with four years' teaching experience, two publications, a good service record to the university, and a pleasant personality applied for a promotion to the rank of associate professor. Since he was well liked and seemed to

show promise as a researcher, the department members were anxious for him to be promoted. The dean called their attention to the discrepancy between their criteria for someone coming from outside the institution and their criteria for someone within the institution. After some discussion, they decided to ask the faculty member to wait another year and work toward coming closer to department standards. In this case, the dean's intervention modified the way in which the department developed and used its human resources.

2. As might be expected in an academic environment, sometimes the dean can rely on the use of research findings or conceptual understandings to help faculty members broaden their perspective on a particular problem. A communications department chairperson was faced with the problem of having too many sections of an extremely popular speech course and too few instructors. The faculty's desire to maintain the twenty-to-one student-faculty ratio in the classroom was opposed by the dean, who said that he simply could not find the additional faculty positions to support so low a student-faculty ratio in a lower-division course. The dean urged the chairperson to review the research on students evaluating their peers' performance, which showed that students' evaluation of their fellow students was reliable and permitted a larger class size by reducing the amount of time the instructor spent on grading. The chairperson shared this information with the faculty members, who were convinced by the evidence. The appeal to research findings was persuasive and allowed the department chairperson both to double her class size and to maintain the faculty members' morale—and the dean was able to protect his budget.

3. Occasionally, help for the dean resides in institutional activities that are germane to a particular problem at just the right time. A new economics department chairperson wished to involve junior faculty members in the department's decision-making process. When he met resistance from the existing oligarchy, he asked the dean for help, and the dean used the occasion of a university self-study to appoint a committee composed of junior and senior faculty members to review the department's decision-making process. The committee concentrated on the methods used to make decisions and, with the

input from the junior faculty members, recommended a revision of the department's decision-making processes. The committee work load was distributed more evenly and the senior faculty members' time used to better advantage, and the new chairperson and the dean both came out winners.

4. Once in a while just changing the environment can help in lowering situational conflict within a group by improving group relationships. The faculty members of an English department were unable to modify their selection of requirements for their undergraduate general education courses. The modernist faction felt that the traditionalists were being stubborn in their devotion to the past, while the traditionalist faction felt that many of the modernists' innovations were too radical and that faculty members who espoused curricular revisions were merely trying to promote their own ends. Tensions had increased to the point that the dean suggested—and paid for—a departmental weekend retreat at the university convention center some twenty-five miles from campus. During the retreat, as the faculty members walked together on the beaches or sat in front of the fire, many of the superficial emotional elements of the conflict were reduced. On the last day of the retreat, the faculty members were able to resolve the problem to everyone's satisfaction.

5. Sometimes if a department can be persuaded to adopt two or more options rather than a single forced choice, new procedures and new ideas can be implemented. This approach is particularly appealing to social science departments that are quantitatively oriented. Although the procedures for comparing courses of action are not scientifically exact, they do add an element of logic to the decision-making process. A graduate psychology department wished to modify its comprehensive-examination procedures by substituting a research project assignment for the written examination. The faculty members disagreed about the appropriateness of this course of action, so the department chairperson allowed one group of doctoral students to select either the examination or the project for one academic year. After the year's experience with both options, the faculty decided to adopt the research project as an option for students.

6. Sometimes departments can be persuaded to accept a not

very attractive course of action simply because all other courses of action seem even worse. This might be called the Hobson's choice (or, even better, the dean's choice) form of intervention. The chairperson of a history department found that she was unable to provide adequate office space for a growing number of faculty members and graduate students. A morale problem developed. The dean made the chairperson an offer that she could have all the office space she wanted in a vacant house on the edge of campus. The chairperson met with the faculty members to explore the advantages of being housed in spacious quarters but away from the center of campus life and the advantages of being housed in cramped quarters but close to the center of campus life. After much discussion, they decided in favor of more cramped quarters closer to classrooms and other students. The intervention resulted in increased understanding of the space problems on campus, thus reducing the morale problem.

7. The strategy of invidious comparisons, provided those comparisons are carefully documented, can usually stimulate a department to change its behavior. One dean urged the geology department chairperson to encourage faculty members to solicit research proposals from outside agencies; it was the dean's belief that not enough sponsored research was being conducted by the faculty of that department. The chairperson conducted a review of outside funding received by the department over the preceding ten years and compared it with research activities and funding both of other science departments within the university and of other geology departments within the university system. The evidence indicated that the department was missing out on some research opportunities. Faculty members began to write proposals and to receive outside funding.

8. Always available to the dean for use in effecting change is the presence of either fiscal constraints (when were they ever absent?) or a handy institutional policy. A humanities department chairperson was challenged by a group of her faculty members for her failure to secure enough travel money for them from the dean to attend a national convention. The department chairperson met with the group and reviewed the board of regents' budgetary procedures, the university's re-

strictions on travel, and appropriations of travel funds throughout the university and, specifically, the dean's travel budget for the college. She was able to demonstrate that while the absolute amount of travel money was ridiculously low, the dean had allocated to the department more than its fair share, given the institutional constraints. She also indicated that those departments that had more travel money usually obtained it from outside sources. By showing the faculty members the structure of the system, she was able to spur their requests for funds from outside agencies.

9. For deans who like paradox, there remains the possibility of using tradition to effect change. Faculty members, it has been said, never like to do anything for the first time; appeals to tradition can therefore be particularly persuasive. A dean of a college of humanities wished to encourage the faculty members in his college to be more active in ordering books for the library. Processing book orders was the responsibility of his staff, and consequently he knew that the faculty had grown lax in ordering books. He also knew from experience that a general request for more book orders would generate little response. He began his strategy by asking students in the college to point out books that were considered basic to areas in various specialties but were unavailable in the library. When student interest in this had gained enough momentum, the dean brought up the whole matter of the library's collections at a meeting of the faculty. At the meeting, the dean spoke of the great libraries at the universities at which many of the faculty members had earned their doctorates. He stated that funds were available to departments for the purchase of books in their respective special fields; thus, a library collection could be built that would at least equal those they had used as students. With the expertise of the faculty mobilized, a first-class collection representing the highest tradition of university scholarship could be amassed. As a result of the discussion, the book-ordering function was taken over by a faculty committee and the orders poured into the dean's office.

Whatever the strategies adopted by the dean, it is clearly important that he or she be ready, willing, and able to engage in the process of change. The change may be major and substantive, or it may be minor and procedural, but it is inevitable that the dean will have to effect change several times during his or her tenure. After all, even the trivium and the quadrivium were subject to change in the medieval period.

Questions and Exercises

1. **a.** List four different types of decisions that deans must make, such as final decisions for action or decisions on what to recommend to the provost. Give specific examples.

   b. For each type of decision listed above, indicate to what extent a faculty committee, a committee of department chairs, or the faculty as a whole should be involved.

   c. What does a dean do when his/her decision or recommendation is inconsistent with the opinion of one or more chairpersons?

2. Review reasons for faculty resistance to change on page 38. Give examples from your experience or observations of specific change situations which have been resisted or would be resisted by members of your college and give reasons why.

3. Review the guidelines for bringing about change listed on page 41. Give examples from experience or observation in your own college of specific change situations in which one or more of the listed guidelines have been tried or could be tried. Indicate whether the guidelines worked or not.

4. Select one of the following case studies, which are representative of real problems that might occur within colleges. For the purpose of the exercise, please assume that the problem in each case is valid and that the dean is interested in trying to bring about a change. To the extent possible, apply the suggested methods in the text, as well as your own ideas, in attempting to reduce resistance to the change. If the case study as described seems to lack details necessary for its resolution, please fill in the missing aspects of the case with hypothetical information based on your own experience.

Case Studies and Exercises

1. EVENING CLASSES

Three departments of a seven-department college at a major multipurpose university in a large northeastern city offer courses in the morning and early afternoon, but very few in the evening. There has been considerable demand for evening courses by individuals who hold full-time jobs during the day and who have enrolled in the three departments as part-time students seeking the master's degree. Many of the faculty, engaged in research activities and in outside consulting, are reluctant to teach evening classes. They complain about their busy schedules and the problems of commuting to their suburban homes. Although the dean and chairpersons of these departments are reluctant to impose teaching assignments in a unilateral manner, they are anxious that evening offerings be expanded as soon as possible to meet the needs of the part-time students. The problem is to get the faculty to accept this responsibility willingly and to see the opportunities that evening classes will afford.

a. Identify the types of faculty who will support the changes and who will resist them.
b. What are the legitimate concerns of the faculty in this issue? What faculty concerns might not be legitimate?
c. What can be done to alleviate faculty concerns?
d. How can faculty be involved in planning and implementing an evening program?

2. A CHANGE IN DEPARTMENTAL EMPHASIS

Since its formation over ten years ago, the criminology department at East Florida University has considered its primary role to be that of training researchers. Although some programs for the training of practitioners are being offered, the recognition and prestige given to faculty who teach in them is less than that given to their researcher colleagues. During the past three years, students and law enforcement agencies have been pressuring the dean and the department to increase the amount of effort spent on the training of practitioners. The academic vice president of the university has transmitted to the dean the results of a study that documented the serious need for additional law enforcement practitioners with graduate training.

The dean and the chairperson of the criminology department feel it is essential that the department respond to this need and increase its emphasis on the training of practitioners. To do this would require diverting some of the research budget to the development of programs for practitioners. The faculty is reluctant to go along with the change in departmental emphasis. The problem is to get the faculty to agree to expand its practitioner training and to develop a plan for implementing changes.

a. Identify the types of faculty who will support the changes and who will resist them.
b. What are the concerns of those who oppose the idea of expanding the training of practitioners?
c. What can be done to alleviate faculty concerns?
d. How might the dean involve the research faculty in planning for an increased emphasis in practitioner training?

3. THE "HIGH FAILURE" MATHEMATICS DEPARTMENT

The mathematics department has an unusually high failure rate in freshman-level mathematics courses. In a meeting called to discuss the problem, the vice president for academic affairs pointed out that he had received numerous complaints from the dean of engineering because too many students were failing the mathematics courses required to enter full-time study in the college of engineering.

The mathematics faculty feels that the high failure rate simply reflects inadequate preparation on the part of entering students. The director of institutional research counters this suggestion by revealing that many students who ranked in the top quartile of the College Board Examination were included in the large number of failing students. The dean of engineering is threatening to develop mathematics courses within the college of engineering if the situation persists any longer. The dean of the College of Arts and Science, in which the mathematics department is located, wants the mathematics faculty to see that a problem exists. He recognizes that they must develop a plan for changing the grading policy or the structure of the freshman mathematics courses.

    a. How can the dean of arts and science get the mathematics department to recognize that the present situation cannot continue?

    b. Identify the types of faculty members who might resist making any changes.

    c. What might be the concerns of those who oppose change?

    d. What can be done to alleviate their concerns?

    e. How might the dean involve faculty in developing a plan for solving the problem?

4. CREATING A MODERN-LANGUAGE DEPARTMENT

    A medium-size university has five language departments—namely, French, Spanish, German, Russian, and Italian. The size of the departments varies from three to seven faculty members. Only one of the departments seems to be managed well. The departments are very competitive, and the conflict between them is affecting faculty morale and productivity. The dean believes that combining the five separate departments into one modern-language department and finding a good chairperson to provide leadership would help solve the problem. The problem is to get the faculty from the departments to recognize the situation and consider the dean's solution. What strategies should the dean follow to persuade the faculty?

    a. Identify the types of faculty who will support the dean's idea and who will oppose it.

    b. What are the concerns of those who oppose the idea?

    c. What can be done to alleviate faculty concerns?

    d. How might the dean involve faculty in planning for a merger of departments?

5. CREATE YOUR OWN CASE STUDY

You may create your own case study based on your own experience or the experience of one or more of your colleagues. If you decide to do this, state the problem and what kinds of change(s) are needed. Provide answers to the same questions that follow each of the case studies above.

4

Dividing the Budget Among Academic Departments and Programs

There is never enough money. In this imperfect world in which deans live and work, they must plan how to spend the marginal sums of money they are allocated. The first step in planning is setting priorities. This obviously is one of the most important things a dean must do. In this chapter we will focus first on the mechanics of program planning—how a dean generates a plan—and then on how a dean uses criteria to evaluate that plan so that funds can be rationally allocated to departments or programs in a college, school, or division.

Setting Priorities

How does a dean set priorities? The quick and obvious answer is to do so carefully and with a great deal of consultation with his or her department chairpersons and faculty members. But the emphasis in this quick, obvious answer should be on the term consultation. Consultation does not mean taking votes;

priorities cannot be set in town hall meetings. Some one person finally has to act, has to make decisions. That person is the dean; that is what deans are paid to do, and that is why good deans work hard and suffer, at least occasionally, periods of extreme anxiety. It is not possible for a committee of, say, ten or twelve department chairpersons or program leaders to decide which one or two of their respective departments or programs should receive preferential treatment in the allocation of resources. Nor should such a committee be expected to do so. Any chairperson who would voluntarily give up resources from his or her department or withdraw a request for additional resources in favor of another department or program would generally have a great deal of explaining to do to the department's faculty members. The best a chairperson can hope for is the opportunity to present an argument for fair and equitable treatment to a dean who will evaluate that argument alongside all other arguments and, after weighing all relevant considerations, make a decision.

What are those considerations? They cover a broad range: (a) the strengths and weaknesses of the programs in the college; (b) the internal arrangements of the college with other colleges, schools, or units in the institution; (c) the needs of society, which are not necessarily the same as marketplace considerations; (d) the opportunities for the students of the institution; and (e) the desires and aspirations of the faculty. There is no way to put these major considerations into a priority order of themselves, for each institution may present a different array of problems and opportunities that are related to these considerations. Each must be examined within the context of an individual institution. The following sections deal with some of the considerations listed above.

STRENGTHS AND WEAKNESSES OF PROGRAMS

Probably the easiest set of conditions to come to grips with within a college, school, or division are the strengths and weaknesses of the programs in it. Truly great institutions are not supposed to have any weak programs, yet we all know that this is not so. But great institutions have become great because they have built undeniable strength and excellence in at least a

limited number of programs. Thus, the dean, whose responsibility it is to improve the college, must find a way to build,
maintain, or improve upon one or a small number of strong
departments or programs. Where there is strength, it is typically the dean's duty to build upon it. This kind of priority decision is the easiest to make because a strong program in a college is almost always recognized as such by the faculty of the
college and the rest of the institution. For example, a strong
chemistry department is difficult, even perilous, to ignore.
Chemists are quite often among the most aggressive of all academics; perhaps that is why there are so many strong chemistry departments in American higher education. However, the
dean should avoid the temptation *not* to build strength on
strength. Strong programs are normally the result of constant
nourishment given by years of preferential treatment. And
while it takes a long time to establish a strong program, it takes
only a few short years of neglect for strong programs to falter
and grow weak. Key faculty members are often mobile and
generally have little patience with administrators when their
normal expectations are disappointed. Hence, one of the worst
priority decisions a dean can make is to build up a weak program by ignoring a strong program or to fund the strong program at the same level each year, whatever that constant level
may mean in context.

Weak programs exist in every college and in every university. They are the curse of every dean, and their mere existence
becomes an intellectual land mine for all deans. Several things
can be done about weak programs: they can be made strong,
but if strength is infused swiftly it will inevitably be at the expense of other strong or average programs; they can be made
into average programs, but here again if the transformation is
effected rapidly, it will be done at the expense of other programs; they can be ignored and left weak; or they can be abolished. No one likes to have a weak program in an institution,
especially since over the long course of time they may receive
more publicity than strong programs. Hence, it is often dangerous to leave them weak. Unless other considerations such as
societal need and student demand are strongly operative, it is
also not a good idea to make them strong at the expense of
other programs, although, on a short-term basis, resources can

be borrowed from, or denied to, one program in order to help support another, more deserving one.

The dean, then, has three alternatives in dealing with a weak program: (a) provide resources that will gradually improve it to average status; (b) abolish it; or (c) ignore it. Selecting the third alternative is generally least desirable, for to do so is ultimately to cheat students who enroll in the program. Suppose, for the sake of argument, however, the dean identifies a certain program in his college as weak. In this program, the department chairperson provides no leadership or advocacy; the faculty members seem to be content with the status quo; the number of students enrolled meet enrollment criteria; reputation has it that the courses offered lack substance; and the faculty members are easy graders. Not surprisingly, very few complaints have been received from students. In the dean's opinion, the subject matter of the program does not add to, or detract from, the institution's central mission and is therefore not integral to it. He also believes that faculty attitude being what it is, the allocation of additional funds to the program without personnel changes would not bring it up to average status. He has already decided not to provide additional funds and really believes that the best solution as far as the college is concerned is to abolish the program. Upon further reflection and with advice of his academic vice president, he realizes that its abolition at this time could create personnel and other types of problems that might be more costly in terms of human energy and dollars than the resources saved by abolishing the program. What is a dean to do? This dean decides that for the time being, the least harmful decision is to allow the weak program to continue as is. An institution, however, cannot afford to have too many such programs, and eventually a decision will have to be made either to abolish it or to improve it at least to average status.

INTERNAL ARRANGEMENTS WITH OTHER COLLEGES

Another thing that a dean must take into account when establishing priorities for resource allocations is the internal relationships that a college has constructed with other colleges and schools within its institution in terms of the service courses it offers for students of other academic units. This is particularly important for the dean of a college of arts and sciences, a college that is the base for all other colleges in a large institution (and in a small institution it may be the institution itself), for the arts and sciences college not only provides the majority of traditional liberal arts majors, but it is also the feeder of students to other colleges and schools. In a land-grant university or in a university that has a medical school, the arts and sciences dean cannot long neglect the biological science programs in that college. If the university has a major engineering school, the arts and sciences dean cannot neglect the mathematics and physics programs in that college; if the university has a law school, the arts and sciences dean will have to remember the supportive role some of the social sciences play in their relationships with law.

The dean of a fine arts college also has to remember the service role that college plays in the life of a university, that educating painters and pianists is important, but equally important is the offering of a wide array of art history and music appreciation courses for students in the rest of the university. The dean of a college of journalism must remember the service role that the college should play in the life of a university and therefore must make certain that the college's curriculum is not designed solely to train newspaper reporters or TV announcers. And the dean of education must ensure that his or her college makes available professional education courses for those graduates of other colleges who wish to complete requirements for a public school teacher's certificate in their respective fields. Thus, while common wisdom tends to emphasize the service role of the typical arts and sciences college, each professional college in its turn has a special service role to play, and these service roles become important factors in any academic vice president's or dean's decision regarding resource allocations. In a well-organized university, one that offers its students a sound, broadly based educational experience, each college must be an active contributor to that broad program, and the more each college contributes to that program, the easier it is for the individual college dean to gain support for resources from the central administration.

THE CHANGING NEEDS OF SOCIETY

Perhaps the most immediate pressure any dean faces in making priority decisions concerning the allocation of resources stems from the needs—either real or imagined—of society. These needs are most often expressed through regents, trustees, legislators, alumni, and occasionally students themselves. Societal needs are often born of short-term crises; sometimes they relate to the immediate needs of the local or regional marketplace; sometimes they are the result of local or regional political turbulence; and occasionally they are the offspring of a particular *idée fixe* of an individual or a small but vigorous group of the public. Sometimes, of course, they are anything but local or political or idiosyncratic. Anyone who has had to deal with the incredible demand for computer access in a college or university knows that here is a far-reaching legitimate pressure on academic institutions that springs from one of the fastest-moving, fastest-changing technologies in the history of man, a pressure that emanates from virtually every segment of American society, a pressure that cannot be ignored. In this particular case, deans across the country have had to—or shortly will have to—alter the resource allocation priorities of their colleges, as whole institutions attempt laboriously, and in most cases belatedly, to meet the need to prepare students to live and work in a computer age as yet not fully imagined.

OPPORTUNITIES FOR STUDENTS AND STUDENT DEMAND

But potentially the most difficult external need a dean must deal with is student demand, a demand that manifests itself usually in a vast, silent, often sudden shift in student preference for one set of programs over another. In one decade students may enroll in great numbers in such social sciences as sociology and political science; in another decade, without warning, students may swarm into another kind of social science, into economics or business administration, or into engineering and such sciences as chemistry and physics, or more recently, into a glamour field like computer science. These shifts in student preference are of course reflections of the changing value systems of society, and each dean who must make priority decisions must be prepared to take into account these shifts in order to prepare as well as possible for them, yet at the same time protect, as far as is humanly possible, the overall academic integrity of the college's programs. A changing society is really the basis for shifts and changes in student demands and enrollments. One cannot stubbornly resist the pressures of society, because colleges and universities are shaped by society at least as much as they themselves shape society. As an aside, it is interesting to note, in spite of the shifting changes in student demand for courses, how relatively silent many students are about the establishment of academic programs needed to help them flourish in the "real world"; their attacks on their institutions are almost always about policies, not programs.

DESIRES AND ASPIRATIONS OF THE FACULTY: INVOLVING FACULTY AND DEVELOPING A PLAN

How does the dean take into account all of the preceding considerations for each department or program and, at the same time, appropriately involve the faculty of the college or division as resource allocation plans are made for it? Consultation is of course absolutely necessary, not only because of the collegial nature of the decision-making process in a university, but because only a polymath can know all of the forces that should come into play in formulating plans. Few deans are polymaths; this status is reserved for senior professors and university presidents, a set of circumstances that may explain why the dean receives most unsolicited advice from these two quarters.

There are several mechanisms commonly used to fulfill the need for the dean to consult with colleagues in the college before arriving at a set of decisions for establishing priorities for resource allocations. The first mechanism is for the dean's office to develop a rough draft of the grand plan. This draft can be formulated by the dean with or without the help of a very few staff members. Such a draft is then circulated throughout the college for commentary, which commentary will always include revisions, amendments, and outright rejection. The dilemma here is that advice must be sought, but once solicited, it cannot be ignored. Such advice need not be accepted in whole or in part, but it cannot be ignored. If it is rejected, its rejection must be explained in some detail. A second mechanism is the establishment by the dean's office of a planning committee charged with the responsibility of formulating a plan. This has advantages and disadvantages. The planning committee acts somewhat as a buffer between the dean and the college, and the dean tends to take less direct criticism for the sins of commission and omission that every such draft will inevitably contain. Yet, unless the planning committee is democratically elected by the college, an appointed membership— especially if appointed by the dean—will be regarded as simply the dean's stalking horse. But if one thing is certain, it is that a planning committee cannot be democratically elected. First, this is a simple abdication of the leadership role of the dean, and second, no such planning committee can give the dean the kind of advice he or she needs in the establishment of plans for resource allocation. The very act of planning—establishing priorities—means that some departments will get more than others; some will get less than others. Democratically elected committees seldom are capable of making such distinctions.

Perhaps a better way to engage a college in the consultative process is to ask for planning proposals from all of the departments in the college. These proposals can be reviewed and evaluated by department chairpersons and, if appropriate, by a collegewide review committee appointed by the dean. This kind of process, a process that operates essentially from what is commonly called the bottom up, allows all in the college to express their aspirations and their own sense of priorities. Naturally, not all aspirations can be fulfilled, but this process at least allows for all aspirations to be expressed. In any planning process, the expression of aspirations is in many ways as important as their fulfillment. Once these aspirations have been reduced to writing and given a fair review by an appropriate group, the dean must make the final decision. Votes cannot be taken on the establishment of collegewide priorities. If taken, the votes will be split, often badly, and the very act of voting sets into motion a political process that is inimical to the establishment of a rational plan for resource allocation. The dean must make the final decision and, in so doing, establish the fact that the dean is indeed the leader of the college.

The dean has two other important constituencies to consult, namely, fellow deans and the central administration. It does no good in a university whose medical school is the jewel in the university's crown to decide that programs in the biological sciences will be fifth on the list for resource allocations in a college of arts and sciences. That decision will be contested vigorously by the medical dean and surely overturned by the central administration. It does no good for a fine arts dean in a land-grant university to establish a set of priorities that will require that the fine arts college become the premier unit in the university. Such a plan will be treated with bewilderment by the central administration. No college can stand apart from the rest of the colleges in a university; no college can divorce itself from its central administration. Not even, in the long run, a college of law.

Criteria for Evaluating Program Viability

Once a working draft of a plan has been formulated and is in the hands of the dean, certain criteria can be applied that will help assess the viability of each department or program being considered. The results of the assessment will provide a rationale for the dean in making final decisions and in explaining those decisions to the college's department chairpersons and most of their faculties. The following seven criteria have been formulated by Dr. T. A. Emmet* and can be used in a variety of ways: institutional essentiality and centrality; societal need; demand for programs and services; geographical location and environmental and political factors; quality factors; cost; and timing. Not all seven criteria can be applied uniformly to all programs under analysis by the dean, but most of them will be useful most of the time.

---

*T. A. Emmet, unpublished list of criteria for program vitality and evaluation, personal communication, 1983.

INSTITUTIONAL ESSENTIALITY AND CENTRALITY

Consider the criterion of institutional essentiality and centrality. How essential is a particular department's program to the college's and university's mission? What historic value does the department's program have to the college and university? To use a hypothetical example, Krypton Institute of Technology, a famous university located in Silicon Valley and known for its science and engineering programs, has a College of Liberal Arts and Sciences within which college is a Department of Religious Studies. This department was established somewhat whimsically in the turbulent sixties by people who have long since left the university. Clearly this department is not essential to Krypton's mission—unless we rewrite the scenario to note that this Department of Religious Studies was established by Krypton's founder as a counterbalance to the original science and engineering emphasis in 1865 and that the department has been world famous for its studies in Sanskrit and Hebrew for a hundred years. As mentioned previously, the Department of Religious Studies at Krypton is not central but tangential to the mission of the institution. How important currently is the department to the institution? If it also offers elective courses to students majoring in areas other than religious studies and if enrollments in these courses are high, there might be justification for maintaining the department at average status. Or if the department has strong enrollments, is really world famous for its scholarly activities, and is contributing to the institution's national visibility, there might be justification for keeping it at above-average status. On the other hand, if indeed it is not central or essential to the institution's mission, if it offers courses only to its own majors, of which there are very few, and if it has an undistinguished faculty, its abolition might be considered. Its elimination would hardly be noticed, except by its few faculty members, who would become unemployed unless assignments could be found for them elsewhere in the institution.

For another example, a college may maintain a small department or program in an area such as classics with two or three faculty members, even though the number of students who major in this field or take elective courses in it are too few to justify its existence. Classics is retained at this particular college, not because it is central to the college's mission from a curricular point of view, but because there has always been a classics program here and it has become part of the college's tradition. It is perceived as the institution's symbol of culture and scholarship. Yet at other colleges with budget problems, programs such as this, with no traditional value to the institution, might be the first to go.

The matter of the centrality of a particular department's program may at first seem easy to resolve. But the criterion of the centrality of a particular program needs to be applied to both the university and the college, an application that is sometimes less easy to determine. Obviously, in an arts and sciences college, the departments that teach the two languages used throughout the university, English and mathematics, are central to the college and the university. If a university has a medical school or an engineering school, then equally obviously the departments of chemistry and physics are central to the university's mission. But what about political science—does the university have a law school? What about sociology or geology? Here the dean must rely heavily on the criterion of essentiality and centrality and resist the temptation to make every department in the college world renowned. Moreover, in applying this criterion, the dean needs also to consider the concept of evolving essentiality. The obvious example here is computer science, an evolving discipline whose future is at this writing unlimited. Although, as noted earlier, no one likes to have a weak program, it is more important to have at least one or two very strong programs than it is to have no weak programs.

What evidence is available to the dean, other than his or her own common sense, to help determine what is essential and central to the university? Consider the documents that load the shelves in the offices of the central administration of every university. Every institution has a mission statement or master plan; normally these documents are turned out each time a new president or chancellor assumes office and with the decennial visit of every regional accrediting association. Their numbers are legion and their rhetoric prolix. Every university that is governed by a state system—that most dolorous of all innovations in American higher education—has a state master plan for higher education. Most universities constantly measure themselves by analysis of the number and quality of the graduates of all their programs, and most universities attempt to get evaluations of their programs from their alumni. A reading of these documents, plus the dean's experience in the particular institution he or she serves, will produce at least three grades for a program's essentiality and centrality: essential, marginal, or not essential.

SOCIETAL NEED

The criterion of societal need is much more difficult to define than the previous one. Societal need must first be defined as the institution defines it. Thus, the societal need defined by Saint John's University in New York City is bound to be different from societal need as defined by Oklahoma State University in Stillwater. Many universities have very special interpretations of societal need, interpretations based on the following kinds of consideration: the university's perception of the kind and degree of citizen preparation its students need to function intelligently in public policy areas of society; the university's perception of the kind of education its students need in their lifework (are they prepared for multicareers?); the university's perception of its students' need to function effectively in a technological world and to be able to work effectively in foreign countries; and other special needs appropriate to the mission of the university. In assessing the relationships between the college's programs and these societal needs, the dean has available the same kinds of documents that can be used in the application of the first criterion—essentiality and centrality—plus the steady stream of national, regional, and state higher-education reports concerning education and society. The dean has also available the greatest textbook of all—the lessons of history. Again, as with the previous criterion, at least three rather obvious grades for the departmental program under evaluation can be given by the dean: the societal needs for the programs are high, medium, or low.

DEMAND FOR PROGRAMS AND SERVICES

Perhaps the easiest of the seven criteria that the dean can apply in the evaluation of programs is the one concerned with the demand for programs and services. This criterion is easy to use because it involves primarily the application of simple numerical data readily available to the dean. Consider these data: the number of majors enrolled in a program, the number of nonmajors registered for courses in the program, the retention rates of majors in the program, and the number and quality of applicants for enrollment in the program. Other nonnumerically based data that inform this criterion are the employability of graduates of the program, or the marketplace demand for these graduates; the support given the program by business, industry, and government, which need not be solely in the form of grants and/or contracts but, rather, in the form of cooperative job arrangements for the program's students; the support of the program that emanates from other academic programs, which might very well be termed dependency upon the program; the outreach activities of the program. Evidence gathered by the dean for the use of this criterion can again provide at least three grades: high, medium, and low.

GEOGRAPHICAL LOCATION AND ENVIRONMENTAL AND POLITICAL FACTORS

Another criterion available to the dean is based on the university's geographical location and the environmental and political factors attendant upon that location. Is the university an urban university or is it a traditional college-town university? What is the demographic character of the population surrounding the university? What kind of cultural emphasis influences the university's environment? Clearly, Krypton Tech, our hypothetical university emphasizing science and engineering and located in Silicon Valley, has one set of program priorities reinforced by its location and surrounding population, while Mesa University, with a surrounding population that is overwhelmingly Hispanic, has another set. Ethnic and cultural demographics play a role in the application of this criterion, but so do such matters as the kind of clientele served—such as adult students and military personnel who enroll as students. The evidence available to the dean to measure these factors comprise political, demographic, and geographic data derived from such sources as chambers of commerce, state and regional planning offices, and the U.S. Labor Department.

What are some of the political forces at play in most colleges and universities? The concern here is not internal politics (deans versus deans, deans versus vice presidents or provosts, chairpersons versus deans, etc.), for in several of the succeeding chapters these political forces will be dealt with at length. We wish to describe the influences and pressures that are brought to bear on program evaluation and planning by external politics, those movements generated by city, state, and federal levels of government. Urban universities are inevitably caught up in city politics, and many times the urban university can find itself in danger of becoming the focal point of savage municipal political wars. The urban university is almost always an integral part of the city in which it is located, and its programs generally reflect the needs and aspirations of the city. This generally means that urban universities have to take special care of their programs in the social sciences; a program in criminal justice almost always elicits strong support from city government, and a business dean must always have a strong M.B.A. program in an urban university. Such needs cannot be relegated to the second level of importance if an urban university wishes to maintain the support of city government.

State universities generally are a step removed from the hot breath of urban politics, although a state university in a big city has to serve two masters constantly, city government and state government, the locus of which in America is almost always somewhere other than the major urban centers of the state. Generally speaking, state universities draw their students, and thus their constituencies, from every part of the state and therefore are seldom subject to intense local pressures—although traffic problems, competition with local businesses, and student life-styles are major points of friction between any city government and a state university, no matter how small or large the city in which the university is located. But since the constituencies of state universities are broader than those of most urban and urban state universities, the deans in state universities are under less pressure to develop highly specialized programs. The major political forces at play in state universities arise from competition of state university versus state university, and these struggles are played out in the state legislature, where envy and avarice are featured as prominently at times as reason and cooperation. The dean must always take these struggles into consideration in formulating plans for new programs, expansion of old programs, or evaluation of current programs.

The consequences of federal politics are almost beyond a dean's ability to predict. "When the gods are at war, mortals must hide." National clashes over budget deficits, defense preparedness, social programs, agriculture policies, Federal Reserve monetary policies—all play a vital role in the dean's professional life and can make or break the future of a program under the dean's direction. Yet the best a dean can do is to become an astute and well-informed student of federal politics, even though his or her ability to influence the course of such events approaches zero. But a careful student of federal politics can sometimes discern an opportunity to develop a program or change a program's direction and thus attract funding of an almost unreasonable magnitude. It is best, however, to remember that federal initiatives seldom maintain any consistency of thrust or direction, and the dean who builds a program wholly on a current federal initiative risks that program's future four years down the road. When all is said and done, the grades a dean can assign to the criterion of geographical location and environmental and political factors are these: favorable, marginal, or unfavorable. Even these grades, like politics itself, are temporary and subject to change.

QUALITY FACTORS

The most important criterion is, of course, quality. The quality of the students and faculty in the program being evaluated is the most valuable indicator a dean has in making decisions about programs. The quality of the students is easy to assess. The quality of the faculty rests on a number of factors: teaching ability; research ability, including not just number of publications, grants, and contracts, but their nature and relevance to the program; and previous faculty training and education, such as the graduate schools from which they were graduated and the kind of institutions they have served in. How does the program being evaluated compare with other programs of its kind in the state, region, and nation? How does the program compare with other programs in the college and in the university? The dean should study also the pattern and placement of the program's graduates. Sometimes, but not often, the program's ability to meet accrediting association standards can be a quality indicator. Usually, however, these standards are largely self-serving and are only marginally reflective of program quality.

After assessing all the quality indicators, the dean should use them to project the potential quality of the programs over the next three to five years. The evidence available to the dean is plentiful: national studies by field of discipline are standard references these days; contract and grant awards by national agencies involving peer review are excellent indicators of the quality of both individual faculty members and the programs in which they work; and institutional research data are valuable. If funds are available for consultants, they should be hired to evaluate programs. The consultants should be individuals whose opinions are well respected by faculty and administration alike. Generally, the reports of such consultants are one of the most important sources of relevant information and can give the dean virtually unassailable arguments to use in (a) getting more funding from the central administration for the program; (b) convincing the faculty in the program to change emphasis in teaching or research; and (c) convincing the faculty in the program and/or the central administration that the program must be either phased out or radically reconstructed.

The grades the dean can use in assessing quality are essentially those used all over academia: A, B, C, D, or F. But deans should beware of awarding an A in their program evaluations; an excellent program is rare. Excellent programs are generally found in either only the very best universities in the nation—such as law at Harvard, engineering at Stanford, and physics at Berkeley—or in highly specialized universities. Very few deans in this country can honestly award an A to their programs.

COST

Always pressing on the dean in any sort of program evaluation is the matter of cost, another criterion. Program costs can be measured in a wide variety of ways, no one of which is usually conclusive. Consider the following: faculty-student ratios, actual and potential outside funding, comparative costs with other programs within the dean's institution and college, comparative costs with similar programs at other selected institutions, cost to bring the program to a higher level of quality, cost per student credit hour calculated by using all variables, and, finally, the cost-benefit ratio of the program to the college and to the institution. This last factor may be extremely difficult to calculate because it takes into account not just numbers derived from the university's budget but ultimately all seven criteria. But in amassing evidence to use in applying this criterion, the dean is almost overwhelmed with data sources; he or she has available all of the institutional research data and budget analysis data generated by both the central administration and the dean's own college office. The grading system here is the same as in most of the other criteria: favorable, marginal, and unfavorable.

TIMING

The last criterion is simply described as timing and should never be used alone. Philosophically it could be called fate; pragmatically speaking, it comes down to a juncture of circumstance with time. Some times are better than other times to do things about, with, or to a program, and any program evaluation must take the criterion of timing into consideration. If, after applying the previous six criteria, the dean decides it is necessary to try to triple the budget of the physics department at Krypton U. and Krypton has just undergone its second budget rescission in three years, the timing is going to be way off target if the dean tries to convince the central administration to buy into a tripled budget for physics. Thus, in many instances, no matter how high a program has been graded by the dean using the first six criteria, those grades may not be conclusive; the tide has to be coming in, not going out. There are other matters of timing that the dean should consider: vacancies in the leadership of programs, faculty resignations or retirements in sufficient numbers, crisis versus noncrisis situations. Every once in a while timing may be at least as important as quality in the evaluation process. And there is only one grade distribution scheme the dean can use, namely, good or bad. Is it dumb or smart to do x for program y at this time? That means that above all else the dean must have common sense, because all of the elaborate apparatus described in these seven criteria amounts to nothing without common sense.

Case Studies

THE KUDSU UNIVERSITY CASE

It might be useful to construct a case study using these seven criteria with at least two scenarios about one hypothetical university. Let us construct, then, Kudsu University, locate it in a rural southern environment, and give it the following characteristics: Kudsu was founded in the early part of the twentieth century as a university whose emphasis was on agriculture and engineering. As Kudsu grew and matured, its College of Engineering became its strongest program, and by virtue of a whole series of factors, including timing and state politics, its College of Arts and Sciences developed an excellent basic physics department, a department much better than the well-known physics department at the state's flagship university more than a hundred miles away. One of Kudsu's illustrious physics graduates who became science adviser to the president of the United States and later director of the National Science Foundation developed a sudden desire to return to his alma mater and finish out his career—a science career not yet over—at Kudsu. The timing was perfect; the longtime chairperson of the physics department retired at about the time the illustrious alumnus told Kudsu's dean of arts and sciences he wanted to return and, in his words, "pay back what my alma mater has given me." The appropriate university procedures for hiring a new department chairperson were put in motion, and the alumnus was made chairperson of the Department of Physics. Then the problems began.

SCENARIO A. In this version, the illustrious alumnus decides that the best way to help his department and his university is to build a high-energy group in the department. Such a group would make Kudsu famous. The chairperson submits to

his dean a budget for $1.92 million for four new faculty posi-
tions and equipment. The state legislature will meet within two
months and the general revenue estimates for the state for the
coming year project a 2–3 percent decrease over current-year
revenues. Enrollment in Kudsu's College of Arts and Sciences
is stable, as is the enrollment in the College of Engineering.
The enrollment in the Ph.D. programs in both colleges has
dropped off sharply during the past five years. What kind of
answer can the dean give to the department chairperson?

The essentiality and centrality of the proposed new program
are marginal, as is the societal need. The demand would appear to be low. The location and environment are marginal,
and the cost is unfavorable. But the quality of the proposed
program is graded B. The politics seem unfavorable. The timing is bad.

SCENARIO B. In this version, the illustrious alumnus makes
the same decision: Kudsu should have a high-energy group in
the physics department. The $1.92 million cost is the same; the
state legislature is still facing a slight general revenue shortfall
for the coming year. Enrollment in the physics department is
up slightly, and enrollment in the College of Engineering has
increased 10 percent each year for the last two years. Before
the illustrious alumnus left his last Washington post to return
to Kudsu, he and the state's U.S. senator, a veteran of thirty-six
years in the Senate, managed to get a new federally operated
supercomputer located in Pine Bluff, an old ballistics missile
research station about thirty-five miles from Kudsu, and the
Pine Bluff research station has received a large number of federal contracts for work on various Space Defense Initiative
(SDI) projects. Now what does the dean do?

The essentiality and centrality of the proposed new program
is still marginal, but it begins to appear that the societal need
is at least medium. The demand will probably be medium; the
location and environment can probably be rated as favorable.
The cost is unchanging; the quality remains graded as B, but
the geographical and the political factors appear to be favorable, and timing may not be bad.

These two scenarios are barely developed; neither of them
tells us what the dean is trying to do with other programs in

Kudsu's College of Arts and Sciences. Nor do we learn anything from the scenarios about the quality of the mathematics and chemistry departments. We do not know anything about Kudsu's master plan or its private-giving programs. Indeed, to develop a proper scenario, we would need to write a small novel. And that is precisely the point we wish to make: decisions about program development are complicated by a host of factors, and thus, such decisions should never be made on the basis of one criterion—or, as the scenarios point out, one dominant personality. Of course, the cost of perfect information is inaction, but the cost of ignorance is disaster. Somewhere in between lies the the correct course of action for the dean, a course of action tempered by common sense but driven by courage and imagination.

THE CASE OF THE PSYCHOCERAMICS DEPARTMENT AT MIDWESTERN UNIVERSITY

This case study concerns a situation that occurred in 1970 at Midwestern University, a medium-size state institution. The state legislature and the state board of regents charged that the universities were not being managed efficiently. They based their charge on the fact that prior to this time, no program had ever been deliberately abolished in any of the universities in this state. They suggested that if the presidents wanted to demonstrate that they could manage efficiently, they would abolish at least one or two unproductive programs.

The president of one particular university, wanting to gain favor in the eyes of the legislature and the state board of regents, asked his director of institutional research to review all the data that had been submitted by the departments over the past several years and to recommend two or three that might be considered appropriate for abolition. One department in particular seemed to be a likely candidate—the Department of Psychoceramics. The department, located in the College of Fine Arts, was established twenty years before and developed by Dr. Fischer, who became its first chairperson. Over the years it had acquired five faculty members and had graduated about five hundred students with bachelor degrees, most of whom had found satisfying jobs practicing their profession and who still maintained friendly contact with their department and its chairperson. The facts in 1970 were as follows: the number of students enrolled in the program had declined to about five majors; there was no demand by nonmajors to take any of its elective courses. The faculty had decreased in number and now consisted of two faculty members, one of whom was the original chairperson who was planning to retire within the year, and the other, a middle-aged associate professor who was well respected in his field and had competencies that would make him acceptable to several related departments in the college.

The president of the university asked the academic vice president and the dean of fine arts to establish appropriate faculty committees to conduct a thorough study of the department and to make recommendations regarding its future. The committee findings and recommendations are discussed in the following sections in terms of the seven criteria described in this chapter for evaluating viability of departments:

1. *Institutional centrality and essentiality:* The program was not central to the mission of the university, nor was it essential for the well-being of any of the other departments or programs in the college or institution. Grade: not essential.

2. *Societal need:* At that time there appeared to be no great social need for graduates of the program. Grade: low.

3. *Demand for program and services:* Only five students were enrolled as majors. No students outside of the major were taking any courses in it and there were very few admission applications from new students. Grade: low.

4. *Geographical location and environmental and political factors:* There appeared to be no great regional need for the program in the city where the university was located or even in the state. Grade: unfavorable.

5. *Quality factors:* The quality of the program was satisfactory, since the faculty were well qualified. Grade: C.

6. *Cost:* The cost seemed excessive for just five students. Grade: unfavorable.

7. *Timing:* The timing seemed good for abolition. There were very few students who would be affected. One fac-

ulty person, the chairperson, was retiring, whereas the other faculty member could easily be placed in another department for the mutual benefit of both. No serious objections were anticipated from either of the two faculty members. Grade: good timing for abolition.

The committee's final recommendation was that the program be discontinued. The recommendation was considered and approved at all the necessary levels in the university hierarchy and transmitted to the state board of regents, which at this point in time would have been delighted to approve a recommendation for any program to be discontinued. This was the first time that a recommendation for discontinuing a program had ever been received from a university. The board praised the president, the committee, and the university for being able to "face up to the budget crunch." The recommendation to abolish the Department of Psychoceramics was therefore approved, the department was officially abolished by the board of regents, and the university was duly notified of this action. Assessment of the department's viability clearly showed that its abolition was a logical decision that could be easily justified.

At some colleges or universities, this would have been the end of it. But not here. The retiring chairperson, who at first raised no serious objections, started to reminisce, remembering how she had developed the program from its infancy. And now she could see twenty years of her lifework being wiped out before her very eyes by a stroke of the pen. So she wrote letters and made telephone calls to the program's many friends and alumni who had accumulated over the years. Soon large numbers of letters of objection started coming to the president's office, to the office of the board of regents, to offices of state legislators, and even to the office of the governor of the state. The end result was that the board of regents reinstated the program, which still operates today at a level less than adeqate, but of course with a new chairperson. The moral of the story: Do not underestimate the power and influence of a lame-duck retiring department chairperson, and do not underestimate the power and influence of a letter campaign from aroused friends and alumni of an academic program targeted for extinction.

THE CASE OF THE LARGE FOUNDATION GRANT

Deans, like ships' captains, should not try to fill their sails with every wind that comes along. This ancient seaman's axiom holds especially true for the glittering opportunities that occasionally present themselves to a dean through the auspices of a large foundation grant or a substantial cash gift from a private donor. Foundations and donors rarely give money for generalized educational purposes; there is a string attached to almost every gift or grant. It is critical for the dean to decide if the string will free or bind the college or school.

Take, for example, the case of Urbanette College, a small (enrollment five thousand) college founded around the turn of the century downtown in one of America's largest cities. It is a private college that each year receives a small subsidy from the government of the city in which it is located. In the last five years, the relationship between the municipal government and the college has blossomed, and a series of city-financed projects at the college have been authorized by both the city commission and the college's board of trustees, the latter group being enthusiastic about this growing relationship.

World Foundation, whose corporate headquarters are located in the same city, offers Urbanette $3 million over a five-year period to conduct a detailed study of an obscure South American Indian tribe. This gift is being proposed by the foundation because Urbanette has on its faculty a very famous and distinguished anthropologist who has devoted his life to the study of that very same South American Indian tribe, and the foundation has from time to time over a period of fifteen years given this anthropologist small research grants to pursue his lifework. Urbanette has not seen fit, however, to build up its Department of Anthropology around this man, who is the college's most distinguished faculty member, probably because he is an eccentric loner who spends more time in South America than on campus. The college has a doctoral program in cultural anthropology, but it is a tiny, faltering program whose few graduates are the product of the distinguished faculty member's occasional bursts of interest in students who can help him pursue his single-minded quest.

Indeed, shortly before World Foundation's offer, Urbanette

decided that it could not afford a separate anthropology department and, at the urging of the dean of arts and sciences, made plans to merge its departments of anthropology and sociology and to emphasize the subspecialities of urban and medical anthropology and sociology. The $3 million offered by the foundation will force the college to hire with grant money at least three Latin American anthropologists to develop special language courses in Indian dialects and to give up or postpone the development of those promising relationships in urban sociology and anthropology that are emerging from town-gown negotiations.

Hence the problem: Can Urbanette turn down $3 million? Can anyone? Maybe not, but what will happen six years from now? Who will pay for those Latin American anthropologists now on soft money? How will the courses in Indian dialects be financed? How does the college best serve society, the world, and, more important, its students?

The essentiality and centrality of the proposed new program are marginal, as is the societal need. The demand is obviously low. The location and environment are marginal. The initial cost, being essentially zero, is highly favorable, but the future cost is highly unfavorable. The quality of the program is graded B, maybe even B+. The politics are awful and the timing is terrible. So, Urbanette turns down the foundation grant. Five years later, the distinguished anthropologist is still teaching (intermittently) at the college, and anthropology and sociology have been merged. Some of the arrangements between Urbanette and the city have been successful; some have not. And many people still wonder if Urbanette did the right thing in turning away $3 million. This sense of wonder emerges every time a faculty member from Urbanette applies for a grant to World Foundation.

Questions and Exercises

1. For the purpose of this exercise, readers should mentally review all of the departments or programs in their colleges or universities over which they have jurisdiction or with which they have familiarity. Each reader should se-

lect one department or program that, in his or her opinion, is weak and one that is strong.

2. Evaluate the selected department or program in light of each of the seven criteria in the chapter. Do the results of your evaluation reinforce your original opinion of the department or program? Are there other criteria not described in the chapter that might be included?

3. Do you agree or disagree with the procedures in the chapter on how deans can obtain either information or advice from faculty in developing priorities and/or making decisions affecting budget allocation? Explain your answer.

4. What system or systems do you use at your university for dividing budget among departments?

5

The Dean and Department Chairpersons

In very large measure, department chairpersons are critical to the success or failure of the dean's mission, a mission we take to be the constant improvement of the teaching, research, and service activities of the college. It is crucial therefore that the dean make every effort to gain the support of his or her chairpersons. Support from chairpersons does not mean their complete acquiescence to the dean's opinions; but deans should not be reluctant to engage in argument when chairpersons try to persuade them to adopt policies different from those in practice. Chairpersons are naturally expected to voice their opinions and be advocates of their departments. They are expected to test the dean in every possible way, but once a decision is made, they are expected to support its implementation.

Over the long run, it is not possible for deans alone to establish program priorities, implement them, upgrade the faculty, strengthen the curriculum, and increase and improve scholarly activity. They need the willing support of the college's department chairpersons. Gone are the days of the imperial dean whose policies had the force of Hammurabi's code. There are in American universities frequent examples of decanal dictatorships, but in almost every instance, these are short-lived arrangements. And a dean's work is not done in one or two years; in most instances, it takes five years before the results of any efforts are clearly visible. And if the results are indeed successful, one can be sure that willing and cooperative chairpersons were involved every step of the way.

Tasks Shared by Department Chairpersons and Deans*

Deans sometimes take for granted the roles of their department chairpersons. We should pause here to consider how many tasks vital to the academic life of the institution fall squarely on the shoulders of department chairpersons, how closely they must work together with the dean to accomplish those tasks, and, thus, how dependent the dean is upon them. Not all of the tasks described here will be performed by all chairpersons in every institution. The size and administrative organization of the institution sometimes determine which tasks are to be performed. Most deans and chairpersons, however, will be able to identify with many of those tasks contained in the following discussion.

In the area of governance, chairpersons conduct departmental meetings, which can set the tone of the relationship between the whole department and the dean. Chairpersons generally establish all departmental committees, many of which work with other departments in the college to achieve specific goals. In consultation with the dean, they develop long- and short-range departmental program plans and goals, all of which are part of the dean's long- and short-range plans for his or her college or academic unit. Chairpersons then are the chief implementers of these plans; the dean cannot possibly implement all of them himself. In consultation with the dean, chairpersons must determine what services the department should provide to the university, the community or region, and the state. These services, some of which are mandatory in state colleges and universities, are always a function of departmental

---

*A full treatment of the chairperson's job responsibilities can be found in Chapter 1 on roles, functions, and characteristics of department chairpersons in Allan Tucker's *Chairing the Academic Department: Leadership among Peers.*

budgets, which of course are allocated by the dean in consultation with chairpersons. Chairpersons must keep their departments accredited (if they are subject to accreditation) and prepare their departments for institutional and decanal evaluation, a process that occurs at least once every five years. Chairpersons of course serve as advocates of their respective departments to the dean for budgets. This advocacy almost always generates creative tension between them and the dean, but if both are skillful, this kind of tension can only serve to foster close working relationships between the two. Furthermore, chairpersons are the primary initiators of affirmative action. Here again, they and the dean must work together to achieve success in meeting the institution's affirmative-action goals.

As all deans eventually come to realize, department chairpersons bear the primary responsibility for the college's instructional and research programs, and the tasks that must be performed to fulfill this responsibility are myriad in number. Supervising the scheduling of classes is a basic but onerous chore that requires coordination with departmental faculty, the dean's office, and the registrar's office. If the department is large enough to have multisection examinations, chairpersons monitor the scheduling and quality of the examinations. In connection with scheduling classes, they must try to ensure that the enrollment in both undergraduate and graduate courses meet the projections of the dean's office. They sometimes advise undergraduate majors and not only help to recruit graduate students but supervise their assignments as graduate teaching or research assistants. Chairpersons have responsibility for the general welfare of all the graduate students in their departments. They are responsible to the dean for the quality of teaching in the department and, with the help of the dean, must promote, through various incentives, good teaching. Chairpersons are the quality-control officers of their departments for both undergraduates and graduate programs, and must make sure that the course, curriculum configurations, and programs of the department are constantly updated. They must also promote research and, with the help of the dean, promote and encourage contract and grant activity among their faculty members.

Deans should always remember that department chairpersons generally make most of the basic decisions in the college. The unusual decisions, both good and bad, are seldom made without the approval and help of the dean. Chairpersons are at least initially involved in the recruitment of new faculty members and, with the help of the dean, are chiefly involved in the recruitment of special faculty appointments, such as the new superstar of the department. Although the dean generally has final approval of all new faculty appointments, almost always the chairperson's recommendation is the deciding factor. The chairperson assigns all faculty responsibilities, such as teaching, research, and service activities, and generally either makes or approves the assignment of committee memberships and other departmental activities. A good dean stays as far away from these matters as possible unless very unusual circumstances prevail. The chairperson fosters the development of each faculty member's special talents and interest, and often becomes, in some ways, a mentor and development officer for various members of his or her faculty. The chairperson evaluates all the faculty in his or her department, a critically important process that ultimately determines the progress and the quality of the department.* The dean must encourage chairpersons to carry out this important activity with care and courage. Depending upon the resources available, a logical result of this evaluation process is the assignment of annual salary increases, and the chairperson's recommendations to the dean are generally accepted. This responsibility requires, however, close cooperation and mutual respect between the chairperson and the dean.

While in almost all institutions the primary decisions regarding tenure and promotion are made collegially by the department faculty, the chairperson plays a key role in those decisions. In some institutions, the chairperson can reverse a tenure or promotion action by the faculty; in other institutions, the chairperson can only forward the actions of the faculty to the dean. In any event, again the dean and the chairperson must work together in acting upon these critical personnel decisions. The chairperson has the unpleasant duty of dealing

---

*See the chapter on ''Faculty Evaluation,'' in Allan Tucker's *Chairing the Academic Department*.

with unsatisfactory performance on the part of both faculty and nonacademic personnel in the department. If a faculty member's unsatisfactory performance cannot be remedied by actions of the chairperson, the dean is usually called upon to provide assistance. In the event that neither chairperson nor dean can solve the problems created by poor performance of a faculty member and the decision is made to terminate that faculty member, the chairperson must initiate the termination proceedings. In every step of those proceedings, the chairperson and the dean must be of one mind, determined to take one action. Finally, the chairperson has to be both teacher and cheerleader in the department. He or she must keep faculty members informed of department, college, and institutional plans, activities, and operations; must maintain good faculty morale; and must, in so doing, reduce, resolve, and prevent conflict among the department's faculty members, all the while encouraging active faculty participation in all important departmental activities.

In those colleges and universities that operate under a collective bargaining agreement for the faculty, the dean has a very special relationship with the department chairpersons. Salaries, tenure, and promotion are actions regulated—and sometimes tightly constrained—by the collective bargaining contract. While college deans seldom, if ever, are involved with the bargaining process itself, once the contract is agreed to by the university or college and the collective bargaining agent, both the dean and the department chairperson must monitor the provisions of the contract and make sure that both sides, employees and management, comply with all its provisions. Sometimes department chairpersons are included in the contract (that is, they are in the collective bargaining unit); sometimes they are not. But in either case, the chairperson and the dean must both know thoroughly all provisions of the contract and be willing to act in unison to honor those provisions. The penalty for disunity, for misunderstanding, for ignorance of the contract on the part of either chairperson or dean is more than awkwardness and embarrassment and hurt feelings; the penalty can be the filing of formal grievances, which then must be processed up through the chain of command to the central administration. And if a dean's college is the cradle of more than a few grievances, it is a sure sign that either the contract is not being honored or that the dean and the chairperson (or chairpersons) are not very good at solving personnel problems.

Although the dean is the chief spokesperson for the college, the department chairperson is the main communicator for his or her department and is the main link of communication between the faculty and the dean. Through the dean, the chairperson also at times communicates and interacts with vice presidents, provosts, and presidents. Thus, the dean and the chairperson are responsible for improving and maintaining the department's image and reputation not only among upper-level administrators but among governmental and private funding agencies and the general public. The chairperson also represents the departments and, by extension, not only the dean but the college and the university at various meetings and conferences of learned and professional societies. Small wonder, then, that the communication between chairperson and dean must be in every way excellent. Perhaps the most onerous part of the chairperson's role as communicator for the department is the daily round of correspondence, both intramural and extramural, and the endless reports and surveys that must be completed. Much of this correspondence and reporting goes to the dean's office, and from this continuous stream of paper, the dean can form a good idea of how the chairperson performs his or her job.

In many middle-sized and large institutions, the most important area of cooperation between the chairperson and the dean is probably in the formulation of the departmental budget. The chairperson, in consultation with various faculty committees, prepares the annual budget request and maintains primary control over the operating budget. The chairperson is the department's advocate in preparing the request budget, and as noted earlier, it is in this area that there is almost always a creative tension (at least one hopes that the tension is creative) between chairperson and dean. Additionally, the chairperson is usually the leader in seeking outside funding of various kinds for the department as a whole, if not for individual members of the department. The dean, in turn, must fit the funding goals and aspirations of each department into the larger budget request of the college or academic unit over which the dean presides. Obviously, the dean and chairperson must work very closely together in administering the department's operating budget because it and all the other departmental operating budgets become the operating budget of the dean's college or academic unit.

Finally, the dean should expect the department chairperson to be an office manager, a maintenance supervisor, an inventory manager, a building security officer, and a record keeper. The chairperson must not only manage his or her own office but also be generally responsible for the maintenance of all departmental facilities, all equipment (which nowadays is worth literally millions of dollars in large-scale science departments), and in some cases a departmental library. The chairperson, under the authority of the dean and with the help of the campus police, must maintain the security of the department's facilities and equipment. As if all this were not enough, the chairperson's office generally is the central record-keeping unit for all of the department's undergraduate majors and all of the department's graduate students, both those on stipend and those who are not. If these tasks are not performed satisfactorily, the dean's life can become a nightmare. No dean can function properly if the chairpersons in that college or academic unit are unable or unwilling to perform their duties with care and enthusiasm.

The relative importance of all these activities may vary from one department to another, depending on the situation in the department, the priority level of the department in the institution, and the way it fits into the college and university master plan. The dean, whose responsibility it is to provide leadership and guidance to all departments under his or her jurisdiction, probably knows—or should know—better than anyone else the obligations of a department at a given time, and which tasks, duties, and responsibilities described in the preceding paragraphs are most important for that particular department. How well that chairperson performs will therefore depend to a great extent on how clearly the dean communicates what is expected and what departmental tasks need the most attention.

Good communication and a good relationship with department chairpersons will not eliminate all of the dean's problems, but will certainly help keep them to a minimum. If too many chairpersons in a given college are unable or unwilling to provide their dean with the support needed to carry out the functions of the college, it may be necessary to have intransigent chairpersons replaced with more cooperative ones. If this is not feasible, it may be advisable for the dean to consider moving to another line of work. For in the final analysis, the relationships of the dean to the department chairpersons form the nature and character of the dean's working conditions. If those relationships are sour, then so is the dean's professional life. Deans are no different from other people; their professional lives must be as rewarding to them as anyone else's in an academic community. Thus, the dean must ask the same question we all ask ourselves about our work: Is it rewarding, fulfilling, and fun, or not? If not, why not?

Dean's Communication with Department Chairpersons

Viewed from a management perspective, the greatest flaw in the operation of a college or a university is, invariably, poor communication. One would think that an academic community staffed with Ph.D.s, most of whom must earn their livelihood by communication with students and peers, would be the one organization in America where communication is not a problem. In fact, intramural communication is probably more of a problem at University X or College Y than it is at General Motors. There seem to be at least two obvious reasons for this paradox: (a) universities and colleges have perfected that American genius for compartmentalization of work, a compartmentalization enhanced by the myriad of disparate academic disciplines that flourish in academia; (b) academic managers have developed a reluctance to be plain and specific in articulating directions or guidelines for action, for no academic manager wishes to be accused of nit-picking. To state the obvious in an academic community is bad form; one must never appear to be talking down to one's colleagues. There is a third possible reason—namely, that in the experience of the authors, professors almost never read directions.

Thus, the dean, who, above all else, must communicate effectively with department chairpersons and faculty members, is faced with a challenge of significant proportion. How can the dean overcome the casual, thoughtless, sometimes even mindless methods of intramural communication so prevalent in America's universities and colleges? By hard work, careful attention to detail, and acceptance of the general premise—based on the authors' years of observation—that people in academic life are not accustomed to accepting advice or following directions. With this general premise in mind, let us review in some detail the mechanics of the obvious methods used by deans in communicating with their department chairpersons.

The most effective, least ambiguous method of communication is writing. If the dean is careful in phrasing the written message directed to the department chairpersons, the possibility of misunderstanding is reduced to almost zero. But the key to written communication is clarity, and even written messages can be ineffective if ambiguity creeps into letters or memoranda. And ambiguity is most likely to insinuate itself into the message if it contains bad news. Only psychopaths like to purvey bad news, and consequently a fairly normal dean has almost always a tendency to find a way to ameliorate the impact of bad news. Bad news can take many forms: a budget shortfall that results in a rescission or a freeze, a messy and embarrassing personnel problem, a less-than-anticipated salary raise, a reprimand for failure to perform an assigned task. The list, unfortunately, is endless. But the more the dean temporizes the language conveying the bad news, the more likely it is to be misunderstood, either unconsciously or willfully, by its recipient. Thus, the best thing the dean can do is to introduce the subject briefly by expressing regrets for having to do so ("Dear Ed: I regret to tell you that I find your handling of the recent appointment of Professor Strangelove unsatisfactory") and then enumerate as crisply as possible the reasons for the dissatisfaction ("1. You took the letters of recommendation at face value. 2. You did not conduct a telephone check with Strangelove's former employer. 3. You failed to meet with and consult the persons on the departmental appointments committee who were opposed to the selection of Strangelove. 4. You failed to take into account the unfavorable reviews in two journals of Strangelove's latest work"). End with an invitation to the department chairperson to discuss the matter personally ("Please make an appointment with me to discuss this matter. You and I need to find a way to extricate the college from this situation''). In the final analysis, there is no way to get around bad news. It has to be communicated plainly and without rancor or petulance. If bad news is to be directed toward one chairperson and is to be communicated in written form, it should always be sent in the form of a letter, not a memorandum. A letter is a direct, personal form of written communication; a memorandum is impersonal. There is no place for ''Dear Ed'' in the format of a memorandum, and in a certain sense, a memorandum is easier to brush aside than a letter. Indeed, we recommend that in one-to-one written communication, the dean should always write letters. In advising two or more people, however, memoranda may be written. Sometimes a letter to two people is appropriate (''Dear Ed and Sarah''), but writing one letter to three or more people becomes quite awkward.

The dean's memoranda generally address such tasks as information on recent developments in the college or university, or contain requests for information or action from department chairpersons. There are two cardinal rules for writing decanal memoranda. First, always mention the deadline date for submission of requested data or implementation of requested action at least twice in the memorandum, the first time in the subject of the memorandum (''SUBJECT: Board of Regents Program Review Reports, Due April 26, 1986'') and the second time underlined at the end of the memorandum (''Please remember that these reports are due in my office on April 26, 1986''). Even so, the dean will be lucky to get 95 percent compliance with the announced deadline; some people just cannot make deadlines. But the fact that the deadline has been mentioned twice in the memorandum gives the dean extraordinary leverage in whatever subsequent negotiations have to be made with the recalcitrant department chairperson. Second, if at all possible, memoranda should be made brief and interesting, although brevity may be easier to attain than interest. Some subjects of decanal memoranda are simply inherently dull—and their dullness leads to inattention on the part of their recipients. Sometimes the only way to enliven such memoranda is by giving the announcement of the subject a little twist (''SUBJECT: Faculty Parking in the Anderson Hall Lot, Chapter XXXIV'').

A situation that prompted a memorandum with an interesting subject heading arose back in the turbulent late sixties when students tried sporadically to destroy universities and colleges in order to save them. It was faddish for students to bring dogs on campus and either tether them outside classrooms or try to take them into classrooms. This practice led to certain hygienic problems, and one dean we know was directed by the central administration to issue a memorandum exhorting his faculty to help rid the campus of dogs. His memorandum began with the words "SUBJECT: Running Dogs."

There are times when meetings with department chairpersons are more useful and productive than letter writing or memo writing. Meetings are sometimes useful for simply passing on information, but no dean should fall into the habit of using them as a primary method of information distribution; most chairpersons resent meetings at which they are told things they could have learned by reading memoranda. Meetings between deans and department chairpersons should generally be consultative in nature. They are usually held to discuss options in implementing policy, to form policy, to plan for good times or bad times, and, most important, for the dean to receive and to give advice. Each dean will run the meeting according to his or her style, but style aside, no meeting should be held without an agenda. It is always preferable to send out a list of the points to be covered, even for an informal meeting, at least several hours—or, if possible, several days—in advance. A structured meeting always produces more results than an unstructured meeting, and the presence of an agenda gives the meeting, at least at its beginning, some semblance of structure. The very act of listing items to be discussed forces the dean to think about, or at least hope for, certain results. Even with no predetermined result in mind, the preparation of an agenda makes the dean better prepared mentally, with a better chance of performing a leadership role during the course of the meeting.

The greater the attendance, the greater the necessity for preparation and the greater the need for an agenda, for academics are generally intellectually unruly people, often given, particularly in times of stress in their professional lives, to a pursuit of the irrelevant. The smaller the attendance, the less need for structure. If, for example, only four or five chairpersons meet, the dean should prepare an agenda at least for himself or herself, although even here it is probably useful to distribute copies of the agenda to all parties when the meeting convenes. Generally, when one or two chairpersons are involved, it is not necessary to distribute an agenda, but at least the dean should construct a semblance of one in the form of personal notes or have in mind the main points that need to be covered. In one-to-one cases, the better the dean knows the chairperson, the more important it is to be prepared mentally for the meeting, for old friends have a way of slipping off into subjects of mutual interest, gossip, or other generally irrelevant pleasantries.

Some people place a great deal of emphasis upon the site of one-on-one meetings between the dean and the department chairperson. For those who think that site is as important as substance, the generally accepted view goes something like this: a dean should almost always go to the chairperson's office to impart or discuss really bad news, and should always strive to give the chairperson good news in the dean's office. There is some psychological validity to this type of procedure, but it, like any other management technique, can be overdone. Obviously, the dean's presence in the chairperson's office gives, in and of itself, an emphasis to the subject matter being discussed that is absent if the dean and the chairperson are discussing business in the normal environment, which is the dean's office. Visiting the chairperson in his or her office should not be restricted necessarily to times when the dean needs to pass on bad news. It would be unfortunate, indeed, if department staffs became conditioned to expect bad news every time the dean walked into the department office. Occasional visits to the chairperson's office just to chat for a few minutes would demonstrate that the dean is amiable, approachable, and accessible. These visits provide the dean with the opportunity to greet faculty and staff members who happen to be in the department office at the time and have a tendency to promote good morale and friendly feelings toward the dean.

In all meetings, large or small, the dean must strive to avoid ambiguity unless the very nature of the meeting itself demands ambiguity. Meetings between deans and department chairpersons are almost always held for the purpose of reaching agreements on any of a wide variety of topics. If those agreements are reached, it is important for the dean, at the conclusion of the meeting, to state the nature of those agreements as clearly and as plainly as possible. The more complicated the oral summary of the meeting, the greater the chance that exists for multiple interpretations. If agreements are not reached, it is incumbent upon the dean in a summary statement to say clearly that no agreements have been reached. A meeting should not be concluded without a summary statement of what has or has not transpired. If one is not provided, the participants in the meeting will provide their own individual summaries, and all *that* can do is to make the dean's life more complicated. It is therefore important that as soon as possible after the meeting, the dean provide all the participants with a brief written summary of what took place. This summary should take the form of a memorandum.

The most unreliable method of communication between the dean and department chairpersons is the telephone. The telephone should be used to keep in touch with chairpersons in a friendly, personal way ("Just calling to see how things are going, Ed"); to get answers to certain kinds of operational questions ("Who's in charge of the graduate program this month now that Dr. Jetlag has gone to that conference in Tokyo?"); and, most important, to try to ascertain through personal contact *first* if an unsubstantiated horror story about some aspect of the department has any truth to it ("Listen Ed, the people in Finance and Accounting tell me that it looks like Professor Flintlock has been illegally charging the freshmen a breakage fee for lab materials. This can't be right, can it, Ed?"). Deans should never write chairpersons about such matters without first talking personally to them. If the horror story is true and a letter is fired off to the chairperson, the chairperson's natural defense is to write back along these lines: "I have received your letter about Flintlock, and while you have some of the facts right, there are a few things you don't know. I wish you had at least called me before writing that terrible letter about Flintlock." If the horror story is false and the dean fires off a letter to the chairperson, the chairperson has been given enormous leverage in any and all negotiations with the dean for at least two years, no matter how abjectly the dean apologizes. In short, important matters can be discussed on the telephone with a chairperson, but final agreement or resolution of such matters should always be in written form. And the dean should always have the last written word. Always.

Electronic mail has not yet disrupted the fairly serene environment of academic intramural communications. Eventually, of course, it will, and when it does, everyone's life will be made more complicated. Presidents or chancellors will leave messages for vice presidents or vice chancellors, who will leave messages for deans, who will leave messages for department chairpersons, who will leave messages for faculty members, who will, as they have in the past with letters, memoranda, and telephone calls, choose to respond to, respond to after a long time, or ignore these messages. Our only advice to deans at this point in the nascent development of our Orwellian technology is to use electronic mail only as a substitute for the telephone, but never as a substitute for the traditional letter or the important memorandum.

Characteristics of a Good Department Chairperson

The chairperson who is best for a department depends on the place of the department in the matrix of the needs of, and the plans for, all of the departments within the college and on the department's relative importance within the institution's needs and its future plans. Determining the type of chairperson who is best therefore requires a careful examination of the department in question. The department may be nationally recognized, or it may be known as mediocre, even on its own campus; it may be critically important to the mission of the college, or it may be peripheral to the college's mission. No department wants to believe its mission is peripheral, and all professors of knowledge like to believe that their particular subset of knowledge is important not only to their academic institution but to the general welfare of the galaxy; hence, the dean probably should not make too much public noise about the relative importance of the departments under his or her jurisdiction.

Obviously, some departments are more important to the

college's mission than others. In a liberal arts and science college, English and mathematics, the two languages of instruction and research in American universities, have to be strong; if they are not, the whole structure of education in the college and in the university is weakened. If the liberal arts and sciences college is a part of a land-grant university, then chemistry and physics must also be strong, or else the agriculture and engineering colleges will not ultimately flourish. In colleges of engineering, electrical engineering must be strong, for everything now, it seems, is hooked to a computer. In colleges of business, the department of management must be strong in order to attract the best students, even those interested in the rarefied field of econometrics, for in the last analysis, econometrics is a management tool. Ideal chairpersons for the kinds of departments just described are individuals who have good reputations in their respective fields, are aggressive and ambitious for the department, are good managers, can provide the right kind of leadership to achieve the departmental goals within the context of the mission of the university, and—last, but not least—can gain, maintain, or enhance a wide reputation of excellence for the department.

When a department faces a specific problem, the ideal chairperson is one who has whatever special skills are necessary to address that problem. For example, if a mathematics department in a large land-grant institution has been unwittingly allowed to pursue its own internal interests to the detriment of its universitywide service role, the type of chairperson who is best in this situation is one who, through skillful argument and at least a modicum of courage, can bring the department's faculty members back to an understanding of their role as a major service unit to the entire university.

On the other hand, what type of chairperson, for example, is best for a zoology department that is in a medium-sized liberal arts university and is not slated for growth and development as a first-line research department? A few of the younger faculty members would opt for a person of academic stature, someone who might be a member of an organization such as the National Academy of Science, who would try to change the emphasis of the department from whole-organism biology to cellular and molecular biology. Most of the older faculty members who still work in traditional biology would probably prefer a more conservative chairperson, one who is not overly ambitious to change the status quo. The dean moreover would feel more comfortable if the chairperson were an individual who would not aggressively hassle the college for additional money to build up a department that is not high on the institution's and dean's priority list. Let us consider another example. What type of chairperson would be best for a small department of music that must spend one-third of its budget supporting the institution's marching band? Would an individual who is an outstanding music theorist from Juilliard be the best person for this position? Probably not, even if someone with this type of background were willing to accept the position—which is unlikely unless that person's human survival were at stake. The zoology and music departments just described would be better served, at least from the dean's point of view, by chairpersons who are not national figures, who understand the priority position and financial constraints facing their respective departments, who would not create a problem at budget allocation time, and who would be willing and capable of providing leadership to their faculty members within the established priorities of the institution.

Even though the dean might perceive each department at a different priority level in terms of its importance to the mission of the college or institution, chairpersons of low-priority departments must never be treated as second-class citizens, lest they develop feelings of inferiority that might discourage them from being the best advocates they can be. Some chairpersons, by virtue of personality, are less capable of being effective advocates than others. One who does not have the capability of being an aggressive advocate, but who has other desirable characteristics, such as high standards of performance, may be the best type of chairperson for a department that is destined to remain low on the institution's priority list.

The Dean's Role in Selecting Department Chairpersons

Every dean is sooner or later faced with the task of selecting a department chairperson. Indeed, many deans will face this important decision several times during their time in office, for the average national turnover rate of department chairpersons in four-year colleges and universities is from three to six years. As noted earlier, department chairpersons are the most important people in a dean's professional life; hence, the dean will do well to give as much time and effort as possible to their selection and appointment.

How is a chairperson selected for a particular department? At most American institutions of higher learning, the members of the department are involved one way or another in the selection of their chairperson. The standard method for obtaining formal faculty consultation is for the dean to establish a search committee to evaluate the dossiers of all applicants for the position and present a list of candidates from which the dean can select one. Another method frequently used when informal faculty consultation is desired is for the dean to ask members of the department to suggest names of individuals who might be interested in becoming chairperson. The dean selects one from among those suggested. In both preceding situations, the dean, for whatever reasons, may not be satisfied with any of the names presented, and may appoint someone whose name has not been presented either formally or informally. On rare occasions, the dean may appoint a department chairperson without even requesting or receiving any faculty consultation. (This procedure, however rare its use, is not recommended, for it puts a great burden on the person so selected, in terms of his or her relations with the department's faculty.) Two other procedures are also used for selecting chairpersons. One is election by faculty members of the department; the other is the rotation method, in which faculty members take turns being chairperson.

At most medium-to-large-sized institutions, no single standard method must be followed by every department in its search for, and selection of, a chairperson. The method can vary from one department to another, even in the same college within a university. Departments, by themselves or in collaboration with their respective deans, are permitted by some institutions to determine what procedures they wish to follow. The procedures are then included in the departmental regulations and bylaws. Advance approval, of course, must be obtained from their appropriate deans and institutions. If the department or institution has no written rules or regulations for selecting and appointing chairpersons, deans sometimes follow their own procedures. Nor is the department necessarily restricted to the same procedures every time it seeks a new chairperson. It can, with the dean's permission, change procedures from one time to the next. At small institutions, in which departments are not very different from each other, it is not uncommon for a single standard method to be prescribed for all departments. Regardless of which method is used, the dean should keep in close contact with the institution's affirmative-action officer to assure that affirmative-action guidelines are followed before, during, and after the search, selection, and appointment process. These guidelines, as they affect decanal decision making, will be discussed later. The following sections discuss the various methods that are followed in the selection of chairpersons.

APPOINTMENT WITH FORMAL CONSULTATION AND THE USE
OF A SEARCH COMMITTEE

One of the most commonly used methods at many colleges and universities is for the dean to establish a search committee that is assigned the responsibility of reviewing the documents submitted by all applicants and nominees for the position. The search committee is given instructions on how to announce the vacancy, conduct the search within affirmative-action guidelines, evaluate each candidate's documentation, acquire information about the candidate from as many sources as appropriate, and then submit at least two names for the dean's consideration.

Many institutions have bylaws and/or written guidelines for the selection, appointment, and responsibilities of search committees. These may vary somewhat from institution to institution. Regardless of how members are selected for this important committee, it is incumbent upon the dean to give careful instructions to the committee, including a reminder of the mission and goals of the department, the parameters of the position and salary, the institution's and dean's perceptions of the issues and problems with which the new chairperson will be expected to deal, and so forth.*

Most deans can, and sometimes do, reject the recommendation made by the department's search committee, but this does not often happen. A wise dean will know in advance if a candidate objectionable to the dean is going to be presented by the search committee. Thus forewarned, he or she will work diligently within and without the committee to prevent embarassment both to the committee and to the candidate. If dissatisfied, the dean can request the committee to submit one or two more names from the pool of applicants. If none of the candidates is satisfactory, the dean can ask that the time for the search be extended to permit additional individuals to apply or that this search be concluded and another be initiated. If the committee knowingly persists in presenting a candidate objectionable to the dean, the dean must take this action as an early warning that one of two things has gone awry: either the dean has lost credibility with the department or the department needs a major renovation of its value systems in teaching, research, or service, or perhaps all three.

Throughout this whole search process, it is advisable for the dean to spend time with both the departmental faculty at large and with the search committee, explaining the mission of the department, its goals, its weaknesses and strengths, and the way all of these elements fit into the institution's plan for the future. This kind of involvement in the search process, usually a stressful and time-consuming exercise, will help strengthen lines of communication between the faculty and the dean's office and usually help avoid the nomination of an unsuitable candidate. Finally, the dean should not allow the search committee to present only one name. The dean should insist on the presentation of two or more names in almost every circumstance unless, well in advance of the conclusion of the search, the dean, the search committee, and the general departmental faculty are firmly in agreement that there is only one candidate

---

*A detailed description of a model on how to select individuals to be members of a search committee and how to recruit and screen candidates is presented in one of the chapters in Allan Tucker's *Chairing the Academic Department*.

who is just right for the job. It is surprising how often in large departments, particularly those in the sciences and engineering, such consensus occurs; generally, however, the smaller the department, the more intense the internal dissension over the departmental leadership position.

APPOINTMENT WITH INFORMAL FACULTY CONSULTATION

In this scenario, which is quite common in American universities, the dean asks faculty members in the department to suggest names of persons whom they would like considered for the position. Those suggested under this procedure are most often members of the department, but sometimes an outside search is warranted and names of individuals from other institutions may be suggested. The dean reviews the list of those suggested and selects one. On occasion, it may be the case that none on the list meets the dean's criteria in terms of what is best for the department. If the dean has someone better in mind, he or she may discreetly try to influence one or more faculty members to place that person's name on the list. If this is not feasible, the dean's candidate may be appointed regardless.

The procedure of appointment with informal faculty consultation most often occurs at institutions that have no prescribed set of departmental or institutional procedures for selecting a chairperson. If the dean appoints someone who is not on the list, it is usually because conflict has developed among the faculty members, no visible pattern of consensus has arisen, the dean believes that none of the nominees can bring about needed change, or a combination of all these reasons exists. Actually, a dean who appoints someone not on the list does so for the same reasons, and may suffer the same consequences, but perhaps to a lesser degree, as a dean who appoints with no faculty consultation.

APPOINTMENT WITH NO FACULTY CONSULTATION

At some institutions, probably very few, a dean may appoint a chairperson for a particular department without consulting its faculty members. In such cases, the appointee is usually selected from members within the department, but could be someone from another institution. The reasons given by the dean for not consulting with faculty include concerns about a history of strife among faculty members who are never able to agree on anything, the need for a drastic change in the department to bring it in line with existing or revised college and institutional goals, or because dissident faculty members on their own would never agree to the nomination of someone who might be willing or able to change the department.

Faculty members of a department are generally unhappy with this particular procedure, and such a procedure is followed when the dean perceives the department faculty to be sufficiently passive to accept the decision without too much opposition. Deans who make appointments this way are usually authoritarian in their management style, but they are not always correct in how they judge the extent to which faculty members are passive or the effect this type of decision might have on faculty morale. If the dean's judgment is correct, there will probably be little resistance to the appointment. If, however, faculty members are not as passive as the dean perceives them to be, they will create all kinds of problems for the newly appointed chairperson and the dean. Even if the appointed chairperson is competent and could become well liked, he or she may not be given the chance by faculty members who resent not being invited to provide advice in the selection process and do not feel motivated to cooperate or follow the leadership of the appointee. It is the dean's hope that even though opposition and resistance to the appointment may arise initially, over the long run the new chairperson will demonstrate attractive personality traits and effective management styles that will win over the faculty members, who will then work cooperatively with the chairperson. Sometimes this happens, but not always.

ELECTION BY DEPARTMENT FACULTY MEMBERS

In some universities and colleges, a department chairperson is elected. Where this occurs, a detailed set of rules and regulations generally govern the process—rules and regulations that have been developed by the faculty members of the department and approved by the dean. For administrative and legal purposes, however, institutions may require that the dean appoint the elected individual as chairperson. Although the dean has the right to veto the results of the election, he or she very rarely does.

This arrangement works best under the following conditions: The department is of medium to large size, strong, and mature. All of its senior professors are highly respected in their professions and work well together. The department is well funded, either by the institution or grants and contracts, and much of the decision making is done by strong departmental committees. The elected individual is usually someone who has an excellent reputation in the discipline of the department and, as its representative, provides it with local, regional, and national visibility. The term of office is most often three years, but the individual may be elected for additional three-year terms. Although the elected chairperson is expected to provide leadership, the business of the department is often run by an assistant chairperson and/or other well-trained support staff who have spent a number of years as employees in the department. The departmental committees and the support staff provide the department with much of its continuity. But if few or none of these conditions exist, the election method of governing a department works to the department's disadvantage. If, for example, all the senior professors are not highly respected, the election may produce a chairperson who is not highly respected off campus, and the department's reputation both within and without the university will suffer. Unless the support personnel are highly trained, well paid, and dedicated to the welfare of the department, the lack of continuity in the conduct of its business affairs will inevitably hurt the department.

ROTATION AMONG DEPARTMENT FACULTY MEMBERS

In departments using the rotation method, faculty members take turns being chairperson, the term of office typically running two or three years. Most often only senior faculty members are involved in the rotation, but in some smaller colleges and universities virtually all faculty members in the department participate. Where this process takes place, guidelines and regulations have been established for its governance that have been approved by the dean and/or the institution.

The system of rotating chairpersons might work well in small departments that have four to six faculty members. Business is usually conducted, and decisions made, by the entire department acting as a committee of the whole and chaired by the department chairperson. The rotation method in which all faculty members participate does not work well in a large department that has too many faculty members to be able to operate effectively as a single committee of the whole. Moreover, it is unlikely that all members of a large department would have the necessary qualifications to be good department chairs. Under the election system in some large departments, not everyone is given the opportunity to be considered for the chairpersonship. Those not willing to be candidates or those without faculty support are never nominated. This is not truly a rotation system; it more closely approaches an election-by-committee system. Under the rotation system as we define it, every member of the department takes a turn. Schedules are usually drawn up in advance, indicating whose turn it is and when. The rotating chair, perhaps even in the best colleges and universities but most certainly in most other kinds of institutions, often deflates the importance of leadership, turning the position into a kind of thankless and somewhat onerous task, one so uninviting that everyone must be made to share every once in a while so that the misery can be spread around. Also, the rotation concept may put a heavy burden on the dean for providing a sense of continuity in the operating and planning for the department. Thus, except in certain kinds of institutions, the college dean often gets little or no help from rotating chairpersons.

Choices and Options in Selecting Chairpersons

Regardless of whether deans, faculty members, or a combination of both are involved in selecting department chairpersons and regardless of which procedure is followed in making the selection, many candidates will emerge, from which one must be chosen. Some choices will be easier than others, depending on the nature, composition, and bylaws of the department as well as the method used in the search and selection process.

The following are examples of choices that must be considered. Is it better to select someone from the department membership or from another institution? Would a person who is well liked and very popular with the faculty but who possesses no proven managerial skills be a better choice than someone who is less popular but is known to have good administrative skills? Is an appointed candidate more effective than one who is elected? Is it wiser to choose someone with previous administrative experience but no track record as a research scholar than someone with a good record as a research scholar but no previous administrative experience? Will an accomplished researcher and prolific writer make a better chairperson than one who is recognized as an excellent teacher? Would someone with prior experience as a dean or an academic vice president at a four-year college or university be a more effective chairperson than one who has not had administrative experience in a central administration? Should a candidate who does not yet have a full professorship be considered for chairperson? What is the optimum length of time that a chairperson should serve in that office? These questions will be addressed in the following sections.

A CANDIDATE FROM INSIDE VERSUS OUTSIDE THE INSTITUTION

What are the advantages and disadvantages of selecting an inside person to be chairperson rather than searching outside the university? The advantages are clearly on the side of the risk-averse dean. Obviously, the strengths and weaknesses of the inside candidate should be fairly well known to the dean; if they are not, then the aversion of risk cannot be considered a factor, for one can get just as much bad advice about an unknown inside candidate as an unknown outside candidate. Hence, if a chairperson from within the department is to be selected, the dean had better know the possible candidates as thoroughly as it is possible to know them. If, then, the dean knows the inside candidate well when the appointment is made, the advantages are obvious. The inside candidate is going to be more knowledgeable about the department than someone who comes in from outside. It is often very important to know the history of the development of the department, how certain programs within the department came into being, what great or shabby figures have worked in the department, and what, for good or ill, they have left as legacies. Predictably, an inside candidate will operate more efficiently, at least during the first year of his or her tenure as chairperson. Every department in every college in every university has its own peculiarities in the way it does its business, and every institution has a set of procedures that varies from every other institution's. The inside candidate does not have to master this institutional folklore and, as a consequence, can begin work as the department chairperson without a lengthy learning period. Finally, an inside candidate generally lends an air of stability or continuity to the life and work of the department, and stability and continuity are normally of utmost importance. A very strong, well-established, well-respected department, one central to the mission of the college and/or the university, probably needs a sense of continuity more than anything else. Sometimes, at the other end of the spectrum, a young department, with its programs just recently established and its mission finally agreed upon and understood by all, may need a settling-in period to achieve a sense of stability, which an internal appointment can help to provide.

But there are good reasons for going outside to find a departmental chairperson. First, the candidates from inside may not be prepossessing, or if they are, they may not want the job and will not take it. Herein lies another early warning for the dean. If a respected and valuable person in the department will not take the job as department chairperson, even for three years, the chances are high that one of two things has gone wrong: the dean has insufficient credibility with the candidate or some bad trouble is brewing in the department that the dean knows nothing about. Such a set of circumstances literally forces the dean to search outside the department for a chairperson.

A far more likely and common reason for going outside is that both the department faculty and the dean want to bring in new leadership in order to bring new ideas and new insights to the department, bring added prestige to the department by persuading a star or a rising star to become the department's chairperson, or increase the number of faculty positions in the department. This last reason is not usually a compelling one with the faculty, although in recent years many departments have found this to be a way to squeeze the dean. This play can easily be turned aside by the dean's agreeing to provide a new line for an outside chairperson if no vacant position exists in the department and, at the same time, announcing his or her intention to withdraw from the department the next vacant line in payment for the new chairperson's line.

Often there are plenty of good people inside a department who could serve quite well as chairperson, but academics thrive on new ideas and new approaches to old problems. Thus, a fresh start not only in the administration of the department but also in the department's relations with the dean are almost always important to the faculty. And new department chairpersons bring more than fresh ideas about program administration; if they are worth their salt, they bring fresh ideas about the intellectual advances of the academic profession that the department represents. Finally, if a college or a university completely abandons the practice of bringing in department chairpersons from outside, it runs the risk of intellectual stagnation.

The risk factor in going outside for a department chairperson is fairly high. It is certainly higher than going outside just to add a senior professor to the department's roster. The prospective professorial appointee's scholarly credentials are easily checked; his or her published work is easily available; and generally the academic grapevine is proficient enough to provide details on any eccentric or aberrant behavior of the candidate. But hard intelligence about a person's managerial skills is not as easy to come by. Many different things can come into play here. It may be easy enough to find out if the candidate is a good manager, but very difficult to find out if he or she is a bad manager, especially if the candidate's departure from his or her current managerial position is something devoutly wished for by the candidate's home institution. Thus, it is important to obtain information about the outside candidate from as many different sources and people as possible, including employers previous to the current one and individuals who are not on the candidate's list of references but who may be familiar with his or her performance in former positions. But above all else in the search for an outside candidate there looms the operation of Murphy's Law: if anything can go wrong, it will. Samples: the good outside candidate is hired and comes aboard, but the new chairperson's spouse hates the institution and forces the chairperson to return, usually at Christmas time, to the old institution. Or, the good outside candidate is hired, but before arrival, financial considerations at either the old or new institution force the candidate to withdraw. Or a nationally respected scholar is hired to be chairperson but, once on campus, proves rather quickly to be an inept—or undedicated—administrator. These are but three operations of Murphy's Law, all which are enough to throw the department into confusion, cause the academic vice president or provost to look askance at the judgment of the dean, and generally create a bleak ambience in the department for at least a year, maybe longer.

But good deans should not be averse to to risk taking. And if everyone in the search process, including the dean, has worked hard, exhaustively checked references, and carefully researched the records of the candidate, the work and the risk are worth it all, for surely the payoff will be a stronger, better department.

POPULAR VERSUS COMPETENT CANDIDATE

Sometimes a dean must decide between the popular choice of the department and one who is not so popular but is known to be competent. Suppose the dean has concluded through scrupulous research that appointing the popular candidate would result in long-term disaster for the department. Should the dean accept the popular will of the department and trade off short-term serenity for long-term disaster or reject the will of the department, select the candidate who may not be popular but is competent, and thus trade off short-term turbulence for long-term growth and development in terms of productivity and quality? How can the dean be sure which is the right decision in such cases? Is the dean's private prediction of long-term disaster really right? Can a popular appointment that presages trouble be turned to advantage, thereby avoiding anticipated trouble?

We would argue that in the hypothetical case being examined here and with the assumption that there are no other variables, the dean should reject the popular will of the department and choose a new chairperson who will give the department the best chance to grow in productivity and quality. But how can the dean know who is best of the choices available? No appointment, as we all know, is foolproof. Of all the resources available to help the dean accomplish the decanal mission, none is more precious or more valuable than the department chairperson. Now is the time for the dean to analyze carefully the specific department for which a chairperson is being selected and to consider all the variables—such as its priority level within the institution, its strengths, viability, and future plans—and use the best possible judgment to make the decision, on the basis of the information available at the time.

APPOINTED VERSUS ELECTED OR ROTATED CANDIDATE

Behavioral differences exist between appointed and elected chairpersons, especially at the beginning of their terms of office. Which is best for a given department depends on many factors. Advantages and disadvantages accompany each type. The advantages of an appointed chairperson are fairly obvious. Naturally, the dean would choose the person most likely to accept the role planned for the department and one whom the dean could trust to transmit messages to the departmental faculty accurately and faithfully. The disadvantage is that possibly the messages coming the other way may not be either fully or accurately reported, although this should be only a minimal risk if good judgment of character was exercised when making the selection.

The election of a chairperson by the faculty has the advantage that it ensures almost everyone concerned that the person so chosen is liked, or at least respected, by the faculty and has their collective trust. The dean can also be assured that whatever messages come from the faculty through the chairperson to the dean generally carry considerable weight and are accurate readings of the department. Furthermore, as noted earlier, the popular election generally presages at least short-term serenity, for it is very difficult for the departmental faculty under such an arrangement to march on the dean's office to complain about departmental leadership. The responsibility of making hard decisions affecting faculty members may be difficult for the newly elected chairperson at least in the beginning, and even after the first couple of years the difficulty may not go away. As in every kind of politics, logic ultimately ceases to prevail, and after two or three years, the elective process is forgotten by the faculty and the chairperson chosen under that process is as much at risk as one appointed by the dean.

RESEARCH SCHOLAR VERSUS EXPERIENCED ADMINISTRATOR

The criteria for selecting a new chairperson usually include the requirement that the applicant have a good research and publishing record as well as administrative experience. It is often the case, however, that those who have acquired a reputation for being good at administration have done so at the expense of conducting research and publishing. Good administrators who have good track records as researchers probably conducted most of their research prior to entering administration. Many academic administrators claim that they lack time to engage in scholarly activities, that all or most of their professional time is taken up with administrative duties. The problem is that there are few chairpersons and even fewer deans sufficiently committed to research to deliberately take time from their busy administrative schedules to engage in or supervise a research project. One wonders sometimes about the sincerity of administrators who keep saying that they wish they had more time to do research—but never do any. These individuals have really chosen administration over research, and the talk about their strong personal desire for involvement in research is either wishful thinking or uttered for faculty consumption. The truth of the matter is that it is indeed difficult to find time to do a good job both in administration and in research, but few academic administrators are willing to admit openly that they have opted for the administrative route and have, for all practical purposes, disengaged themselves from research activities, even though the yearning may still be there.

Faculty members who expect to find someone to chair their department who will be a good manager and at the same time maintain a heavy research schedule are deluding themselves unless the department can afford an excellent, well-financed support staff to perform most of the routine administrative chores that usually fall to the chairperson. If both administrative experience and a good research record are prerequisites for the job, the faculty may have to settle for a research record that is no longer current, but was achieved sometime earlier in the candidate's career. This type of individual will at least have an appreciation for what is involved in helping faculty members conduct research. If the choice is limited to one or the other of two candidates, there may be less risk in choosing a person with the right kind of administrative experience who has no research record over one with a good research record but without previous administrative experience. Persons currently involved in heavy research schedules who decide to become candidates for a department chair may have to curtail many of their personal research activities if they are appointed to the position. Therefore, before making a selection, the dean should find out whether these candidates realize this possibility and the extent to which they are willing to make an advance commitment to administration.

EXCELLENT RESEARCHER VERSUS EXCELLENT TEACHER

In searching for a new department chairperson, whether from within the department or from another institution, if none of the candidates being considered has had prior administrative experience, more weight is often given to the candidate's research and scholarly record than to the teaching record. Many faculty members believe that a great scholar is better qualified to be chairperson than one who is not. Experience has shown that a great researcher and scholar who happens not to be a good teacher does not always make a great manager; in fact, very few great scholars even think briefly about becoming academic managers. The very qualities that generally are found in great scholars—introversion, intense concentration upon a single aspect of a single topic, jealous, almost selfish protection of their time—are not the usual hallmarks of a good academic manager. A great teacher has a generally better chance of becoming a good academic manager, because the qualities of good teaching—empathy, enthusiasm, good organizational skills, rapport with colleagues and students, a public presence, and a willingness to work hard at repetitive tasks—generally are the same qualities that one finds in good department chairpersons and good deans. The ideal candidate would be one who is both an outstanding teacher and an outstanding scholar. Not many candidates have both sets of qualifications. Unfortunately some have neither.

FORMER DEAN OR ACADEMIC VICE PRESIDENT VERSUS A CANDIDATE WITHOUT SUCH PRIOR EXPERIENCE

More frequently now than before, an individual who has had prior experience as a dean or an academic vice president of a small college or university may apply for the position of department chairperson at a larger institution. Such a vita is impressive in terms of administrative experience. Faculty members think that a candidate with this background will certainly know how to deal with deans and how to be effective in obtaining maximum resources for the department. In some cases, this is true. Sometimes, however, a chairperson who has been a dean or an academic vice president is detrimental to the department. Former deans and academic vice presidents tend to have a more global philosophy about the institution than candidates who have not held a deanship or been in the central administration. They can understand why deans make certain decisions. This understanding and empathy may make them less aggressive advocates for their own departments. If an aggressive advocate is wanted as a department chairperson, someone who has prior experience as a dean or central administrator may not be the best choice.

CANDIDATE WHO IS A FULL PROFESSOR VERSUS ONE WHO IS NOT

The professorial rank and tenure of a chairperson constitute a characteristic that generally affects how departmental business is conducted. A member of a department who is appointed its chairperson before achieving full professorship will usually not have time after the appointment to perform the scholarly tasks necessary to meet the institution's criteria for promotion. Unless there is a record of scholarly achievement prior to the appointment, the members of the departmental promotion committee will vote negatively. They seldom recommend promotion to anyone just for being a good chairperson. Chairpersons who are not familiar with this problem will certainly learn about it at promotion time. They will also learn that certain members will vote against a chairperson who has made a departmental decision that might have had a detrimental effect on them. Being apprehensive about this possibility may deter a chairperson who is still working toward promotion from making important and difficult departmental decisions. Another problem may develop for the department chairperson whose academic rank is lower than that of some of his or her faculty colleagues. The chairperson may be overly permissive in giving them assignments and evaluating their performance, and conversely, faculty members who are full professors may resent following the lead of a chairperson whose professional rank is lower than theirs. Except for unusual circumstances, individuals who are not professors should not be asked to take the position of chairperson. Nevertheless, faculty members of a department who are not professors do sometimes become chairperson of their respective departments. When this occurs, the dean should do as much as possible to prevent the individual from being professionally penalized for sacrificing two to five years of personal academic opportunity for the administrative good of the institution. But whatever the case, it is not advisable for an institution, be it large or small, public or private, to appoint a nontenured person to an academic administrative position.

If the decision is made to go off campus to find a new chairperson, it is quite likely that the candidate will probably want a commitment from the university that tenure as a full professor will be granted before he or she assumes the chairpersonship, or at least within one year from the beginning date. If the dean is seriously considering finding a good candidate from off campus and this intent is agreeable to the department concerned, the dean must be prepared to find a way to give the recruit instant tenure as a professor or something close to it.

SHORT-TERM VERSUS LONG-TERM APPOINTMENTS

After all the decisions about procedures for selecting a department chairperson have been made, after the inside versus the outside questions have been resolved, and the dean is about to make the appointment, the next set of considerations involve the length of time the new chairperson will serve in that office. In some departments, chairpersons are appointed for an unspecified period of time with the understanding that they will remain in the position as long as their performance is considered satisfactory and will be asked to step down when this is no longer the case. At many institutions the length of time of a chairperson's appointment may vary from department to department or from time to time in the same department, ranging from two to five years with or without renewal possibilities. Many smaller institutions have a standard period of appointment for all departments. What is the optimum length of time that the chairperson should serve? Should it be for life? For one term? For two terms? If so, how long should a term be? What are the boundary conditions a dean must consider in setting a chairperson's term of office?

In general, department chairpersons, once almost universally called department heads, no longer serve in their chairs for fifteen to twenty years. To be sure, there are some of these durable figures left here and there around the country, mostly in colleges of agriculture or engineering, but by and large, the average tenure for a department chairperson is from three to six years. The reasons for this are fairly obvious: the startling increase in the indicia of bureaucracy—reports of every kind on every subject and audits of every kind on every activity imaginable—have made the chairperson's job less and less attractive to academicians, almost all of whom choose an academic career to escape the mind-numbing drudgery of bureaucracy that is part of middle management in almost any enterprise in America today. This is also why it is increasingly difficult to find good deans. But, as long as there are academic departments, there will have to be department chairpersons, and their terms of office will have to be dealt with.

Term appointments of department chairpersons may create complications and problems under certain circumstances and yet, under different circumstances, may be the saving grace of a department. If, for example, the dean has decided to recruit a department chairperson from outside the university or college, the recruitment process is immediately complicated by a term appointment. In addition to wanting assurance of receiving tenure as a full professor, as described in the previous section, the recruit will want to know the length of the term of appointment; he or she will in all likelihood want to negotiate over the length of the term; he or she will want to know if the term of appointment is renewable, and if so, renewable once, twice, or more than twice. If resources are available, the university may find it advisable, for the sake of the department, to offer a term of appointment that is renewable at least once with an initial term of somewhere between three and five years and a renewal term of the same length. Generally speaking, somewhere between six and ten years is the optimum tenure of office for a department chairperson. In most cases, it takes at least five years for a chairperson to make a positive impact on the life of an academic department; new people must be hired, new programs started or old ones improved and changed, and new budgets established after the usual wars of attrition are waged against the dean or with the dean against the central administration.

Lack of continuity can become a problem as a consequence of certain types of term appointments. Some sense of continuity or stability in the life of an academic department is a real necessity. Academic life, even in fast-changing disciplines like engineering, requires a degree of intellectual serenity, a chance for contemplation, an opportunity for the development and growth of new ideas in both teaching and research. If a policy of term appointments for departmental chairpersons permits only short-term nonrenewable appointments, the natural growth and development of the intellectual life of the department may be disrupted. As stated earlier in the chapter, the potential problems and conditions of success here are similar to those for departments that follow the election or rotation method in selecting chairpersons. Again, as mentioned in these earlier descriptions, only in the best departments in the best universities and colleges in the nation can a department survive constantly revolving change in department chairpersons. The characteristics of these truly great departments are that the senior professors are, without exception, distinguished in their fields of intellectual endeavor and the staff support for the departmental chairperson is richly supported by the university or college with longtime senior staff administrators, a plethora of secretaries and fiscal assistants, and an expensive computer support system. In such cases, short nonrenewable term appointments of department chairpersons will work, because here the departmental chair is reduced to a clerkship with ceremonial overtones, and the intellectual leadership of the department rests safely in the hands and minds of a peerless senior professoriate. But in all other cases, short nonrenewable term appointments are dangerous to the health of the department.

The obvious compromise between the revolving department chair and the generation-long dinosaur of a department chairperson is the term appointment that is renewable once or twice for a maximum of about nine or ten years' duration for a chairperson. The dinosaur chairperson is to be avoided if at all possible, and if a dean is newly appointed, one of the first and most difficult decanal tasks is to remove this ancient mariner and whatever others are in office before they cast a spell over the judgment of the dean. Twenty-year chairpersons, unless they are fantastically imaginative and vigorous, cannot be good for the growth and development of a department. In twenty years, such people generally have been able to build a protective cocoon of loyalists whom the chairperson hired, tenured, and promoted years ago. Twenty years as the chairperson will in all likelihood have given the incumbent plenty of university-wide visibility; such a chairperson has seen presidents, vice presidents, and deans come and go, and has gotten a sense of both immortality and infallibility. Such people are bound to be dangerous, or if not dangerous, they are silent and hidden anchors that tug against the movement of the department, the college, and sometimes even the university.

But with the renewable term appointments such hazards are removed. The best policy is one that gives the dean the ultimate amount of flexibility in the matter of appointments of department chairpersons. Such a policy might designate the term of appointment as three years and allow department chairpersons to be eligible for two renewable terms of appointment rather than just one. In this way, the dean can take full advantage of the leadership of an excellent chairperson and, if necessary, send back to the faculty after one term of office a chairperson whose leadership was acceptable but not extraordinary.

All terms of appointment must be at the pleasure of the dean; if an appointment of a chairperson turns out to be a disaster, the appointment should be terminated as quickly as practicable. In such cases, it is better done immediately with the appointment of an acting chairperson and the initiation of the long search for a successor. Searches are painful and full of risk, but failure to remove a bad chairperson quickly is even more painful and more risky. Renewable term appointments give the dean the chance constantly to renew the intellectual life of the department, build strength in the faculty, and make the college a generally more vigorous and exciting place in which to live and work.

Affirmative Action Considerations

While the dean must consider a whole range of options about how to choose a chairperson—if, indeed, the dean exercises the prerogative of choosing—these options must take into account the whole matter of affirmative action. The underrepresentation of minorities and women on the faculties and administrative staffs of American universities and colleges is a reality; it is not a hypothesis that is given form and substance by federal regulation. It is a fact of the dean's life, an aspect of the recruitment and appointment of chairpersons and faculty members that must be dealt with daily, weekly, monthly, and annually. Everyone cries out for progress: the federal government, state legislatures, boards of trustees and regents, various organizations (both local and national, both on campus and off campus), vice presidents of academic affairs, provosts, chancellors, presidents, and the faculty themselves. Yet another indestructible reality, another fact that simply will not go away, is the astonishingly small pool of minorities to draw from when looking for a department chairperson in almost every discipline. This small pool is a reflection of a very small national pool of minorities who have the standard credentials necessary for employment as faculty members. We are all familiar with the basic configuration of the problem: that pool gets progressively smaller as one moves from education to the social sciences to the humanities, grows slightly larger in fine arts, but almost vanishes as one calculates the numbers in the physical and life sciences, in law, and in medicine. In the case of women, the problem is not as difficult. Unlike the minority pool, the pool of women who can be employed on the nation's university and college faculties has begun to increase at an encouraging rate.

But there is no immediate solution at hand for the dean who is searching for a department chairperson and who is mindful of the need to employ representatives of various minority groups. The dilemma—pressure to hire minorities from a pool so small that there are simply not enough minority candidates for most universities and colleges to hire—will not go away in this generation. The enlargement of the national pool can only be effected by vigorous recruitment into the nation's graduate and professional schools of the best minds among the country's minorities, an expensive but worthwhile enterprise that takes time, more time than most either realize or are willing to recognize. Thus, the dean must recognize the fact that the recruitment of minorities—and to a lesser extent, of women—is extremely difficult, but must not abandon either hope or effort.

What, then, can the dean do? The search committees for departmental chairpersons must make every effort to place representatives of minority groups and women on both the long and short lists of candidates for departmental chairperson. The dean must be active in encouraging search committees to find suitable candidates from minority groups and to find women who can be considered. It is true that often these efforts are no more than elaborate games. If there is a general belief that such games are played, the sensibilities of both the search committee and the dean may be blunted to the presence of a truly viable candidate who is either a woman or a representative of a particular minority group.

The best way to prevent game playing is to include women and minority persons on all search committees. One criterion generally followed in establishing a search committee is that all members, including women and individuals from minorities, should have some familiarity with the discipline of the department for which a chairperson is being sought or some familiarity with the administrative environment in which the department is located. As has been mentioned, some disciplines have very small pools of women or minority members trained in that discipline, and it may be difficult to find one who meets the familiarity criterion. In such circumstances, it is still better to have at least one woman and one minority member from the faculty or administration of the institution—or perhaps from another institution—than not to have them represented on the committee at all. Even without specific training in the discipline, their presence is useful in raising the level of commitment to search vigorously for a member of the protected classes who will compete for an opening for the chairpersonship. Such members may also be able to provide new suggestions and ideas on where to look for qualified candidates from minority groups.

And if the composition of the search committee is elective and if no woman or minority member is elected, then the dean must appoint such a person to the committee. This is one of the times when the dean must be imperial and take direct and decisive action. And should the search committee discover a viable candidate who is either a woman or a representative of a minority group, the dean, in analyzing that candidate's potential, should be willing to take a higher degree of risk than normal in deciding upon the appointment. Every appointment made by a dean involves risk; just as there is no such thing as a free lunch, there is no such thing as a safe appointment. No dean should throw caution to the wind simply because among the viable candidates for the position of chairperson there exists a woman or a minority group member. But no dean should think that risk is found only in the appointment of women or minorities. *Any* human being is a risk.

Questions

The questions below intended to help deans analyze the situation at their respective institutions with regard to the selection and appointment of department chairpersons.

1. To what extent is the dean involved in the search, selection, and appointment of department chairpersons at your institution?
2. To what extent are faculty members consulted formally or informally? Or are they not consulted at all?

3. To what extent do departments at your institution have election or rotation systems for department chairperson? Do these systems seem to be satisfactory for those departments that follow them?

4. How frequently do departments search off campus for chairpersons?

5. At your institution, how long is the period of appointment for a chairperson? Two years? Three years? Indefinitely? Are terms renewable?

6. What weaknesses exist at your institution in the system for selecting and appointing chairpersons?

7. What systems, in your opinion, would be best for your institution?

6

Performance and Evaluation of Chairpersons Through the Dean's Eyes

The dean always hopes that chairpersons he or she appoints approach the perfection described in chapter 1, a perfection that reflects the utopian university or college and a perfection embodied in the infallible dean described in that chapter. But just as there are no utopian universities or colleges and no infallible deans, so there are no perfect chairpersons. Innocence left the world when Adam left paradise, and deans, like the rest of us, must deal with postlapsarian reality. Hence, the dean needs to watch chairpersons constantly for behavior patterns that are going to cause trouble. During the recruitment period, a dean should watch for warning flags that will help screen candidates. Also, these warning signals must be heeded if they surface among any of the chairpersons the dean has inherited.

Problem Areas in Performance

Generally stated, the major problem areas in the performance of chairpersons as we have observed them are as follows: lack

116

of courage, lack of flexibility, irresponsibility, lack of planning ability, game playing to squeeze the dean, and plain ignorance of effective management techniques. Some of these problem areas are relatively easy to remedy; others are rooted, unfortunately, in human nature itself.

LACK OF COURAGE: FEAR OF TAKING A STAND

Perhaps the most common fault found in any academic administrator, be that person president, vice president, dean, or department chairperson, is the fear of taking a stand, or more simply, lack of courage. This flaw appears to be more prevalent in managers of academia than in managers of industry and business. Perhaps it is due to the fact that academic employees of universities are more intimidating to their administrators than employees of business or industry. Most faculty members invariably believe that they know as much about running the business of the institution as those appointed to do so. Any stand taken by an academic administrator, therefore, has potential for becoming controversial and subject to criticism by faculty members. Academic administrators try to avoid as much controversy as possible and so are sometimes reluctant to take a stand. Although understandable and occasionally necessary for survival, reluctance to take a position on an issue is often detrimental to the progress and development of academic programs and departments.

This type of behavior occurs more often in universities than in business and industry, perhaps because, as noted in chapter 1, the management structure of a university or college is an inversion of the management structure of American business or industrial organizations. At Boeing Aircraft Company, for example, it is assumed that the higher one goes in the management structure, the greater the chances are that one will encounter deep knowledge, wide experience, great wisdom, and impressive intellectual ability. It is a given fact that the president of Boeing knows more about building and selling aircraft than the assembly-line worker. In an academic organization, however, the newest assistant professor has a Ph.D. just like the dean's or the provost's or, in many cases, like the president's. There is as much formal knowledge at the bottom of the organization as there is at the top. As already suggested, it is habitual for assistant professors to believe that they know as much about running a university or college as a president. And it is an article of faith for professors to believe that they know as much about academic management as a president, a dean, or a department chairperson. Generally speaking, this set of beliefs is most fervently held by faculty in the humanities and the social sciences; as the academic discipline becomes more technical and professional, the fervency of those beliefs tends to decrease. But no faculty member is entirely exempt from those beliefs, particularly as they apply to parking, student affairs, and manipulation of the alumni. No wonder, then, that the department chairperson, no matter how filled with certitude and self-confidence, approaches the job of leadership with some degree of hesitancy.

RELUCTANCE TO EVALUATE FACULTY MEMBERS. The evaluation of the faculty performance in the department is at best a difficult undertaking, and the chairperson who lacks nerve is often tempted, particularly when addressing the senior members of the department, to make the evaluation as perfunctory as possible. Yet criteria are at hand for the chairperson to make the evaluation a meaningful and constructive one. Areas that can be evaluated are teaching performance as judged by the faculty member's peers and students; the number and, more important, the quality of publications or creative works; when appropriate, the number, quality, and dollar value of the faculty member's research contracts and grants; and, finally, the quantity and quality of the faculty member's service activities. Any dean interested in the performance of his or her department chairpersons must become immediately alarmed if evaluations of the faculty in a given chairperson's department are generalized, vague, and filled with benign personal references and/or anecdotes. The chairperson's failure to use available criteria to evaluate performance of faculty members in the department is generally an unmistakable clue that the chairperson has a failure of nerve.

The dean has a particularly difficult problem with the chairperson who passes along a bad decision that has been made on tenure or promotion though fully aware that the decision was bad. This can happen in two ways: the departmental tenure and promotion committee can deny tenure or promotion to a person who obviously has earned and deserves one or the other, or the committee can recommend tenure or promotion to an undeserving candidate. The chairperson, afraid to challenge the obviously bad decision of the committee (or the voting members of the faculty), simply passes the decision on to the dean in order to avoid taking a stand. The dean cannot allow this kind of behavior to persist, for it in effect makes the dean the chairperson. Such behavior must be modified, or if it persists, a new chairperson must be appointed.

FAILURE TO ESTABLISH BUDGET PRIORITIES. Another warning signal that indicates a fear of taking a stand can be found in the departmental budget. If the resources given to the chairperson by the dean are spread equitably over all specialty areas or activities, then there are no departmental priorities. And if there are no priorities, there is almost always a failure of nerve. Here the dean must rigorously examine the department's budget and find out why nonpriority or low-priority activities received the same resources as those with high priority. In such a case, something is clearly awry, and generally the answer lies in a department chairperson who cannot or will not take a stand.

FAILURE TO ASSIGN FACULTY WORK LOADS ACCORDING TO INTERESTS AND COMPETENCIES. The same cautionary review must be undertaken by the dean if it appears that the departmental work load has been assigned equitably across all members of the department—or perhaps *mindlessly* is a better word. To be sure, all persons in the department should work equally hard, but the nature and quality of the task assigned to each person should be appropriate to that person's experience, specialty, strengths, and weaknesses. At most universities, junior professors teach more freshman and sophomore courses than do senior professors. Senior professors are not exempt from teaching lower-division students, but their load of freshman and sophomore courses is usually not equal to that of the junior faculty. Occasionally, a junior faculty member should be given a light teaching load so that he or she will be able to finish or start a research or special project—but not all junior faculty members should be given such assignments simply because one of their number was given such relief. Some professors are better at teaching graduates than undergraduates; some are better at teaching large classes than small classes; some are better at research than others; some are better at committee work than others. Although equity is important, what counts more than equity, or at least as much, in the assignments of work loads is what is appropriate to the person receiving the work assignment. This calls for the department chairperson to exercise individual judgment, a function of courage and conviction.

TENDENCY TO BLAME HIGHER AUTHORITIES FOR ONE'S OWN UNPOPULAR DECISIONS. Finally, the dean must beware of repeated instances of poor communication between the faculty members of a particular department and the dean's office. This is almost always a sign that the chairperson has decided to blame higher authority for unpleasant, uncomfortable, or unpopular decisions that the chairperson has made. Fear of taking a stand is a malady most easily remedied by taking a stand but blaming that action on someone else. The familiar expression "The devil made me do it" conveys an attitude common to those with a lack of nerve. The problem is that usually in such situations it is the dean who becomes the devil. The more straightforward course for the chairperson who does not like or agree with a particular measure that the dean believes must be taken is one of two options: argue vigorously with the dean in an attempt to change the dean's mind, and if unsuccessful, carry the dean's measure to the department and defend it as well as possible; or simply resign as chairperson. In either case, honesty demands that the dean's decision be given a fair hearing before the departmental faculty. Simply passing on a decanal decision with no explanation or commentary except as to its stupidity, tyrannical nature, or ignorance is very bad form. No dean can long tolerate such behavior. The dean in turn has to be flexible when confronted with an argument or a set of logic that is clearly unassailable, but that is a subject for entirely separate treatment.

LACK OF FLEXIBILITY

Because of the unfamiliarity of new departmental chairpersons with departmental rules and procedures, one of the most common flaws found among them is a lack of flexibility, but this flaw is not restricted to neophyte chairpersons. Some chairpersons long in service have perfected inflexibility to a very high form of art. Their rigidity in interpreting rules and regulations, for example, is usually generated by ignorance of the rules and regulations that govern a university or college and a consequent fear of challenging, bending, or creatively interpreting them in the name of common sense and logic. Clerks usually follow regulations strictly and literally without exception, but chairpersons are not clerks. Thus, when certain regulations create problems or provide obstacles in the way of resolution, the department chairperson is expected to be sufficiently flexible to make or recommend exceptions. Some chairpersons will arbitrarily quote a nonexisting institutional regulation in order to prevent a faculty person from doing something that might result in a change from the routine activities of the department. The dean's first warning of this sort of behavior usually comes in the form of a puzzled complaint from a faculty member in the new chairperson's department: "I always used to double up my graduate seminar classes and teach one night for three hours instead of two afternoons for an hour and a half. What's this rule about not changing class schedules after the term begins?" Or, "Why can't I teach an overload in the fall term so that I can have more time for my special research project in the spring term?" Sometimes the complaint will come from students who are prevented from substituting a course required for the departmental major or from a staff member who had been denied permission to extend a holiday in return for overtime work in the laboratory or in the accounting office. Department chairs are often concerned about how much power they have and whether they are authorized to make exceptions to rules or to make certain decisions for which there are no rules for guidance. Unless there are specific written rules strictly forbidding a certain action, the chairperson should feel free to use his or her best judgment in making or recommending a decision regarding a requested action or exception and to challenge the written rule if it appears to be too oppressive. Any decision made by the chairperson must take into account the current or potential availability of resources for implementation. Imagination and creativity are desirable attributes in a chairperson, but the creative solution of problems that require additional funding demands a prudent as well as an imaginative chairperson.

The dean must not permit rigid and inflexible behavior on the part of the chairperson to go unchallenged. Any delay in counseling chairpersons who habitually exhibit rigid behavior simply makes such behavior more difficult to modify, and can, if left unattended, finally put the dean in the awkward position of urging the practice of rule bending.

PROFESSIONAL BIAS RIGIDITY. Rigidity in a department chairperson is also generated by a professional bias against parts of one's own discipline. There are those professors of English who regard the term *American literature* as an oxymoron and constantly find ways to denigrate graduate courses in that subdiscipline. The warfare between whole-organism biologists and their colleagues in cellular and molecular biology is well known and has resulted not infrequently in the formation of new departments simply to avoid the sometimes bitter conflict that erupts when the equipment budget is discussed in a faculty meeting of a biology department. Tensions exist in engineering colleges between electrical engineers and civil engineers, between pathologists and gynecologists in medical colleges, between economists and marketing professors in business colleges; indeed, few colleges are without some form of rivalry among the faculty in various disciplines and subdisciplines in their departments. The dean needs to learn about these rivalries and be alert to the rigidity they can engender in some department chairpersons. The key to thwarting overt rigidity on the part of the department chairperson who is driven by professional bias is to make sure that the program priorities within the department are funded appropriately. If, to use an earlier example, the departmental library budget for American literature in the English department reveals a history of continued deprivation and/or if resources allocated for staff support to the division of American literature are curiously depleted over a reasonable period of time, and if American literature has been deemed to be the showcase division of the English department, things are badly out of alignment. The first place to look for an explanation is the department chairperson, and the first prejudices to examine are the chairperson's own. Zealous protection of small pieces of departmental turf, insularity of mind, and intellectual tunnel vision are the very sources of intransigence.

PERSONAL BIAS RIGIDITY. A dark side exists in human nature that most deans at some point must confront: the department chairperson whose biases and rigidities are not born of lack of nerve or ignorance of rules or fear of failure or professional dislikes, but instead are stimulated by plain and simple dislike of certain people in the department. All of us have encountered persons we did not like; most of us have managed to temper that dislike with tolerance or avoidance of the object of our dislike. But a chairperson, like a dean, must have some of the qualities of a saint in order to treat fairly and rationally those persons in a department for whom he or she has a fundamental dislike. If the chairperson cannot temper an active dislike into a passive and controllable emotion, the dean will soon learn about this most unfortunate set of circumstances. A chairperson who acts against one of the departmental faculty members because of personal bias presents the dean with one of the most difficult personnel problems that a dean will ever face. Sometimes the person disliked by the chairperson has earned that dislike through irresponsible or ethically questionable actions. In such cases, the dean's focus must be on the person who has misbehaved. But sometimes the individuals disliked by the chairperson are simply socially inept, naive persons who always seem to make inappropriate, irrelevant, or even bizarre comments when involved in conversations outside of their academic disciplines, even though in matters of their discipline they are usually brilliant and highly productive. Academia is a haven for brilliant and aberrant people; generally these people contribute substantially to the vitality and intellectual worth of the institution where they teach and work. These people often need protection from themselves and sometimes from their chairperson—and occasionally from their dean or even their president. If the chairperson can be made to recognize that aberrant behavior, no matter how gratingly egotistical, is often a hallmark of brilliance and if that behavior in the long run benefits the department's students and/or its research program, then the dean has earned his or her salary for the month or possibly the year. There is no excuse or defense for harmful irresponsibility or questionable ethical behavior or simple-minded actions; not even intellectual brilliance can compensate for these flaws. But if a faculty member is a good teacher and a tireless discoverer of knowledge, then much in the way of nonstandard behavior needs to be tolerated by the chairperson. Tolerance, not dislike, is desirable; the suppression of dislike, however, is necessary. And here, perhaps more than in any other decanal duty, the dean comes closest to being a judge of human behavior.

IRRESPONSIBILITY

One of the most nettlesome aspects of the dean's professional life is the irresponsible department chairperson. The definition of irresponsibility covers a wide range of factors, from forgetfulness and inattention to detail to deliberate avoidance of rules, regulations, and laws that govern the life of the institution. We begin with the minor sins, inability to meet deadlines of all sorts—for reports, data requests, and other bureaucratic indicia. Generally speaking, everyone misses a deadline now and then. Sometimes there are solid reasons for failure to observe a deadline. Sometimes, however, this failure is the result of forgetfulness or even deliberate stalling tactics in order to avoid the revelation of unpleasant news. If this particular shortcoming persists, the dean needs to gain an understanding of the basic reasons for its persistence. Oftentimes, the missing of deadlines is simply the result of an inability to focus on details. The irony here is that academicians are trained in their graduate school experiences to pay attention to detail. Few scholarly reputations have ever been built around inattention to detail. Yet when academics become managers, one of the most common faults of their managerial behavior is inattention to detail. The reason for this seeming contradiction is pretty clear: the scholar can seldom, if ever, be brought to believe that the quarterly fiscal report on equipment expenditure or the request for an updated list of prospective graduate students is as important as the complicated calculations of a laboratory experiment in analytical chemistry or the conflicting evidence presented by two contemporary sources regarding the historical significance of the importation of tanned hides in seventeenth-century England. This particular failing on the part of the chairperson can generally be remedied by persistent counseling by the dean, although sometimes the forwarding of a sharp memorandum from the central administration, whether solicited or unsolicited by the dean, can be very helpful.

LACK OF PLANNING ABILITY

A more basic flaw in department chairpersons that the dean occasionally confronts is an utter lack of planning by the department chairperson. Generally this deficiency is the result of unfamiliarity with the concept of planning itself. Some department chairpersons operate on the belief that their planning is done for them by the dean and the rest of the university. Such people understand the function of planning as it relates to the basic events of their departmental lives—the opening and closing of each term, the dates for commencement, the deadlines for submission of student grades, even the necessity to draw up a budget request for the next year—but the concept of planning for contingencies seems beyond their comprehension. Such chairpersons refuse to acknowledge the necessity for a further plan in the event that the enrollment projections dramatically increase or decrease; the equipment budget is suddenly cut or improved substantially; the salary budget is cut or improved; student demand for courses and programs within the department is quickly and significantly altered; or the star professor in the department is abruptly hired away by another university, industry, or government. Chairpersons of this stripe cannot be made to believe that there is any utility in projecting five years into the future what the department will be doing. This particular failing requires patience, time, and energy on the part of the dean. The department chairperson must essentially go to school to the dean; the dean must conduct private seminars for the chairperson and, then, to reinforce those lessons, meet with the faculty of the department along with the chairperson and conduct more seminars and engage in constructing scenarios for the future. If all else fails, the dean must prevail upon the chairperson to appoint a planning committee for the department and require from the department annual updates of the department's plan for the future. Eventually, a persistent dean will prevail in this regard.

DELAYED SPENDING, A CONSEQUENCE OF FAILURE TO PLAN. An unfortunate consequence of the lack of planning ability or planning consciousness by a department chairperson is the phenomenon of delayed spending. Sometimes a chairperson, either through unwillingness to spend out his or her budget—miserliness or, put more benignly, squirreling—or an inability to understand that planned spending is better than unplanned spending, will delay the allocation of large parts of the departmental budget until various deadlines established by the college confront him or her and the money is spent in one great spate of activity. Money spent swiftly is usually money spent thoughtlessly, and no dean can long afford a department chairperson with habits like these. However, this habit is easily overcome with the aid of computer printouts and ceaseless reminders attached to them by a persistent dean. If these measures fail to produce results within two years, the department needs a new chairperson.

SQUEEZE PLAY

Just about everyone in academic life likes to play games. Professors engage in "what if" games in their classrooms and in their research; case studies, a form of "what if" scenarios, form a major part of the curriculum in some departments and some schools. But some department chairpersons occasionally play a serious game that has as its target the college dean. The game is called the squeeze play, and in its most dangerous form, it can jeopardize students' programs and alter the dean's financial plans for the academic term or the academic year.

SQUEEZING THE DEAN FOR MORE MONEY. In one form, the squeeze play is presented to the dean as follows: just before the opening of the academic term—the timing is exquisitely handled by practiced squeeze-play artists—the dean is notified by the chairperson that the department has run out of money for graduate students and/or adjunct faculty. Scores, even hundreds, of students will be unable to enroll in the courses they need to continue their planned programs. Immediately the pressure is put on the dean, who has visions of sensational headlines in the student newspaper (MATH DEPARTMENT TURNS AWAY 600 STUDENTS), quizzical or acerbic memos from the central administration, and distant rumblings from trustees or state legislators. The true squeeze play is not the result of a department chairperson's inability to plan: indeed, it is just the reverse. It is a deliberate attempt to squeeze more money from the dean in order to build a bigger base for the departmental budget. It is accomplished by passing off inaccurate enrollment projections on any unwary dean or at the last minute changing faculty teaching assignments to other duties so that classes do not have instructors. Sometimes the same effect can be achieved by the last-minute addition of new sections to high-demand courses without sufficient faculty to teach the new sections and still provide instruction for the department's regular program. The dean has three choices: give in to this particular form of extortion for at least one semester in order to avoid unpleasant publicity and criticism; tough it out and simply tell the department chairperson—and the world—that there is no money left in the college to handle this "unprecedented demand"; or, as a last resort, ask the central administration for temporary relief. If the squeeze play is the first in the dean's experience, it is probably safe to ask for emergency aid from the central administration, but the dean who asks for this help should understand that a very large blue chip has just been cashed in, with the result that it will be very difficult to seek help again from the central administration when and if a true, rather than a manufactured, fiscal crisis arises. Moreover, the dean who decides to give in to the extortion should remember the multiplier effect: if one squeeze play can work, why not two or more next term? If the dean decides to tough it out, he or she must make sure, if such a thing is possible, that the students are not penalized by the decision. In any event, no dean should be burned twice by the same hot stove, and the chairperson who has attempted the squeeze play should not be allowed to succeed again. Preventive measures that the dean can employ include improving enrollment projection techniques, seeking moratoriums on last-minute course additions, and utilizing clear, unambiguous procedures in the allocation of departmental budgets. A college policy, or even a policy for one or more particular departments, that gives overriding priority to teaching all courses before any other activity, including research and service, is considered will discourage even the boldest squeeze-play artist.

SQUEEZING THE DEAN FOR AN ADDITIONAL FACULTY POSITION. There are other forms of the squeeze play that are more subtle, variations that can pose very difficult dilemmas for the dean. Consider the following scenario: The Department of Chemistry has been given a new faculty line, and the dean and the department chairperson have agreed that the line will be reserved for an analytical chemist. The search for the great mind or the young phenomenon ensues, and just before its conclusion, the department chairperson reports to the dean that during the course of identifying an excellent analytical chemist, who has been offered and has accepted the job, a truly outstanding organic chemist applied, not fully understanding that the position was reserved for an analytical chemist. The department is very excited about the prospects of securing the organic chemist, and the chairperson, driven by the enthusiasm of the department's faculty, has gone so far as to make a tentative offer of employment. Nothing binding, mind you; the chairperson knows better than to do that, but then again, the department's credibility is really on the line. The department could not refuse to interview the organic chemist when she expressed an interest in joining the department; to refuse an interview request would have been extremely bad form. So the dean is put in a vise.

It does not take too much imagination to see how this game can be played over and over again with endless variations: in the history department, the new position is reserved for an American historian, but in searching for the right person, the department chairperson finds a bright young black woman with a Ph.D. from Stanford in French history. Of course, the American historian has been offered the job, but this person from Stanford would come ("She says she'd rather come here than anywhere else") if the department only had another line. Or, the Department of Electrical Engineering has an opening for an assistant professor, and the search process discovers an associate professor of great promise who has expressed great interest in the department. It will take another $15,000 to make the salary attractive to the rising young star, but, the department chairperson argues, $15,000 is a great investment if the young star will join the department. Or, the chairperson of music has been given $30,000 to find an associate professor to fill a vacant position for which the old salary was $25,000; that is why the line is vacant. The department chairperson has found a superb replacement, but it will take $35,000 to bring in this paragon. Actually, there is no one out there who could be brought in for $30,000, at least no one of whom the dean would be proud—or so says the department chairperson.

As in the case of the enrollment-driven squeeze play, the dean has three choices: (a) find the money in the college budget and hire the unscheduled addition, be he bright organic chemist or be she attractive affirmative-action hire in history, or budding genius in electrical engineering, or promising artist in music; (b) hang tough and say no, although saying no to the affirmative-action opportunity approaches lunacy; (c) go to the central administration for help. In all likelihood, the dean should go to the central administration for help on the affirmative-action hire; indeed, the dean can simply play his or her version of the squeeze play on the central administration, and the odds are that the central administration will be a willing player in this particular game. In the other examples just described, going to the central administration may produce positive results, but a lot will depend upon the program priorities of the institution. If the institution's highest priorities are on the sciences and engineering and if departments in those disciplines are involved, the chances are that the dean will get help, that the help will not be of a grudging kind, and that the central administration will be glad to help. Hanging tough is probably not the correct response, because although these are squeeze plays, they are also opportunities to improve the programs in the departments for which the dean has responsibility. Of course, if the dean has the resources in the college budget to take advantage of these opportunities, he or she should do so. In such cases, the dean looks good; everyone benefits, and the stories all have happy endings. But squeeze plays like these cannot become standard operating procedure. Remember, the dean's first and most important lesson is that there is never enough money.

ACCREDITATION SQUEEZE PLAY. Sometimes a chairperson will come to the dean's office with the bad news that a team from an accrediting agency has just completed its visit to the campus and one or two members of the team are alleged to have hinted that unless the university provides the department with additional equipment, or an additional faculty line, or more space, the program is in danger of losing its accreditation or at least being put on probation. The department chairperson pleads that additional resources should be provided as soon as possible because loss of accreditation for this program could be disastrous to the university, the college, the department, the current faculty, the students, and the alumni. The department chair, hoping to frighten the dean into providing more resources, may be using a passing negative comment of one of the accreditation team members. In some cases, one or two disgruntled faculty members may try to influence their colleagues on the visitation team to criticize the institution for failing to provide the department with the resources needed to meet what they perceive to be minimum accreditation standards, and occasionally such criticisms appear in accreditation reports prepared by members of the visitation team for transmission to the accrediting agency. These reports are often shared with the department chairperson prior to being sent to the agency, which of course gives the chairperson ammunition for squeezing the dean to get additional resources. Academic vice presidents hear these kinds of requests quite often. Deans hear them less frequently and are more likely to be traumatized by them. The first thing a dean should do before taking any action is to check personally with the officials of the accrediting agency or commission to assess the validity of the allegation that accreditation is in danger. The entire membership of the accreditation commission meets annually to review and act on reports from visitation teams. Criticisms by visitation teams that appear overly harsh and unjustified or that are improper and deal with elements outside the jurisdiction of the accrediting agency are often softened, modified, or eliminated from the official commission reports transmitted to the presidents of the institutions concerned. If such is the case, the dean need not act on the request of the department chair. If, however, it turns out that the program truly is in danger of losing its accreditation, the dean must discuss the matter with the academic vice president and decide what steps the institution is willing to take. If the program is important to the university, additional resources might be provided. If it is not important, the program might be allowed to continue indefinitely without accreditation for as long as there is student enrollment. The main point is that the dean should not respond hurriedly to any informal reports about the accreditation review, but should wait until the final and official recommendations arrive from the accrediting agency.

IGNORANCE OF EFFECTIVE MANAGEMENT TECHNIQUES

New department chairpersons often come to their first jobs in academic management without any knowledge whatsoever of simple, effective management techniques. New chairpersons have generally established themselves as good teachers and good scholars. These ingredients of their academic success will help them to become good chairpersons, for good teaching generally presages good interpersonal skills, and good interpersonal skills and good scholarship generally presage strong analytical powers and emphasize, at least theoretically, an ability to give attention to detail. But the dean cannot take for granted that his or her new chairpersons will possess the basic attributes of an effective manager. Those basic attributes are ability to delegate authority and tasks; ability to be discreet; ability to follow through and make sure that a project, once started, is brought to a satisfactory conclusion; and ability to involve the faculty members of the department in decision making.

ABILITY TO DELEGATE. The ability to delegate is essentially the ability to share power, authority, and knowledge. In a collegial ambience, such as an academic department, it is critical that the chairperson delegate authority and work assignments. If the chairperson keeps all authority to himself or herself and tries to do all of the administrative work of the department, representatives of faculty will soon be found in the dean's office firing questions about the department's budget, hiring plans, enrollment plans, and all other vital departmental interests. Sometimes the dean will pick up an early warning at a social event when a faculty member drops a casual question about his or her department's enrollment projection or about the fate of a proposed new departmental program. Of course some people never get the word, as they say, but a casual encounter of this kind should be enough to warn the dean that the new department chairperson may need a seminar in how to be a manager of people.

ABILITY TO BE DISCREET. Department chairpersons must learn the value of discretion. A department, no matter how large, is much like a family. It has its internal quarrels and jealousies, its failures and successes, but all in the department—or almost all—are bound by one common goal: to improve the department by teaching better to better students, conducting better research, and performing better service. And like all families, there are family secrets, most of which revolve around fundamental issues of tenure, promotion, personal problems, and personal successes. The department chairperson needs to share these secrets with the dean, but generally with no one else. If, through the indiscretion of the chairperson, everyone's personal life is an open book, life in the department can become oppressive. Chairpersons also need to remember that they represent the policies of the dean and the college to which their departments belong. A chairperson who is constantly quoted in the student newspaper or local press about policy issues can quickly become a liability to the dean, the college, and even the institution. The dean needs to make sure that his or her chairpersons understand the sometimes delicate balance between First Amendment rights and public relations disasters. Once more, we see the dean as counselor, guide, and mentor.

ABILITY TO FOLLOW THROUGH. Some chairpersons have the ability to delegate authority and to share power and knowledge but cannot follow a project through to a conclusion. It does no good to be able to delegate work if once the task is delegated to someone else, the chairperson forgets about it until too late. Usually, the inability to follow through is rooted in the inability of the chairperson to organize his or her work and to establish priorities and deadlines for those priorities. An early warning signal for the dean is the chairperson's inability to return telephone calls, either to the dean or to the departmental faculty members. While the advent of electronic mail may render this early warning signal obsolete, technology cannot, in the last analysis, overcome the human condition. The best remedy the dean can offer the chairperson who cannot follow through is to take the chairperson's work in hand and organize it—at least for a short, experimental period. If the experiment fails, the dean needs to begin a search for a new chairperson, to develop an inordinate amount of patience and tolerance, or to act as a surrogate chairperson. This last option is clearly not recommended.

ABILITY TO INVOLVE FACULTY MEMBERS IN DECISION MAKING. Whatever other faults the chairperson may have, he or she simply must not fail to involve the faculty members of the department in decision making. The working life of a professor is a very personal thing, perhaps more personally oriented than in most other occupations. Except for the large, multisectioned introductory courses, the professor's courses are almost personal property; the books, the experiments, the assignments are all chosen by him or her; the design of the course and the manner in which it is taught are decided by the professor. The professor is, in short, monarch. The professor generally holds the same status in relation to his or her research work, although some teamwork frequently occurs in the sciences and, to a lesser extent, in the humanities. Nonetheless, the individual faculty member has a very substantial amount of control over how to go about the performance of his or her professional work. Thus, when department chairpersons make decisions about programs, courses, research enterprises, and various service missions of the department, it is critical that the faculty be heavily involved in those decisions. The dean must be sensitive to this important aspect of departmental life, and not put the chairperson in a position where consultation with the faculty is either useless or meaningless. The dean is not only the leader of the college faculty but also an agent of that faculty, and department chairpersons must be given full and unfiltered opportunity to inform the dean of the faculty's needs and aspirations. Thus, just as the dean must encourage chairpersons to consult with him or her, so must the chairperson actively seek the advice of the department's faculty members.

How to Evaluate Department Chairpersons

Now that we have surveyed the possible shortcomings of department chairpersons and suggested various remedial actions to deal with those shortcomings, we must consider how the dean should evaluate chairpersons. In most state universities and colleges, annual evaluations of administrators by their superiors are mandated; many private universities and colleges have also instituted annual evaluation requirements. If an institution does not require annual evaluations of its administrators, it should. Our advice to the dean is that even if that requirement does not exist at his or her institution, the dean should institute annual evaluations of all department chairpersons in the college. They are important for the dean and must be taken with complete seriousness and given careful preparation and analysis. Ideally, an annual evaluation of a department chairperson is a two-step process; first, the dean confers privately with the chairperson being evaluated, a conference that typically lasts at least an hour; and second, the main issues discussed in the conference are summarized by the dean in a letter to the chairperson, a letter that should be sent within a week of the conference. Anything less than this recommended procedure can quickly become perfunctory and routinized into ritual activity that serves no good purpose for either of the participants. The conference itself is, naturally, susceptible to awkwardness, but if both parties view it as a chance to improve whatever needs improvement, the conference can be interesting, even exciting. If the focus of the evaluation conference is on improvement of the department, its programs, its faculty and staff, as well as on the relationships between the dean and the chairperson and the rest of the department, the conference has a very good chance of being successful. However, if the conference's focus is on determining the degree to which the chairperson's salary will be increased for the following year, the chances are not good for an improved department, an improved chairperson, or an improved dean.

There are any number of ways to structure the evaluation conference so that good communication and clear understanding between the dean and the chairperson are achieved. The following outline suggests one way in which all of the major aspects of the work of the chairperson and the life of the department can be discussed and analyzed. Basically, the chairperson is responsible for four aspects of the department's activities: personnel management, program management, fiscal management, and development and long-range planning. The dean should have at hand all necessary data to be able to formulate judgments about the chairperson's management of the personnel in the department. There should be available to the dean a detailed record of all departmental actions regarding tenure, promotion, and salary decisions. The dean needs to determine if the tenure recommendations of the department have been sound. Has the department sent strong recommendations for tenure to the college office or to the college tenure and promotion committee, if there is one? If there is not, a tenure and promotion committee needs to be established to provide the dean with advice and counsel. To be sure, no department chairperson has control over the secret votes of the faculty on tenure matters; but if the voting seems awry, the chairperson has the duty to override the faculty vote, if this is possible under the governance system of that particular institution; or, if a chairperson's override is not possible, then the chairperson's duty is to submit a detailed analysis of why, in the chairperson's judgment, the vote is not sound. Regarding departmental recommendations for promotion, the dean must ask the same questions as those regarding tenure. And finally, if the chairperson has salary allocation responsibilities, the chairperson's salary allocation policy must be reviewed and analyzed. Has the chairperson rewarded good work? Do the salary allocations reflect any evidence of cronyism? Have the women in the department been treated fairly? Obviously, this analysis can afford the dean very good insight into the problems, the failures, and the successes of the departmental faculty members—and the way the chairperson deals with these matters.

Also readily available to the dean are the data on the general health of the department's instruction and research programs. If enrollment in one or more of the department's courses has been increased, the dean needs to know why. Not all the reasons for increased enrollment in particular courses or majors are necessarily good. Conversely, decreasing enrollments need to be analyzed by the dean and the chairperson. The annual production of baccalaureate, masters (if any), and doctoral (if any) degrees must be reviewed and understood. The dean should review the publications of the department in terms of both quantity and quality, with emphasis, quite naturally, on the latter. While no dean is a polymath who can judge quality in all the separate disciplines and subdisciplines in his or her college, every dean can request basic analyses from the chairperson about the quality of the research done in those disciplines and subdisciplines. And most deans can understand those analyses. If a department has a significant service mission, data on that mission should be readily available. Who was served? How many were served? By what means and programs? What have been the reactions of those served? Through all these analyses the dean is afforded another opportunity to learn about the department and the way it is managed.

While it will seem obvious that the fiscal data available to the dean might be the easiest to analyze and understand, it is always important to remember that in the academic enterprise, figures can and do mislead, if not lie. The act of education is resistant to cost analysis. In research particularly, today's failure might well be tomorrow's triumph. Hence, the dean should be especially careful about arriving at judgments when it comes time to sit down with the department chairperson and review the way last year's budget was both allocated and then actually spent. Nonetheless, with these caveats in mind, the dean must determine whether the department was prudent or reckless; whether the money was spent on high or low department priorities; whether, in the last analysis, the money produced what it was designed to help produce. By attentive listening to the chairperson as the department's expenditure patterns are explained, the dean can get yet another kind of education about both the department and its chairperson.

Most chairpersons are not ultimately held responsible for either the long-range planning activity of the department or raising money from private, if not state and federal, sources. These are some of the primary responsibilities of the dean. But the dean alone cannot plan the department's future or raise money from private sources for the department. Both activities must be jointly undertaken, and for them to be successful, constant and clear communications must occur between the dean and the chairperson. Thus, when the dean examines the chairperson's record in planning and in development, the cooperative nature of the two endeavors must be kept constantly in focus. Even so, there are obvious questions that the dean should pursue. Does the department have a long-range plan? Has the department kept to it? If not, why not? Does the plan need revision? What are the obstacles that may prevent the plan from becoming future reality? How effective has the chairperson been in helping to raise money from private sources? Has the chairperson shown the requisite initiative in raising money from the private sector? And, equally important, has the money been raised for the right purposes?

A conference that deals with these four main issues can be highly illuminating to the dean and, on the surface, very successful in the eyes of both the dean and the department chairperson. If appropriate, during the course of the discussion, both the dean and the chairperson can make constructive suggestions on actions that might be taken or new strategies followed by the chairperson to improve his or her leadership and management effectiveness. But unless the dean follows up with a letter to the chairperson summarizing the findings of the conference, within a week if possible, not only is a record of a very important meeting lost to the memories of the participants, but a sense of its importance is also lost, at least to the chairperson. And unless the dean is possessed of total recall, a good deal of what transpired in the conference is lost also. And, equally important, unless the follow-up letter is written, next year's conference is very likely to be less meaningful and more perfunctory. The letter should be as accurate as it is possible to be, and the letter should never contain material that was not discussed in the conference.

In summary, the dean must spend a great deal of time and energy in the care, nourishment, guidance, and instruction of department chairpersons in the college. Since chairpersons are the dean's major constituency, they are more important to him or her than deans of other colleges, vice presidents, or presidents. It is through the department chairpersons that the dean learns the most about the faculty in the college and about the welfare of the students enrolled in the college's programs. Without the support and understanding of the department chairpersons, the dean can, in the final analysis, accomplish very little. But with the support and understanding of those chairpersons, the dean can sometimes move mountains.

FOLLOW-UP LETTERS TO PERFORMANCE
EVALUATION CONFERENCES

In the preceding section, it is suggested that the dean schedule at least one conference a year with each chairperson to discuss the chairperson's performance and that a follow-up letter be sent within one week following the conference to summarize the main points discussed. If a chairperson has performed exceedingly well during the past year, the conference will probably be an enjoyable one, and writing a follow-up letter within one week after the meeting expressing the dean's pleasure and satisfaction with the chairperson's performance will be a relatively easy and pleasant task. On the other hand, if a chairperson's performance has been exceedingly bad, the conference with that chairperson could become quite uncomfortable. Writing a letter to anyone describing shortcomings, errors, and inadequacies in performance is stressful, to say the least, and procrastination can overcome a dean who must write such a letter to a department chairperson. Nevertheless, it must be written; not writing it might create more severe problems in the future. The tone of follow-up letters should match the degree to which the chairperson's performance was either very good or very bad. Extremes in performance are easy to identify, and straightforward letters of praise or criticism can be composed without too much difficulty. Effective letters to chairpersons who perform in a mediocre or average manner, however, are more difficult to write, and the dean must use good judgment in deciding what could be said that might improve the performance and not make it worse.

Following are two examples of letters that a dean might write summarizing a performance evaluation conference. One is to Dr. Margaret Melanesia, chairperson of anthropology, who has performed in an exemplary manner during the past year; the other is to Dr. Steven O. Spanner, chairperson of mechanical engineering, who has performed so badly that his job as chairperson may be in jeopardy if no improvement is shown during the next year.

Dear Margaret:

I write to confirm the substance of our conference of April 22, 1985, concerning your job performance as chairperson of Anthropology during academic year 1984–85. As I told you then, you have provided splendid leadership for the department, and the college is grateful for that leadership. A summary of your service follows.

1. *Program Management:* The programs, both undergraduate and graduate, in the department are strong and nationally recognized, and they provide excellent educational experiences for the college's students.

2. *Personnel Management:* You have recruited very well these past three years. The tenure and promotions recommendations from the department continue to be first-rate.

3. *Fiscal Management:* The fiscal management of the department is sound. You have spent your resources prudently and wisely.

4. *Long-Range Planning and Development:* I think the revisions you have submitted to your department's five-year plan are realistic and sound. I hope we can make them come true.

In summary, I am delighted that you are willing to be the chairperson of the department and that we are going to have the opportunity to work together for another year.

Cordially yours,

Stuart Patience
Dean

Dear Steve:

I write to confirm the substance of our conference of April 24, 1985, concerning your job performance as chairperson of

Mechanical Engineering during academic year 1984–85. As I told you then, while your previous three years as chairperson were quite good, this past year has been, in some respects, disappointing and discouraging. Permit me to comment on various aspects of your performance as follows.

1. *Program Management:* Since your arrival as chairperson, the undergraduate curriculum in the department has been modernized, reorganized for greater efficiency for both students and faculty, and considerably strengthened. Our undergraduates now receive a better education. But we have again failed to send to the board of regents our proposal to implement a Ph.D. in Robotics. We agreed two years ago to get this done by spring 1984, and we are now a year late. That proposal, Steve, must leave this campus no later than November 1, 1985. I will help you meet this deadline in whatever way I can.

2. *Personnel Management:* The three open positions you have had the past three years have been filled with what appear to be excellent young recruits, all from strong schools, all showing good promise. Your handling of John Smith's tenure case last month, however, was not professional, nor did you follow the procedures of this university in terminating nontenured faculty. I am aware that you were personally involved in helping Smith deal with his family's crisis two years ago, but that is no excuse for ignoring university rules and regulations in these matters. We are fortunate that Smith decided to go with Mechotechtron, for if he had wished to do so, he could have generated some difficult legal problems for us. You simply cannot ignore personnel rules; you cannot put this college and this university at risk again.

3. *Fiscal Management:* The fiscal management of the department is sound. You have spent your resources prudently and wisely.

4. *Long-Range Planning and Development:* Although we have had several good discussions in the past two years about the department's future, I have yet to receive a draft of a departmental plan. You have not convened a meeting of your planning committee in more than eighteen months, and several faculty in your department have made a point of noting this lack of action. I simply must have a draft of a departmental plan from you before school starts this fall. My staff and I will

be glad to help you with whatever data requests you make to us.

In summary, this past year has not been a good one for you. I repeat what I told you in our conference. I am ready to help you in whatever way I can. If no improvement is evident by this time next year, you and I will need to consider another way for you to serve this college and the Department of Mechanical Engineering.

Cordially yours,

Stuart Patience
Dean

We hope that not too many chairpersons in the college will be as disappointing as was Dr. Steven O. Spanner to Dean Patience and that most follow-up letters will need to contain only praise and/or suggestions for improvement, with no ultimatums or deadline dates for a demonstration of improved performance.

Both sample letters deal with the four important evaluation areas as described in the preceding section—namely, program management, personnel management, fiscal management, and long-range planning and development. Some deans may prefer to deal with areas of performance in addition to, or other than, those contained in the letters. These examples are included primarily to demonstrate one style of writing candid, straightforward summary letters covering the main points discussed in an evaluation conference. Because of personal style, some deans are less direct in their letter writing than they should be. The important point, however, is that a summary letter be written as soon as possible after the evaluation conference, in whatever style the dean chooses, covering whatever areas the dean selects, and in such a manner that the chairperson has no doubt as to what the dean thinks.

REWARDING GOOD DEPARTMENT CHAIRPERSONS

Chairpersons frequently despair that no one ever tells them whether they are doing a good job. They operate under the assumption that they are performing well unless they hear otherwise from the dean. The lack of sufficient and appropriate commentary from deans to chairpersons about their job performance seems to be a common phenomenon among our institutions of higher learning. And unfortunately, even the assumption that one is doing well unless he or she hears otherwise is not always valid. Some deans may be too shy to praise good achievement or too insecure to criticize unsatisfactory performance. Perhaps even more than administrators at other levels, chairpersons need positive reinforcement from the dean for good achievement. The absence of negative feedback may be enough of a reward for some, but not enough to build self-confidence in relatively new chairpersons who want to know not just that they are doing well, but *how* well they are doing. Whatever can be done tangibly to reward good performance should be done. Rewards can be in several forms, including salary increases and expenses for travel to national meetings if funds are available; personal invitations to special and important functions; nomination to important, powerful, and prestigious institutional committees, such as the university or college budget committee or athletic board; and, nomination to important offices and committees in national professional associations. In addition to whatever tangible rewards may be available, honest and sincere praise as well as recognition should be given to deserving chairpersons as often as possible, in private and/or in front of peers and other members of the academic community whenever opportunities present themselves. Special effort should be made to create opportunities for this purpose. By rewarding effective chairpersons, deans will make them even more effective and set an example for chairpersons to follow in rewarding good performance on the part of faculty members.

DIAGNOSING THE SHORTCOMINGS OF MALFUNCTIONING CHAIRPERSONS

A dean can usually tell when all is not well in one of the academic departments under his or her jurisdiction. The clues are numerous and obvious, but the most reliable warning signal is a gradual increase in the number of faculty members from a department who visit the dean's office. Usually they do not complain openly; sometimes they seek reassurance from the dean that the department is still favored by the dean, that the department's budget is not endangered, or that the plans laid for the department's future development are still in place. Some disgruntled faculty members will complain to the dean about unhappiness with their chairperson's management style. More frequently, however, faculty will first voice their complaints to colleagues outside of their department. The academic grapevine is a marvelous thing, and the dean will quickly learn from outside sources about the distress of the afflicted department. On occasion, the dean may personally observe a problem or issue that was mishandled by the chairperson. But the dean should be wary of overreaction to such an observation or to an unexamined faculty complaint. Overreaction can create a problem where none previously existed, or it might magnify trivial problems into mountainous ones. While a department whose members continually complain is usually one that is unproductive, a department that seems serene may not necessarily be a highly productive department. Faculty members who do not intend or do not have the potential to be productive are not likely to complain about an easygoing chairperson who is not exhorting them to improve their performance. Nonproductive faculty members, however, might complain about a chairperson who keeps insisting on greater faculty effort, and their complaints of alleged tyranny would probably reach the dean. Faculty complaints are symptoms of problems that can emanate from the chairperson or reside with the faculty itself. For whatever reason, the dean is obligated to review and analyze them.

But how should the dean conduct such an analysis and review? In the medical profession, whenever a family or a patient has health problems, doctors do what is known as a differential diagnosis. On the basis of symptoms that can be observed or described, the doctor requires tests to be performed on a variety of possible conditions or maladies that might directly or indirectly be responsible for the symptoms. A separate test is conducted for each suspected malady to determine whether it is present, and if not, it is eliminated as a possible cause. The hope is to rule out as many of the maladies as possible. Those not ruled out are treated.

This process of differential diagnosis may be a model for the dean to follow in examining a chairperson about whom complaints have been made. A review of a composite list of possible shortcomings and inadequacies that might be responsible for a chairperson's malfunctioning may be useful to the dean, first, in determining whether the complaints are justified and, second, in diagnosing the cause of a management problem if one exists. The purpose of such a review is not to attribute a large number of shortcomings to a particular chairperson, but rather to rule out as many as possible so that those remaining can be evaluated and treated. After employing this method of diagnosis, the dean can determine whether counseling might help the chairperson overcome whatever shortcomings are found to be present or whether the situation is sufficiently serious to warrant some other type of remedial action.

In health care, individuals are advised not to wait for symptoms to appear before going to their doctors, but rather to have periodic, preferably annual, physical checkups. No specific maladies are suspected, but tests are conducted on each of a long list of them, with the expectation and hope that none will be found and the patient can be given a clean bill of health. Early detection of an unanticipated malady allows early treatment and provides a better chance for cure.

This medical model can be used in reviewing the management behavior of department chairpersons on an annual basis, even if no shortcomings are apparent. The checkup will either verify that no serious shortcomings are present or perhaps pinpoint a potential shortcoming that can be treated with counseling, thus possibly preventing the occurrence of a problem that might otherwise have emerged.

Directions for Making a Diagnosis

The following diagnostic checklist presents possible shortcomings and inadequacies, one or more of which may cause a department chairperson to perform poorly.

MAKING THE DIAGNOSIS

Beside each shortcoming on the list is a true-false scale for rating the extent to which each shortcoming is perceived to exist in the chairperson being reviewed. By placing an X beside each shortcoming in the appropriate column, and by counting the number of Xs in each of the first five columns, the dean can obtain a general idea about the effectiveness of a chairperson's management style. If X appears too often in column 7, the dean needs more knowledge about the chairperson's behavior and performance, and should obtain it as discreetly as possible by talking informally to faculty members and other appropriate individuals. The list is designed solely for use of the dean and should never be shared with chairpersons.

DIAGNOSTIC CHECKLIST

	TRUE			FALSE			
	True	More true than false	Half true	More false than true	False	Not applicable	Applicable, but don't know
	1	2	3	4	5	6	7
1. Rigid and inflexible in interpreting rules and regulations							
2. Prejudiced or biased for and against certain programs							
3. Prejudiced or biased for and against certain faculty members							
4. Difficult to communicate with							
5. Indiscreet							
6. Lacks courage							
7. Blames higher-ups for unpopular decisions							
8. Does not delegate anything							
9. Always delegates everything							
10. Lazy							
11. Does not follow through on things							
12. Does not submit reports on time or meet deadlines							
13. Does not involve faculty members in decision making							

(Continued)

(Diagnostic checklist continued)

	TRUE			FALSE			
	True	More true than false	Half true	More false than true	False	Not applicable	Applicable, but don't know
	1	2	3	4	5	6	7
14. Uses poor judgment in personnel decisions							
15. Provides poor support documentation for those recommended for tenure and promotion							
16. Has not developed a long-range plan for the department							
17. Does not follow a long-range plan that has been developed							
18. Does not become personally involved in evaluating faculty performance; depends completely on a committee for this function							
19. Does not establish department priorities for expenditure of faculty time and effort							
20. Does not establish department priorities for expenditure of department budget							
21. Poor advocate for the department							
22. Creates conflict among faculty members							
23. Unwilling to take any action without first checking with the dean							
24. Cannot make up his or her mind and changes each decision several times							
25. Afraid to confront faculty members who are violating a college regulation, missing classes, or not living up to their teaching responsibilities							
26. Cultivates close social and professional relationships with higher-level administrators to whom the dean reports and uses the relationships to circumvent the dean							
27. Has played the squeeze game on the dean to extract additional funds for the departmental budget							

(Continued)

(*Diagnostic checklist continued*)

	True	More true than false	Half true	More false than true	False	Not applicable	Applicable, but don't know
	TRUE			**FALSE**			
	1	2	3	4	5	6	7
28. Has played the squeeze game on the dean to extract an additional faculty position for the department							
29. Has funds left in the departmental budget at the end of the fiscal year and spends those funds hurriedly and in an unplanned manner							
30. Does not keep the dean informed on what is going on in the department							
31. Does not personally make a decision; always depends on a departmental committee to make a recommendation that is followed without challenge							
32. Passes departmental problems to the dean for resolution							
33. Unfamiliar with university and college rules and regulations, and because of this, sometimes violates those rules and regulations							
34. Knowingly violates regulations and rules, thus creating problems for the dean							
35. Uses poor judgment in determining for which existing regulations and rules exceptions might be made							
36. Takes pride in never doing paperwork							
37. Asks for more resources from the dean than the dean has to give; is insensitive to the total amount of resources that the dean has available for distribution							
38. Asks the dean to make decisions for which the dean does not have final authority							
39. Makes promises to the dean, faculty, and students that are never kept							

(*Continued*)

(Diagnostic checklist continued)

	True (1)	More true than false (2)	Half true (3)	More false than true (4)	False (5)	Not applicable (6)	Applicable, but don't know (7)
	TRUE			**FALSE**			
40. Does not express an interest in, or does nothing to develop, programs for professional growth of faculty members							
41. Unwilling or unable to give nonacademic support staff clear, precise instructions on what they are expected to do							
42. Seldom available to meet with students							
43. Seldom available to meet with faculty							
44. Spends considerable time traveling off campus and is thus personally unavailable to provide the department with adequate leadership							
45. Spends considerable time on projects not directly related to the management and leadership of the department and is thus unavailable to provide the department with adequate leadership							

Questions

1. Think about the individual whom you consider the best chairperson in your school or college. Review that chairperson's behavior patterns using the diagnostic checklist in this chapter. How does it come out?

2. Think about the individual whom you consider the worst chairperson in your school or college. Review that chairperson's behavior patterns using the diagnostic checklist in this chapter. How does it come out?

3. Select several characteristics from the list that you have observed in one or more of your department chairpersons. What strategies do you personally use in dealing with chairpersons having these characteristics?

7

Dealing with the Faculty

It is a truism in American higher education that its managers—department chairpersons, deans, and academic vice presidents—almost always come from faculty ranks. Presidents and chancellors have sometimes proved the exception, having come from the ranks of lawyers, physicians, professional politicians, or even businessmen. Thus, aside from those who have not come up from the faculty, academic managers generally have quite a close professional relationship with their faculty colleagues. Once a person becomes a dean, how much and in what way can he or she deal directly with the faculty of the college? And how do faculty members deal with their deans? Is there a significant difference between small and large colleges regarding such relationships? These are some of the issues treated in this chapter, a chapter that attempts to give advice on how to form a useful and reasonably happy relationship with the faculty for whom the college dean must provide leadership.

The dean's relationship with the faculty is defined first and foremost by the presence of departmental chairpersons, who in many ways act for the dean. If the dean tries to function as a department chairperson, then obviously there is no need for chairpersons. But even in a very small college with only three departments, it is almost impossible for the dean to do both jobs. Hence, he or she must limit by careful definition the nature of the relationships that can, or should, be developed. Clearly, the dean should not deal with faculty members in general budgetary matters and must be very careful about dealing directly with them in specific budget allocations. The larger the college, the more categorical this imperative becomes. Generally speaking, dealing directly on personnel issues, such as salary, tenure, and promotion, should be avoided, although there may be times when the dean must deal directly with one or more faculty members on these matters.

The dean's relationship with faculty members manifests itself mostly through committee work. The dean must often meet with committees that perform work critical to the life of the college. Such committees are generally policy committees, most of which are advisory in nature, although there are always in motion several special action-oriented task forces or committees designed to treat special projects. Some operationally oriented committees—for example, the college student petitions committee or the college curriculum committee—should be allowed to function with as little interference from the dean as possible. Other committees, however, absolutely demand not only the presence but the active participation of the dean, especially those concerned with the college's long-range planning. Through these kinds of committees the dean has the best chance for fruitful and important direct interaction with the faculty.

There are other, less formal ways to establish direct contact with faculty members, such as hosting informal luncheons or breakfasts during the academic year for small groups to discuss various aspects of the health and welfare of the college and/or the university. The makeup of these groups requires careful attention. Any number of options are available: the groups can be made up of humanists, biological or physical scientists, clinicians, or whatever disciplinary subsets exist in the dean's college. Or the dean can invite to such a meeting the newest group of assistant professors or a group of senior professors. The important thing in constructing the membership of the group is to avoid, unless special circumstances prevail, persons from just one academic department. If, however, it is decided to convene members from only one department, it is important to be sure that the department's chairperson is a guest; otherwise, all sorts of ominous readings can be constructed because of his or her absence. Another example of establishing direct contact is to pay an occasional visit to a faculty member's office or to walk the corridors holding brief informal chats with faculty members. This sort of activity can be dangerous, for conducting business in the hallways with individual faculty members or in the faculty member's office can lead to vast and sometimes very expensive misunderstandings. Most deans and vice presidents shudder when they learn that their president, in an attempt to "get to know the faculty," has taken to touring the corridors once or twice a month. Very little good comes of such public relations efforts on the part of the president. Budgets are upset, priorities are deformed, and levels of expectation surge upward unrealistically.

The Dean's Role in the Recruitment of Faculty

How, then, does the dean get to know faculty, aside from the methods just outlined? The most obvious way is through the process of recruiting new faculty members, whether they are assistant professors or stars brought in at the senior level. We hold that no matter how large and diverse the college, the dean should be personally involved in the recruiting of every new faculty member, from the newest assistant professor to the senior star. In a small college, the dean's involvement in faculty recruiting is almost always high. Yet, in either small or large colleges, deans should never serve on a search committee for a new faculty member, but neither should they accept a search committee's recommendation without personal knowledge of the candidate. This means, of course, that they must personally interview each and every candidate brought to campus. In a large college, this can result in a substantial commitment of time and energy. But perhaps the most important single aspect of the dean's job is the recruitment of the best faculty that the college's resources will allow. After five years—the shortest length of time most deans willingly hold their jobs—a dean in a large college will have been involved in the recruitment of about a hundred faculty members; in a small college, about fifteen to twenty. These are significant numbers, and their magnitude suggests the potential impact that the recruitment process will have on the future strength or weakness of a college.

While the dean should always interview each assistant professor candidate, scrutinize credentials, and, if possible, do some telephone checks, the recruitment of senior faculty members requires far more involvement. Adding a new senior faculty member necessitates a substantial investment of dollars, space, and staff support, even in the least expensive academic disciplines. For these reasons, the dean, along with the chairperson and members of the department seeking to fill the position, must come to a clearly understood agreement about the nature of the appointment before the recruitment process begins. The priorities, plans, and general mission of the university, college, and department must be taken into account. The type of person to be recruited must be settled on. Even the procedures of recruitment may have unusual aspects that must be understood by all concerned. And, as always in these matters, affirmative-action considerations must be carefully planned. Nothing should be allowed to go wrong in this process. The dean should actively help in the search for a senior faculty member by submitting to the search committee names gained from personal knowledge of individuals in the appropriate field or names that have been collected through telephone calls and conferences with graduate deans, people in national professional organizations, or members of the dean's personal network. These names should be submitted in such a way that individuals named do not become "the dean's candidates"; no personal preference for any of the potential candidates should be shown in any way.

When the list is narrowed to those senior faculty members who will be invited to campus, the dean will need to schedule more than one personal interview. Informal breakfasts or luncheons should be scheduled for candidates and members of the appropriate department; evening social events involving the department and its candidates are also necessary. Meetings should be arranged for the candidates with the university's chief academic officer and, if possible, the university's president. Other senior professors in related fields inside and outside the college should be afforded an opportunity to interact with the candidates, and the dean should provide the leadership in planning these agendas. At the end of the process, the chairperson will make the recommendation about who is to be employed. In the final stages of the process, the dean should avoid meeting with the search committee as it prepares its recommendation to the chairperson. But if the dean has taken an active personal role early in the recruitment enterprise, all should go well.

As already noted, all of this activity presents a real challenge; the time and energy spent in these pursuits, although mind-numbing, is nevertheless justified. Not only is time being invested in a top-priority activity, but the dean is learning a great deal about individual members of the faculty, both those already employed and those to be employed. The faculty, in turn, is learning a great deal about the dean.

The Dean's Communication with the Faculty

In an earlier chapter, we discussed the mechanics of the dean's communications, written, verbal, and electronic, with department chairpersons. The generalizations pertaining to those mechanics apply equally to communications with the faculty. But, mechanics aside, there remains the question of the degree to which communication with the faculty is appropriate and the nature of the direct communication. When, why, and under what circumstances should there be direct communication with the faculty?

Whether communicating by memorandum or general assemblies, the dean should always remember the axiom "If it ain't broke, don't fix it." A constant flood of decanal memoranda to the general faculty will invariably produce inattention born of ennui or outright contempt. Not every new development, not every new decanal idea, not every new triumph of decanal policy has to be announced to the general faculty in the form of a memorandum. Conversely, not all alarums and excursions need to be detailed either fearfully or petulantly across the pages of memoranda from the dean. The inevitable result of such ill-conceived practices will be some version of the scrawled graffito discovered next to a hot-air dryer for wet hands in the men's restroom: "Push button for message from the dean.'' The distribution of almost all routine items of information regarding the operational life of the college should be transmitted through department chairpersons. Only really big-ticket items containing either very bad news, such as a budget rescission, or very good news, such as larger-than-expected salary raises, should be the subject of decanal memoranda to the general faculty.

Collegewide meetings of the faculty should also be held to a minimum, even in small colleges. Only the most important business affecting the fundamental aspects of the college's life should bring all faculty members together in a meeting presided over by the dean. There are, of course, those ritual collegewide meetings that no dean and only a few faculty can escape: the beginning-of-the-year meeting and the end-of-the-year meeting, both generally joyful occasions but for different reasons. In presiding over these meetings, the dean, in his or her messages to the faculty, should strive for brevity, but not at the expense of clarity, simply because the attention span of the vast majority of faculty members is considerably less than the standard fifty minutes they expect of their students.

Direct communication with faculty members of one or more specific departments is a different matter. Generally speaking, as has been pointed out many times earlier, most communication with faculty in the college takes place through the various department chairpersons in that college. There are perhaps only two times when a dean needs to communicate and interact directly with faculty members of one or more specific departments. First, there are those events or occasions that come under the category of normal relations. The dean asks, or is asked, to visit with members of the department to discuss plans, to listen to analyses of various operational problems, or to learn more about the department, what it tries to do, what it has accomplished, what it plans to accomplish. Almost always these meetings are conducted with the presence or at least the full knowledge of the chairperson. Many deans encourage this sort of interaction with the faculty and schedule regular visits to each department in their college to learn more about the department and its faculty and to give that faculty a chance to learn more about the dean and the dean's ways of thinking about the department, the college, and/or the university. Second, there are unfortunately those times of crisis when a dean must sit down and deal directly with all of the department's faculty members, or at least the leaders among them. Such crises are almost always brought on by a lazy, incompetent, or sometimes psychotic department chairperson. In such cases, the chairperson has to be bypassed during the period of time pending removal from the chair. Sometimes a chairperson should be removed with lightning swiftness; sometimes an incompetent chairperson has to be tolerated for most of an academic year. But in such times of stress, including the incapacitation or sudden death of a chairperson, the dean must become the surrogate chairperson and deal directly with the faculty on almost all matters until such time as a mutually satisfactory interregnum is established. Nevertheless, once a new chairperson, even on a temporary basis, is in place, the dean should back away and, just as important, should convince the faculty in the department to back away; otherwise, the dean becomes an ex officio chairperson, a status that makes it difficult to convince a new chairperson either to take the position or to stay in it once appointed.

Of course, the best, the most relaxed, and the most interesting relationships are developed in the formal and informal committee structures of the college. The dean can, and should, select faculty members from all over the college to serve on special task forces. Examples of these kinds of relationships are numerous: a special task force of senior professors to review the college's tenure and promotion criteria; a special task force of junior professors to examine ways and means to increase the research support budget of the college; a special task force to upgrade the curriculum in a subset of departments or to raise or lower admission standards in the college. In addition to these special activities, the dean should make sure that he or she is an ex officio member of every standing collegewide committee. It is probably unwise to attend even once a year a meeting of each of these standing committees; in some cases, the committee's work will be done more efficiently if the dean never appears. But the dean has to be an active, if not ever-present, participant in the work of the college's long-range planning committee, its tenure and promotion committees, and, if the college has one, its budget advisory committee. These three committees are pivotal to the college's future.

Thus, there are plenty of ways for the dean to communicate and interact directly with the faculty of the college. It is best, however, to repeat our earlier words of caution: overexposure in the form of too many memoranda or meetings will result in a paling of leadership. And the dean who tries to act for a department chairperson too often has simply added another set of responsibilities to an already complicated job.

Dealing with the Faculty One-On-One

No matter how conscientious the dean may be in making sure that chairpersons are the primary means for interaction with faculty members, there are times when an individual faculty member must be dealt with directly. Life in academe, as everywhere else, is not smooth; disappointment, frustration, rage, envy, tragedy, are just as much a part of the ivory tower as they are a part of Madison Avenue. In fact, nowhere in America are individualism and intellectual entrepreneurship as rampant as in the academy. Thus, the dean must be generally available to discuss, negotiate, and ultimately solve the problems of individual faculty members in the college. Department chairpersons can do only so much in dealing with the ambitions and the frustrations of their faculty; a faculty member who is determined and persistent will eventually be seated in front of the dean pressing his or her case. And if the dean refuses to see such faculty members on the ground that "the buck stops on the department chairperson's desk," they will eventually find their way to the office of the chief academic officer of the university or college or, alas, the office of the president or chancellor.

Almost always these one-on-one meetings are initiated by the faculty member. Indeed, only in special cases should the dean do the initiating. The initiation of such a meeting by the dean automatically raises in the faculty member's mind unrealistic expectations that whatever the problem happens to be, it is going to be solved by some kind of decanal deus ex machina.

Sometimes the dean can indeed solve individual faculty problems; sometimes those problems cannot be solved by anyone—not the dean, not anyone in the central administration. Before any meeting with a faculty member, the dean should always discuss that person's problem, whether real or perceived, with the department chairperson. Let us consider next the kinds of problems presented by individual faculty members as they seek advice, redress, or maybe just reassurance.

Probably the issues that individual faculty members most frequently take up with the dean have to do with tenure, promotion, or salary. Of these, easily the most critical is tenure. In most universities and colleges, tenure is fundamentally a departmental matter. The department is the first and most important body to recommend or deny tenure for a faculty member. To be sure, there are generally a series of checks and balances against this initial decision; colleges usually have their own tenure and promotion committees; the dean generally has the authority to override the decisions of either the departmental or college tenure and promotion committees; and beyond the dean, there is a universitywide tenure and promotion committee, as well as an override authority of the chief academic officer and/or the president or chancellor. In many cases, tenure is not even awarded at the university level; it is finally and in a pro forma, bureaucratic manner awarded by regents or trustees.

Thus, in dealing with tenure issues, the dean must always bear in mind that his or her decision may not be the final one, that the decision is appealable within the institution and possibly by agencies outside the institution, such as the board of trustees or, in very rare instances, a federal court. And if the college or university has a collective bargaining agreement, the dean's decision may well be appealed to an extramural professional arbiter. Most collective bargaining agreements do not, however, allow an arbiter to award tenure; not even federal courts have done this. But both federal courts and arbiters have directed colleges and universities to award back pay or damages or to give the person denied tenure another chance to earn it. Consequently, individual appeals must be handled with the greatest of care, not only in the name of fairness and justice but because the dean's decision likely will be reviewed by a number of other parties and interests. The dean, therefore, should be as fully prepared as possible *before* the faculty member arrives to discuss a tenure denial; rarely does a faculty member want to discuss a tenure approval. Neither a positive nor a negative decision should be made during any meeting with the individual faculty member. The dean should listen carefully for as long as necessary to the faculty member's case. If there is not enough time to listen to the case at the first meeting, it should be continued into a second or third meeting. After the faculty member has had ample time to present his or her case, the dean, *without expressing an opinion of what the decision might ultimately be*, should promise the faculty member a written decision within a very short time. Upon further investigation—which should include personal conferences with not only the department chairperson but key figures in the department—a written decision should be prepared in the form of a personal letter to the faculty member, with copies to a number of appropriate people. The letter should be presented to the faculty member at yet another personal conference. This conference will not be pleasant if the decision is negative, but the conference will indicate the dean's concern about the issues that led to the decision and about the faculty member personally. This conference may result in an argument, at least on the part of the disappointed faculty member, and the dean must be prepared to listen to the argument, yet not get drawn into it. If the faculty member is determined, there will be plenty of opportunities for argument at other times and in other forums.

Those who come to the dean's office to seek decanal intervention in a failed attempt to receive promotion present a far less complicated problem than those who fail to get a recommendation for tenure. Promotion, first of all, is a much more intramural matter than tenure, and while the primary and most important decision rests in the department, the chances of reversal by the central administration are not very high. If the department and the college committee (if there is one) and the dean all agree on a promotion decision, it is difficult to overturn. Most boards of regents or trustees no longer even review faculty promotions. But promotion is a very serious matter, for each promotion in academic rank says a great deal about the standards of the college and sends a message to faculty throughout the college. Here again, the dean must be as fully prepared as possible *before* meeting with the faculty member who wishes to discuss or appeal a promotion decision. And again, an opinion should never be given while meeting with the faculty member. After thorough investigation, a decision should be prepared in writing and presented to the faculty member during a second conference. While this second conference is likely to be unpleasant if the decision is a negative one, negative decisions about promotion do not have the finality that negative tenure decisions possess. A negative decision may well give the dean an opportunity to give very constructive advice to the faculty member about how to improve his or her performance. If the faculty member has good but unrealized potential, hope and encouragement should be held out, but no guarantee. Since disappointed petitioners have a tendency to interpret encouragement as a form of guaranteed action, care should be taken during this conference to stick closely to the contents of the written decision that was presented to this faculty member during the conference.

Finally, there is the sticky matter of salaries. The dean will be approached by a greater number of individual faculty members with salary problems than with problems of tenure or promotion. Salary adjustments are, after all, annual events for each faculty member; tenure and promotion decisions are not. While the college or university has virtually complete control over tenure and promotion criteria and the decisions stemming from those criteria, colleges and universities have little or no control over the amount of money annually available for salary adjustments. Colleges and universities are hostages to the financial health of the endowment, the rise or fall of the state's general revenue receipts, the price of a barrel of oil, the balance or imbalance of trade, and other far more arcane economic indicia. Since faculty members are so firmly in control of the rest of their professional lives and since only a very few of them are trained economists, they exhibit very little patience or understanding regarding the fiscal vagaries that impact their own salaries. But, then, where in America is there a group of salaried professionals who are patient and understanding about such matters? Hence, the dean can expect every spring or fall, depending upon when annual salary adjustments are announced, to have a number of faculty members request personal conferences for the purpose of complaining in one way or another about salaries. Even if each department chairperson in the college is a veritable Solomon, there will be individual unhappiness in the faculty. The presence of a collective bargaining agreement in the college or university will not deter this annual pilgrimage to the dean's office; many, but not all collective bargaining agreements give management the right and authority to assign a portion of each annual salary distribution for merit, market adjustment, or other discretionary purposes. The fact of the matter is that no matter what the institutional arrangement, the dean often has control of some, albeit limited, funds used for salary adjustments, and faculty members driven by a sense of injured merit will seek out the dean.

Yet again we have to insist that the dean be fully prepared for a conference with a faculty member about that person's salary adjustment. Preparation includes careful consultation with the department chairperson and a study of the salary schedule of the department as a whole and of each member of the department. In such discussions, it is important that the dean be confronted with no surprises such as the fact that the complaining faculty member's salary is below that of a colleague whose publication record, teaching evaluations, and service record are demonstrably inferior to the plaintiff's. If such is the case, there has to be a good reason; if there is no good reason, the dean and the department chairperson need to be very limber. And as always, a decision should never be made during the conference with the faculty member. After the customary thorough investigation, a letter should be written to either the department chairperson or the faculty member. If the decision is positive, the letter should be written to the chairperson, based, of course, on the premise that the chairperson agrees with the positive decision; the chairperson should then inform the faculty member of the good news. Only in rare instances should the dean override a chairperson's recommendation on salary; the circumstances have to be unusual—either a clear injustice is evident or the chairperson's recommendation has been based on complicated and subjective grounds, which may mean that a new chairperson is needed. If the decision is negative, the dean should write to the faculty member directly. A second conference with the faculty member may be useful, during which time reasons are given for the negative decision, and as in the case of the denied promotion, an opportunity becomes available to counsel the faculty member and indicate ways in which the person's performance can be improved. The dean should remember, however, that salary adjustments are annual events; like the ebb and flow of the tide, there is an inevitability about them, and discussions held with faculty members about salary adjustments this year will almost surely be revisited next year.

Close on the heels of the problems brought to the dean by individual faculty members concerning tenure, promotion, and salary issues is the problem of a faculty member with his or her chairperson. This should not be surprising; in many cases, the tenure, promotion, and salary issues are linked with real or perceived conflict or tension between faculty members and their chairpersons. The sources of these conflicts and tension are manifold: (a) age or sex differentials (Young Turks versus old guard, militant feminism versus the good old boys); (b) new knowledge versus old knowledge (''What! You really believe we should hire another whole organism biologist instead of that young molecular biologist from Michigan?''); (c) new techniques or technologies versus old techniques or technologies (''You're crazy; we can't teach modern business administration to these kids unless they've had three courses in calculus and two courses in advanced computer information sciences!''); (d) political ideological differences (contrary to popular myth, professors are not objective, as is evident in the intellectual chaos rampant in many philosophy departments throughout America); (e) the clash of personalities, the most difficult of all forms of conflict (''Dean, I can't tell you exactly why I dislike him. All I know is that the guy is an egregious ass'').

There is probably very little that the dean can do to prepare for this sort of conference, particularly if the source of conflict between the chairperson and the faculty member is a personality conflict. Generally, faculty members seeking appointments to discuss the various shortcomings of their department chairpersons are not going to announce the specific subject to be discussed during the conference. Instead, the faculty mem-

ber will tell the dean's secretary that the purpose of the conference is "highly important," "urgent," an "emergency," or
simply state that the matter to be discussed is "personal."
While sometimes these adjectives are accurate and have nothing to do with the faculty member's relationship with the chairperson, generally they are not. Most often, they are code words
used to gain access to a private audience with the dean. Since
one can never tell whether a matter is truly urgent or personal
instead of postponable or conspiratorial, all that can be done is
to tell the secretary to schedule the conference. A wise dean,
one who is quite familiar with the faculty members and the
chairpersons in the college, can sometimes get a little background information by calling the department chairperson and
making inquiries about that person's health, state of mind, or,
if pertinent, most recently thwarted ambition. This should be
done only if the chairperson can be trusted to be discreet.
When in doubt, however, the dean should not call, but just be
braced for the storm and resolve to get through it in the best
possible way. Usually the faculty member wants the dean
either to discipline or to fire the department chairperson.

Most of these conflicts are never fully or satisfactorily resolved, since few chairpersons give up the position because of
a conflict with one faculty member, and few faculty members
leave their positions because they dislike their chairperson;
they just wait for the chairperson to leave, resign, or be promoted to dean. But the dean must act whenever possible. Sex
or age discrimination in the department cannot be permitted;
new knowledge cannot be stifled but must be given a chance
to flourish, just as new techniques and technologies must be
used or at least tested. We are, after all, talking about life in a
college or university. If ideological conflict is adversely affecting the educational experience of the students in the department, that conflict must be stopped or at least ameliorated to
the point where the students are not pawns in professorial
chess games. Sometimes a dean can even resolve a personality
conflict, but not often. The best that can be hoped for is that
the personality conflict between the faculty member and the
chairperson is contained in such a way that neither the rest of
the department's faculty nor its students are adversely affected.

During the conference, the dean should listen carefully to the faculty member, trying all the while to avoid an argument or taking sides. Nine times out of ten, the faculty member will be distraught, and only a practiced, canny old dean is likely to be calm and discreet under such circumstances. In about 50 percent of such cases, the faculty member will end the conference by stating that no immediate action is requested, that the purpose of the conference is simply to inform the dean about the inequities of the chairperson and the parlous consequences of those inequities that are evident in the department. Sometimes, these visits are nothing more than an opportunity for faculty members to discuss their accomplishments with the dean in preparation for imminent decisions relating to promotion or salary adjustments. It is a dumb dean indeed who takes no action at all after such a conference.

The very least that must be done after an appropriate interval is to inform the chairperson that there are some rumors of certain problems in his or her department. Unless it is absolutely necessary for special reasons, the name of the complaining faculty member should not be revealed, at least not after the first conference. If the faculty member persists in presenting complaints, the dean, the chairperson, and the faculty member will simply have to sit together and attempt to resolve whatever issues are capable of resolution. After the dean has informed the chairperson about the possibilities of certain problems in the department, it will be necessary for both to sit down and decide (a) if there are any problems that need resolution, and (b) what kind of resolutions are best and under what circumstances they should be enacted. If there are truly no problems such as the ones described by the faculty member, then the dean can relax. The important thing is not to think ill of the complaining faculty member—not the first time. Everyone is entitled to misperception; no one is omniscient. And there is no real need to have a second conference with the faculty member to announce that there is, after all, no problem. If indeed there is no problem, that will become evident to the faculty member who, in most cases, will eventually get around to writing the dean a note of semi-apology.

But what to do with the faculty member who at the end of the conference requests immediate or swift action against the chairperson to remedy the wrongs that have just been placed in the dean's lap? Except under rare and extreme circumstances, immediate action is not only unwise but probably impossible. The faculty member can be promised that action will be taken *if warranted.* There are always two sides to every academic story; actually most have eleven, and the dean has heard only one side. An investigation must be conducted as discreetly as possible of the various aspects of the faculty member's complaint, beginning with the chairperson and with other individuals if more information is necessary. Generally, however, the dean's first instinct should be to trust the chairperson. If the chairperson is not trustworthy, then one has to wonder why the dean has allowed the chairperson to continue in that position. As noted earlier, real problems demand real solutions, and such solutions must be pursued. But personality conflicts, while real, cannot always be resolved. Sometimes the passage of time mitigates the conflict; sometimes better and deeper knowledge of each other's personality can eradicate the conflict between faculty member and chairperson; sometimes time and greater knowledge just make the conflict worse. In situations like this, the dean must be psychiatrist, priest, and king. These are not easy roles to fulfill in a modern American college or university.

There are other times when the dean becomes, if not the priest, at least a confessor; if not the psychiatrist, at least a counselor; and if not the king, at least a judge. Sometimes faculty members are unwilling to discuss ethical problems, student-related problems, family matters, or business matters with their chairpersons. Sometimes, these discussions with their chairpersons are not satisfactory. A dean should not be distressed by visits from faculty members that deal with such matters, but should instead feel complimented. The faculty member's visit to talk about personal matters indicates a great deal of trust and respect in the dean's discretion and judgment. Not many faculty members will ever make such a visit, for not many get into the sort of personal difficulties that can be discussed with a dean, and even fewer ever think of a dean as a source of comfort and aid. But when such an event occurs, there is every reason to react as positively and generously as possible, even though sometimes the problems presented are difficult and complex.

Consider first the kinds of ethical problems related to a faculty member's professional life that may occasionally be presented to the dean for either advice or solutions. Nowadays, faculty members, particularly in the sciences and engineering, find themselves drawn more and more into situations that can pose conflict-of-interest problems. Faculty members are increasingly becoming business enterpreneurs, owning all or parts of companies that manufacture and/or market products that are the result of the faculty member's own research, carried on—originally, at least—under university or college auspices. More and more faculty members are sought after by both government and private enterprise to act as consultants, often at very high fees. While virtually all universities and colleges have established rules and regulations regarding the conduct of faculty members in these and other related situations, most universities and colleges have not refined and made precise such rules and regulations. The faculty entrepreneurial activity increases; the complexity of the arrangements and the possible variations of arrangements relating to this activity increase, and so does the bewilderment of the faculty and the administration. Sometimes the faculty member will come to the dean not so much to seek advice about the ethical propriety or legality of a given arrangement, but rather to enlist the dean as an ally in either a real or imagined struggle with the central administration over the university's or college's rights in that arrangement.

Again, two cardinal rules must be observed by the dean: (a) prepare, if possible, for the meeting and check with the department chairperson in order to gain as full an understanding of the matter as possible; (b) never make a decision during the conference itself unless the circumstances are so clearly unambiguous and the relevant rules and regulations are so plainly applicable that no further analysis is needed. Seldom in these situations will that be the case. The advice given the faculty member must, of course, be informed and guided by the rules, regulations, and policies of the college or university. The faculty member who seeks purely legal advice should be referred to the university or college legal staff. Only law deans are competent to give legal advice to their own faculty members. In giving advice, every attempt should be made to protect the university, but there is seldom a need to choose between the university and the faculty member in protecting one from another. Common sense, patience, and the awareness on the part of the dean that such matters will become increasingly commonplace are absolutely necessary attributes for rendering a decision or giving advice. Decisions should always be conveyed to the faculty member in writing after the conference, with copies to appropriate individuals. Advice need not be rendered in written form, but should be given to the faculty member during a second conference or at another suitable time and place.

Sometimes the dean is presented by a faculty member with problems involving affairs of the heart—and the rest of the body. Unfortunately, these affairs are seldom related to persons outside the college or university to which the faculty member belongs, but instead deal directly with one of the faculty member's students, a student currently enrolled in one of the faculty member's classes or recently enrolled in one of those classes. While such problems are far from commonplace on a campus, no one should be surprised by the fact that they do indeed exist. Most faculty members are older than most students, and this keeps most of the students and faculty on their respective sides of the desk. But some students and some faculty are drawn to each other for a host of reasons, such as hero or heroine worship, the exercise of power, the mere presence of physical beauty and handsomeness, and, regrettably, plain old lechery. Very seldom does the dean learn about a faculty-student love affair from the faculty member; the dean is much more likely to learn about it from the student, the president's office, the student counseling office, or the student's parents. But if the dean is fortunate enough to learn first about it from the faculty member, then his or her clear duty is to try to discourage its continuance. It is true that faculty members occasionally marry their students, and it is also true that some of these marriages turn out to be astonishingly successful. But most of these affairs are built on quicksand, and the odds are against a lasting faculty-student marriage. Hence, the dean's duty is to play the odds and counsel immediate dissolution of the relationship. Almost always it is the student who must be protected both from personal folly and from the folly of the faculty member.

Generally the dean can use to advantage some rule or regulation of the university or college that either forbids or discourages intimate relationships between faculty and student, a directive that has the force and solemnity of the institution behind it. Of course, faculty lechers are to be punished, not counseled, and the best punishment is firing—if the dean can make the case stand up in any subsequent forum of inquiry. The dean must always remember that every once in a while the college will enroll a student who is either lecherous or scheming or both, and that a professor can be victimized by such students. But in conferences between the dean and the faculty member about such matters, we depart from our advice given throughout this chapter. This is one kind of conference during which an immediate decision must be rendered or instant advice be given. There is no need to check with the department chairperson, no need to render a decision in writing at a subsequent conference. If a faculty member trusts and respects the dean enough to bring such a matter directly to his or her personal attention, there is no room left for delay or temporizing; the dean has to follow instinct and do the best that can be done without delay.

Even rarer in its occurrence is the request by a faculty member for an appointment to discuss "a personal matter" that turns out to be truly personal, such as a death in the family, an impending divorce, or a fiscal crisis. Once again, the dean should not be distressed to be asked for counsel on such matters. The faculty member's request for help is in and of itself a sign of respect and trust. How much can actually be done in such matters depends entirely upon the circumstances of each individual case. Sometimes about all that can be offered is sympathy. At other times, various agencies in the university or the college can be called on to give aid and comfort to the faculty member. The dean should generally exercise whatever power may be available to provide relief, such as granting time off because of a death or suggesting the name of a good lawyer in an impending divorce or the name of a good counselor in the case of fiscal crisis. In the matter of a fiscal crisis, the dean should give advice, if competent to do so, but should never, ever, lend money to a professional colleague. After the conference, and after everything has been done within the bounds of reason and common sense, the faculty member's chairperson should be fully informed as to the nature of the faculty member's distress unless it has been requested that the subject of the conference be kept confidential. Everyone must rally around the faculty member in trouble and try to give him or her all possible support.

Some faculty members who get appointments with the dean for "personal" or "confidential" reasons turn out to be people who have no great personal disaster to discuss, no real issue with a department chairperson, and certainly no desire to receive advice of any kind. These people are in the dean's office for one reason and one reason only: to be told how wonderful they are, how truly important their work is to the college, the university, the nation, the world, even to the galaxy. The truly amazing thing about such people is that they are almost always first-class faculty members with excellent reputations for the work they have done in their field. Generally they are senior professors who are in full stride as they attempt to rise to the top rank in their profession or who have already achieved that rank. One would think that such a man or woman would not need any kind of reassurance from a dean, particularly one who is not even familiar with the field of study in which this kind of faculty member has flourished. Yet, in virtually every college and university there exists at least one or more of these people who have a great need to be loved and appreciated in as many outward ways as possible. They actively campaign for all the honors a university or college has to bestow, and having garnered them, often look to the college and university to invent new honors that they can win. Almost always, such individuals deserve every honor they receive, but the baffling part is that no honor, no recognition, no reward can ultimately satisfy them. When a faculty member like this shows up in the dean's office on a "personal matter," the dean will have very little work to do unless listening to long monologues without being able to say a word is work for the dean. Eventually, the faculty member will wind down, but never on time; if the appointment for the dean has been scheduled for an hour, the faculty member will not get through his or her speech until sixty-five minutes have elapsed. It is then that the dean must do what is expected: praise the achievement, insight, wisdom,

and brilliance of the faculty member as lavishly as conscien
and sense of good form will permit. It is totally counterproduc-
tive to try to teach such a faculty member manners or a sense
of humility. Only radical surgery can change the personality of
a successful fifty-year-old man or woman; and if that personality, with all of its selfishness, involution, and narrow-mind-
edness, has produced new knowledge and new insights, why
should anyone even want to change it? The task in such matters is to encourage the faculty member to continue believing
that his or her work is extremely good, extremely important,
and extremely valuable. This is what the faculty member wants
to hear from the dean, and if it is essentially accurate, then the
dean's job is to play back for the faculty member a version of
that person's own self-esteem. No harm can come from it, and
in the long run, some good may come of it.

Social Interactions with the Faculty

While the saying "It's lonely at the top" has become a mocking
cliché used to puncture the self-importance of high-level execu-
tives from various walks of life, the cliché has a strong core of
hard truth to it as applied to decanal positions. Despite the fact
that some faculty members may regard the position of dean as
being at the bottom of the college instead of the at the top, it
is a position that requires a certain amount of dispassionate
detachment from the individual desires and aspirations of the
college's department chairpersons and general faculty. Not all
their desires can be met or all their aspirations fulfilled; thus,
the dean should not be emotionally identified with any of
them. While some degree of neutrality on such matters is fairly
easy to maintain during working hours, it is much more difficult to avoid letting one's emotions come into play when one
is among close friends. Indeed, that is what close friends are
for—to share confidences, to seek advice, to reveal one's mind
to others. But that is exactly what a dean cannot do among
friends unless those friends—or, more likely, that friend—can
be totally and utterly discreet. A totally and utterly discreet person is hard to find, and a totally and utterly discreet person
who can be a close friend of a dean is even harder to find. Thus,

it is reasonable to assume that even if the dean has spent a number of years at the college as a faculty member before receiving the decanal appointment, old friendships may be difficult to maintain at their former level of intensity. Indeed, the very worst thing that can be done to relationships with the college's department chairpersons is to form, however unwittingly or unconsciously, a kitchen cabinet of friends who appear to, or actually do, advise on matters of college policy and practice. Friends are generally chosen because they are like-minded; the last thing a dean needs is a coterie of like-minded friends reinforcing every thought he or she has. Thus, old friendships will grow increasingly distant, and if the dean is newly imported from another college or university, it will be difficult, perhaps impossible, to form new friendships that will be as satisfying as the old ones left behind. If having one or two close friends is absolutely necessary, they should be sought from either outside the college in another unit of the university or outside the college among people in the surrounding town or city. The new dean, whether promoted from within or imported from without, is going to have to accept the truth: it is, in fact, lonely at the top.

But being lonely does not mean being neglected socially. The college dean generally has more social functions to attend than anyone else on campus, for invitations are received not only from all the departments in the college but from the central administration and from decanal colleagues in other colleges to some of their events. If the institution in which the dean serves is made up of a single college, then he or she, like the institution's president, is invited to every social event connected, however remotely, with the college. The majority of these invitations must be accepted, no matter how inconvenient it may seem. Social functions afford one of the best ways to learn more about the college's faculty members without having to conduct business with them. Of course, nearly every social event will have at least one person among its guests who will want to conduct business with the dean. There is not much that can or should be done under such circumstances, except to listen politely and disengage from the enterpreneur as quickly as possible. When at social functions, the dean should make no commitment, except a promise to "look into the matter'' at an early date. The dean should mainly be a listener at social events. Some deans approach social functions in much the same manner as professional diplomats do: a party or a dinner is an event during which a lot can be learned about the other fellow and during which, if necessary, a discreet message can be dropped in the right place. This is a good way to approach the social duties that must be performed; while no business should be conducted, some business will be conducted; while no one is supposed to learn anything from a social event, almost everything can be learned there. In other words, when going to a social event, the dean can relax, but not completely; social events can turn out to be work.

In summary, there are all sorts of ways that deans can deal with faculty members without usurping the authority and responsibilities of department chairpersons. The extent to which deans relate with faculty members depends on their personality and nervous systems, the degree to which they actually wish to relate, and the number of faculty members in the college.

Questions and Exercises*

Following are examples of a few of the more frequent faculty problems and concerns facing deans. What would you do in these situations?

1. A faculty member in the fourth year as a member of a department in your college has not been reappointed. The appropriate evaluation procedures and nonrenewal procedures have been followed. You (the dean) have written the letter of nonrenewal, based upon the evaluative materials received from the faculty, the students, and the chairperson. The faculty member does not understand why he was not given the opportunity to be considered for tenure in his fifth year, which he believes

---

*Developed for use in seminar discussions for deans and other university administrators by Catherine Archibald Longstreth, associate vice president for academic affairs, University of Florida, with James Parry, associate vice chancellor and other staff members from the Office of Human Resources, Florida Board of Regents.

is his right. He makes an appointment to discuss this with you.

2. The reports you have received regarding a tenured faculty member's performance in teaching indicate that some problems exist. You and the chairperson have discussed the problems that the chairperson has heard from other faculty and students and has observed from the evaluation information received from students. The faculty member continues to deny that there are problems and refuses to accept any criticism. His annual letters of evaluation are poor, and he does not receive merit salary increases. The problems persist for several more years and finally reach a point at which it is imperative that some corrective action take place if the faculty member is to continue as an employee of the university. You and the chairperson have documented the complaints over the years, sending the faculty member a copy and indicating that a copy has been placed in his personnel file. The faculty member files a formal complaint with the vice president. You and the chairperson receive a copy of the allegations, which state that the administration has interfered with his academic freedom, continually imposed disciplinary action on him, and withheld merit salary increases without just cause.

3. A tenured faculty member of long standing who has always been outstanding in his work has begun to have problems, possibly emotional, that are affecting the performance of his assigned duties. You and his colleagues have attempted to assist him in every possible way during the past year. However, his performance has become so poor that appropriate actions must be taken. He has been warned in his evaluation letters and in other communications and by many other means, but the situation does not improve.

4. An attorney calls you and asks for an appointment to discuss a matter dealing with a student and a faculty member in one of your college programs.

5. A faculty member in your college claims that her chairperson did not give her the raise she deserved. Further,

she accuses you of limiting her raise because of her husband's income. Her charge centers on some casual remarks that you had made in her presence to another faculty member regarding her husband's income.

6. You have become aware unofficially that students have continually complained about the conduct of one of the faculty members in your college. You have learned that some students have unofficially informed the office of student affairs that a particular faculty member has had parties at which illegal substances were available. Furthermore, the students claim they were encouraged to use them. You have also been told that the students said they would not lodge a formal complaint (at least for now) because of fear of reprisal.

7. A faculty member is arrested by city police for the possession and distribution of child pornography (photos and motion pictures of teenagers). He is released on bail; a trial date is set for a date six months after the arrest. What would you do prior to the trial? The faculty member then pleads ''no contest'' to the charges. Adjudication of guilt is withheld, and all the records relating to the arrest and charges are sealed by the court. What now?

8. One of your chairpersons comes to you to seek your support for not renewing an instructor who, he claims, ''just does not fit in.'' She is not disruptive at faculty meetings, but she takes the opposite point of view on most issues. She is a fairly good teacher, but does not go out of her way to help students. While she has done an adequate job in performing her assigned duties, he wishes she would just leave. She has already told the chairperson that you do not like her and want to see her fired. She claims that any actions taken against her would be made on the basis of sex.

9. A tenured faculty member in your college will reach the age of sixty-five within a year. You want him to retire so that you can replace him with a faculty person who can contribute more to the research role of the department. You arrange a meeting with him to inform him of your

decision. Based upon the discussion, he files a charge of age discrimination with the coordinator for affirmative action.

10. A faculty member has demanded a copy of the following materials:

   a. current résumés of all members of the mathematics department

   b. all evaluations that you, as dean, have made regarding these faculty members' performance

   c. any grant applications these faculty members may have submitted, and any correspondence regarding the approval of such applications

   d. all documents relating to your college's budget for the past five years

You have conservatively estimated that a response would consume fifty hours of staff time and involve copying over two thousand pages, and you know, of course, that you cannot release your evaluations of another person's performance to anyone except officers of the institution. What are your options?

8

Dealing with the Students

One would think that a dean who supervises an academic or instructional unit consisting of two or more programs, departments, or divisions would be heavily involved with students, the prime reason for the existence of academic or instructional programs. After all, back in 1908, Charles Eliot, president of Harvard, wrote that the dean is "responsible for the discipline of students. In the undergraduate departments much of his time is given to intercourse with students who need advice or pecuniary aid, or who neglect their opportunities, or become dangerous to their associates."[*] But in American higher education times have changed. Of all the officers of a college—its faculty, program directors, department chairpersons, assistant and associate deans, and dean—the dean is likely to have less to do with students than anyone else when performing the routine duties of the office. Deans, generally speaking, do not spend much time with students; the amount of time spent with them probably takes up less than 10 percent of a working day. Why does this state of affairs generally obtain throughout higher education?

In most universities and colleges, there has been established

---

[*]Charles W. Eliot, *University Administration* (Boston: Houghton Mifflin, 1908), p. 242.

175

for many years an Office of Student Affairs with institution-wide responsibilities. In larger universities the director of this office is titled vice president for student affairs, and in smaller universities and colleges the title is either dean or director of student affairs. This office has its roots in pre–World War II days in something that used to be called dean of students or, variously, dean of men and dean of women. The typical modern Office of Student Affairs, which began as a kind of benign monitor of student conduct, now has a large array of services and responsibilities, all directed toward promoting the welfare of students. The conduct-monitoring function is still in place, although greatly attenuated since the demise of the in loco parentis philosophy that once informed virtually all colleges and universities in America. There are now offices that offer various kinds of counseling for the different types of student needs. In most institutions, career counseling is provided by the student affairs office, as are psychological counseling and special programs in sex therapy, such as rape awareness and rape counseling. There are programs in student affairs to regulate and provide guidance for campus fraternities and sororities, where they exist, and for a host of other kinds of student societies. The rise of student unions, at many colleges and universities the most imposing building on campus, has led to a proliferation of services ranging from quasi-academic noncredit courses (with titles such as Aerobics Are for You!) to just plain organized zaniness (Frisbees Are Freedom). Special programs generally located in the Office of Student Affairs include aid for handicapped students and honorary tutoring services or societies. The Office of Student Affairs may have abandoned the philosophy of in loco parentis, but it has substituted for that philosophy an imposing array of services that replace, in a truly operational sense, not only what parents once did for students before they came to college but also what the students' home environment provided them before they left home.

Deans of academic or instructional units such as arts and sciences, business, and education are not figures generally sought after by the students enrolled in those academic units. Furthermore, in all but the very smallest of these, the dean is further removed from the students by the presence in his or her office of a part- or full-time person, generally carrying the title of assistant or associate dean, who serves essentially as that academic unit's student personnel officer. This individual has primary responsibility for dealing with the many and varied aspects of student academic life in the college or division: course scheduling and advising, the latter encompassing not only degree program guidance but also matters relating to academic failure or success and academic probation, as well as problems relating to student-faculty interaction. Currently student consumerism is a rising tide, and the job of the dean's student personnel officer is a full-time occupation; the student personnel officer generally has a support staff of from one to ten people, depending on the size of enrollment in the academic or instructional unit, and has general supervision of all faculty members in that unit who are assigned on a part-time or full-time basis to academic advising activities. If the dean has a good assistant or associate dean in charge of these activities, the chances are slim that a student will ever get as far as the dean's office to discuss such matters.

The presence of an active, energetic Office of Student Affairs with institutionwide responsibilities, coupled with a well-functioning student personnel officer in each of the academic units within the institution, leads generally to only one conclusion: deans will see only the best and the worst students in programs under their supervision unless they make a conscious effort to become involved in at least a few aspects of student life. The very great majority of students have no reason to present themselves to the dean; only those in dire straits or those whose accomplishments are extraordinary will receive attention as individual cases, except as deans arrange their work schedules in order to interact with student honor societies, standard student committees, councils that are a part of the college's life, special student task forces, or special student concerns.

But eventually some individual students with cases that are so bad that the academic dean's personnel officer either cannot (or sometimes simply will not) deal with them find their way to the dean's office. The most common of such cases generally involve students seeking waivers to the various rules and regulations of the college or university. These requests for waivers vary widely in nature and in degree of importance. The most common request is a waiver of a particular course requirement: "I had that in high school." "I simply can't do calculus, and besides, I won't need it as a TV broadcaster." These requests almost always occur near the very end of the student's degree program, very shortly before graduation, and their roots can be traced back through the student's transcript, which will contain a history of delay and sometimes artful dodging. Sometimes the waiver involves, not the course requirement itself, but the professor who regularly teaches it: "He doesn't like sorority women and won't grade me fairly. I'd take the course if only someone else taught it." Sometimes the waiver involves a grade point average prerequisite for graduation or a grade point average requirement: "I have only one D in my major. I made C's or B's, plus two A's in all the other courses in my major. I have an overall grade point average of 1.98 and that's really the same as a 2.0."

Sometimes a student will take an answer of "No, you can't do it" only from the dean, despite what such a student has been told by the faculty adviser, the department chairperson, or the assistant or associate dean. In listening to such a student's petition or argument, the dean must be wary; the student as con artist is a figure upon which countless campus legends have been based. In the very great majority of cases, deans who have before them a string of negative decisions from faculty advisers, chairpersons, and student personnel officers will also have to say to the student, "No, you can't do it." If deans get in the habit of reversing decisions made by their associates who deal with students, then the deans will quickly become their own student personnel officers, a function not found in many academic deans' job descriptions. Only in cases where there is incontrovertible evidence of a miscarriage of justice should there be a reversal of decisions made previously by others.

A more difficult problem is posed for the dean if, let us say, the faculty adviser approves a student's request, the chairperson disapproves it, and the assistant dean says to the dean, "I don't know; you figure it out." In other words, if the decision-making chain below the dean is not in agreement about what to do in a particular case where a student seeks a waiver of an academic rule or regulation or policy, the dean has to act like a dean and make a decision. Obvious rules to be observed in such cases are: (a) Never punt; sometimes delay is necessary in order to gather more data or let emotions cool, but eventually the dean must act, or someone else such as the vice president or provost or president will act for the dean. (b) Never worry about having a decision in such cases overturned by higher authority; it is better to act and be overturned than to have someone else act for the dean. (c) In the great majority of cases the student should not be given the waiver because in a well-run institution rules and regulations are not mindless; they generally serve real and useful academic purposes. (d) Never worry about precedent setting, also known as the domino theory of decision making; decanal decisions in such cases can almost always be fashioned in such a way as to avoid precedent setting. (e) Cling to common sense; in the last analysis common sense should prevail over policy. This suggests that sometimes academic policy is not fully informed by common sense. (f) Whatever decision is made, it is incumbent upon the dean to explain as clearly and in as much detail as necessary why the decision was made. Without explanation, even the most Solomonic decision can appear tyrannical to the mind of a disappointed young man or woman.

Given the fact that a college or university is a thoroughly meritocratic organization, that students, like their faculty, advance through a well-defined grading system (although the faculty's system may not be as well defined as that of the students), it should come as no surprise to the dean that occasionally it becomes necessary to deal with a student's grade appeal. A wise dean ensures from the outset that a grade appeal process is in place in the college in order that students may, in unusual cases, have a forum in which to explain to others besides their professor that a particular grade was inaccurately, perhaps even unfairly, assigned. Such a process should never become a regular and oft-used mechanism. If it does, something is wrong with either the faculty or the student admissions standards. Nevertheless, it is important to have the mechanism in place, and it is equally important that the workings of that process stay as close to the faculty as possible. Departmental faculty committees are the proper locus of such activities; the dean's office is not. The farther away from the faculty such mechanisms are located, the more dangerous they become. That's why a president or chancellor should never hear a grade appeal. And no matter what mechanism is put in place and no matter where it is located, the cardinal rule in any grade appeal process is that a professor's grade cannot be changed by anyone except the professor. The appeal process thus has to be designed to identify any deviations from the announced criteria or process to be followed in assigning a grade and to allow the student to identify any unfairness in the assignment of that grade. But while inaccuracies in following the criteria and/or process can almost always be identified with a high degree of objectivity, fairness is almost always in the eyes of the beholder. Very few faculty members will hold fast to an assigned grade when presented with objective evidence of inaccuracies, but very few faculty members will accept either a student's or a third party's definition of fairness. Thus, at best, a grade appeal process can only present evidence and/or opinion to a professor; it is the professor, and only the professor, who can change the grade. As always, the rule of common sense must prevail; the grade assignment of a certifiably ill and mentally incompetent professor should not be allowed to stand, not only for the petitioning student but for all the students in that class.

Hence, when confronted with a student petitioning for a grade change, there is little the dean can do except listen to the student, review the evidence, and if it is believed that either inaccuracy or unfairness has played a part in the assignment of the grade, talk to the chairperson of the professor's department. If a grade appeal mechanism is not in place, a single experience with one petitioning student in a grade appeal case will be enough to convince the dean that such mechanisms are necessary. Deans should not change the grade under appeal, nor should they recommend to the appropriate department chairperson that the grade be changed. The dean can, if he or she believes it is right to do so, recommend to the faculty member that the grade be changed. But if the faculty member refuses to do so and if the faculty member is not ill, then there is nothing more that can be done.

Finally, the dean will occasionally find in his or her office a student who has a horror story to tell. Almost always, these horror stories turn out upon close examination not to be as horrible as they were when they were first heard. Sometimes, during the course of the dean's interrogation of the bearer of the horror story, the story itself loses some of its color and alarm and is reduced to something more rational. Sometimes, it takes a few days of investigation to bring the story into focus and make it fit more nearly with reality. Bearers of horror stories are more likely to recite their tales in the Office of Student Affairs than in the academic dean's office, and that is because there is not much room for horror to develop in a classroom or a faculty member's office; it is much more likely to develop in dormitories and in other forms of student residences.

In the past, however, there was a kind of horror that sometimes took place in the classroom, and its most distressing and painful form was discrimination against students based on either race or sex. Nowadays, it is relatively rare for a dean to encounter an obvious example of racial discrimination in the classroom. Unfortunately, subtle forms do continue and probably will continue for a long time. But very few faculty members intentionally make racial slurs or tell insulting racist jokes in the classroom. When they do, and when the dean is confronted with complaints, swift but carefully thought-out action is necessary. Long-drawn-out investigations should be avoided, for the longer the situation goes without resolution, the more it festers; and the more it festers, the more likely it is to turn into an ugly semipublic or public episode. The dean generally has all the necessary apparatus available to him or her to bring the matter to resolution, and every effort should be made to settle the matter within the confines of the college. Sometimes the participants on either or both sides will not let the dean settle the matter but insist upon taking the issue to higher levels, namely, the president and/or the university's or college's attorneys. If possible, these excursions into the public or semipublic arena should be avoided, for unless the faculty member is a habitual offender or an unreconstructed racist, resolution can be found without extramural assistance. If the report of racial discrimination is validated by an investigation, the punishment must be severe enough to act as a deterrent against repeated incidents. A message must be sent to the offender and others who might be potential offenders.

Sex discrimination is generally more prevalent than race discrimination in the classroom, and the former takes on many more different forms than the latter. Generally, women are more often the victims of tasteless jokes, of generalized and cavalier references about the alleged foibles of the "weaker sex," and, occasionally, of unwanted and unsolicited propositions. If students report such incidents, the dean's reaction to them must be the same as to racial discrimination—action must be swiftly but carefully executed. Most universities and colleges now have special officers, usually located in the Office of Student Affairs, to deal with such problems; more often than not, the dean of an academic unit is among the last to know that one of his or her faculty members has been charged with sex discrimination. But whether the dean is the first or last to know, corrective and preventative action must be taken. Again, if a report of such activity is proven to be valid, a firm, unambiguous message must be sent to the offender.

Fortunately the academic dean is not often presented with cases of students victimized by racial or sex discrimination; however, horror stories about poor teaching are regularly presented by students. Under the dolorous category of poor teaching are subsumed a host of sins: unfair grading (the most common student complaint), boring lectures, irrelevant lectures, tasteless, scatological lectures. When a dean receives what appears to be a rational complaint about a faculty member's poor classroom performance or unfair grading, certain factors must be immediately assessed. Is the course in question a required course for all students? For premed students? For prelaw students? With this information as background, the dean should then find out whether the accused instructor has a history of such complaints. Required courses, particularly those in chemistry and calculus, are often regarded by students not majoring in those fields as unfair impositions; no grading system other than a guaranteed pass will satisfy some students who are required to take such courses. Students in professional schools such as law and medicine are subjected to many pressures to achieve a high grade point average, not the least of which is the pressure they generate on themselves. These pressures make many of them believe that virtually any course they are required to take is presided over by a poor teacher who is an unfair grader. Thus, the dean needs to be very cautious about such allegations. A fairly consistent history of complaints about unfair grading does warrant investigation and, if possible, remedial but not necessarily punitive action. Generally, such complaints are launched by students in certain professional schools or programs against professors who teach required courses located in the arts and sciences. This happens frequently in departments such as chemistry. Why? Because professors of chemistry are more apt to be unfair? Not at all. But professors of chemistry care a very great deal about their subject matter, and some of them eventually become at least a little embittered over having to teach hordes of students who have no interest whatsoever in chemistry and can hardly wait to get a passing grade and leave chemistry behind forever. Bitterness can generate rigidity and rigidity can easily be translated by an unhappy student into unfairness. In such cases, the dean has to hope that the grade appeal mechanisms established in the departments will draw the attention of the department chairperson and the departmental faculty to the fact that an unusual number of complaints have been lodged against a particular professor. If this attention has not been generated, and it is the dean's unhappy lot to have to deal with the problem, the sole expedient is to force the problem and its solution back on the department. Solutions are available to the department: personal counseling of the professor by the chairperson, workshops or short courses in teaching effectiveness put on by one or more agencies within the university or college (seldom, however, can a senior professor be made to believe that he or she is in need of such services), or finally, relief from an assignment to teach a particular required course. It is interesting to note that students rarely lodge charges of unfair grading against faculty members teaching junior- and senior-level courses in the professional schools or departments in which the students are majoring. In such environments, the professor and the students are more apt to be of one mind: both parties like the subject matter, the students are enrolled in the course because they want to be there, and the faculty member is teaching a course he or she likes to teach.

Complaints about professors who are boring, irrelevant, or incompetent are often the most frustrating kinds of student complaints that the dean experiences. Some faculty members, while highly competent in their subject, are simply incapable of being interesting, much less exciting as they go about their classroom work. Such problems should remain, if at all possible, the province of the department chairperson and of colleagues within the department. Sometimes personal counseling will help, but that kind of counseling is generally much more effective when it comes from the faculty member's department chairperson than from the dean. The dean should always remember, however, who is calling whom boring or irrelevant; what may be boring or irrelevant to some students may be absorbing to other students. If student complaints about professional incompetence turn out to be valid (for example, "Doesn't know the subject matter"; "Doesn't know how to assign grades"; "Can't speak understandable English"), then everyone is embarrassed because the whole system has obviously broken down. The department did a poor job in hiring this particular faculty member in the first place; the evaluation process was badly flawed; someone somewhere was not truthful in writing a letter of reference. Incompetence cannot be tolerated, and the dean must take whatever action is possible to upgrade, isolate or terminate the faculty member in question. After this painful process has been observed, the dean needs next to decide whether the department chairperson who recommended the hiring of this faculty member should be replaced.

Of course, the easiest problem to solve is one in which complaints have been lodged against a faculty member for tasteless conduct in class, such conduct usually taking the form of off-color jokes, scatological language, and frenzied behavior. Generally such conduct is exhibited by the young tyro who, in a misguided attempt to be the students' friend or to be thought of as just another student, engages in what is essentially sophomoric behavior. Personal counseling by both the dean and the department chairperson is usually very effective in such cases provided that counseling is not delayed to the point where the faculty member becomes a cause célèbre among some equally sophomoric students. If the behavior described above is manifested in an older, more seasoned professor, then personal counseling is generally insufficient because the behavior is

probably symptomatic of a deeper malady rather than a mani-
festation of poor judgment or naïveté. In such cases, the dean
is well advised to seek professional counseling for the faculty
member; a midlife crisis is not a trivial matter that can be
treated by avuncular advice from a dean.

As noted earlier, just as the worst students appear in the
dean's office, so do the best. It is the appearance of this latter
group that makes the day livable. After a week of melancholy
budget hearings, scientific equipment failure, savage interne-
cine wars over space allocations, the appearance in the dean's
office of an outstanding student who has come to be presented
with a medal, a plaque, or a scholarship can have an indescrib-
ably salutary effect on the dean's view of the world, the institution, and the job itself. The perfect dean in the perfect world,
we remember, would have as students only Merit Scholars and
other outstanding intellectual stars. Thus, the appearance of a
few students representing an honor society, or even just one
truly outstanding student-scholar, gives a glimpse of the para-
digm of excellence. The trick here is to let that sense of decanal
joy and, sometimes, relief shine forth while the student or students are present. These occasions must never become routine,
no matter how many years the dean has welcomed, honored,
and praised those good students. Excellent students are the
very lifeblood of the academic enterprise, and it is a cynical and
soon-to-be-retired dean who cannot rise to the occasion to
make such students feel welcome and important to the life of
the institution. On such occasions, the dean should ask the students not only about their achievements, but about their academic experiences: "Who was your best teacher this year?"
"What was your favorite course?" "Why did you choose a major in this program?" These bright students can sometimes tell
a dean as much about life in the institution as the department
chairperson can. If an academic unit within the institution has
some kind of newsletter or promotional publication, these excellent students should be featured prominently in each appropriate issue of the publication. This means posing for pictures,
and that means being patient and being willing to spend time
with the students. Bright students can tell the difference between a dean who schedules fifteen minutes for a congratulatory presentation and one who schedules an hour for the same

ceremony. And an hour spent in the observance of such activities is worth it, not only for the students but for the dean.

Most universities and colleges have something called student government, an entity that is generally irrelevant to the
institution's various and diverse academic enterprises. Student
government is an institutionwide organization primarily concerned with the general welfare of students. It provides ambitious young men and women with opportunities to run for office and acquire experience in student politics. Academic deans
generally have little to do with student government. Presided
over by students who stay in office for a year or less, student
government has no institutional memory or stability, and its
participants almost always have to be taught the same lessons
in governance, finance, and decorum over and over again.
Such instruction is usually provided by the people in the Office
of Student Affairs, not the academic dean.

But the dean of an academic unit should have an advisory
board in the form of a student council or a student committee
to serve as a mechanism for communication with the students
in that unit whether it be a division, school, or college within
the institution. The student council acts as an antidote to an
institutionwide student government and provides an arena for
students to become interested in, and participate in, the academic life of the unit over which the dean presides. Student
councils serve a good purpose for the dean; they furnish information on how the students are faring; they give the dean a
chance to explain in person the various academic policies; and
they are a constant, living reminder of the original and main
purpose of the division, school, or college—to educate students. Generally, students who serve on councils or committees are among the best. They serve not for political purposes
or to pad a resume, but to try in various ways to advance the
educational purposes of the various academic programs. Idealistic and sometimes impatient, they can, and do, serve as a
goad to the dean, stimulating action toward reform and innovation that is healthy for the general welfare of the institution
and its programs. Students are not professional academics, and
consequently, there are times when their perspective about academic life brings an uncluttered and fresh insight to both old

and new problems that every educational institution experiences.

Of course, such councils or committees should be advisory; no one wants American higher education to be subject to the student tyranny experienced by Latin American colleges and universities, a special kind of egalitarian tyranny that has in some ways prevented the improvement of the curriculum in Latin America and, lately, in some European universities. But simply because a student council or committee is advisory is no reason for its advice to be treated lightly. Its advice can be rejected, but only upon careful, detailed explanation of the reasons why the advice was rejected. In fashioning such explanations, the dean and his or her staff are forced to analyze why certain policies should remain in effect or why they should or should not be implemented. This kind of process can only strengthen academic programs and help improve the leadership of the dean. There are many different ways to establish the membership of a student council or committee, but perhaps the most efficient is to ask for recommendations for appointment from the department chairpersons. In this way, proper representation of all of the programs is guaranteed, although elections by categories of the disciplines or departments can accomplish the same purpose. Once established and properly utilized, student councils can provide substantial benefit to an academic unit or program.

Occasionally the dean may encounter a situation in which it is desirable to appoint special student committees or task forces to provide advice. New curriculum policies under consideration might benefit from suggestions given by a specially formed student task force. New criteria for evaluating classroom teaching performance would certainly benefit from student analysis and advice. Indeed, many colleges and universities across the land have special student committees that elect or help elect annually the award for the best teaching performance. "Teacher of the Year" is a term widely used. New degree programs, either graduate or undergraduate, can generally benefit from student opinion, and it never hurts when presenting a proposal for the establishment of a new degree program to be able to indicate enthusiastic student support for such a program. In short, students should always be looked upon as allies, as people just as vitally concerned with the improvement of the institution and its programs as the dean and the faculty.

Finally, one should never forget that students become alumni. The better the students are treated by the institution, the better they will treat the institution when they become alumni. While wealth may make an institution powerful and strong, the love of its alumni will make it great.

Questions

The following questions are intended to help deans analyze the situation at their respective institutions regarding the extent to which, and in what ways, deans are involved with student problems and activities.

1. Exclusive of formally scheduled functions or ceremonies, how much time does the dean spend (average number of hours per week) talking with one student at a time? With a group of students?

2. How much time (average number of hours per week) is spent on formally scheduled functions or ceremonies for students?

3. What proportion of time spent on student problems as opposed to proportion of time spent on friendly communication for the sake of communication?

4. Do deans feel that more time should be spent with students for the sake of friendly communications? Please expand on a yes or no response.

5. What are some suggestions for the types of student activities and events in which deans should become more involved than they are at present?

6. Are there statements in this chapter that you disagree with? If so, which ones and why?

9

Relations with Presidents, Provosts, Vice Presidents, and Other Deans

The administrative organization of most universities and colleges consists of a tripartite structure, namely, academic affairs, administrative affairs, and student affairs. Thus far in this book, our concern has been mostly with the academic affairs portion of the structure and with the academic units in it that are supervised by deans, such as colleges, schools, or divisions. We have spent considerable time discussing relationships that the dean has developed in his or her own academic unit. Within academic affairs there may be two or three, sometimes fifteen or twenty, other academic deans to work with, live with, and build with. Each supervises a college, school, or division within academic affairs and generally has responsibility for two or more programs or departments. All spend most of their time dealing with the internal matters of whatever academic unit happens to be under their supervision, including faculty, department chairpersons, curricula, degree programs, budget, and physical facilities. A number of institutions have academic deans who preside over single-discipline or nondepartmentalized units. Some deans have institutionwide responsibilities, such as continuing education, undergraduate studies, and graduate studies. Deans must deal with each other and provide the same kind of attention and analysis given to internal matters. They must also deal with a president or a chancellor and an academic vice president or a provost or both, as well as with appropriate individuals in the administrative and student affairs portions of the tripartite structure.

The Dean and The President

The dean's relationship with the president or chancellor generally follows a simple rule: the larger the institution, the less likely the dean is to interact with the president; the smaller the institution, the greater the chances for a close working relationship. In one large midwestern university, a newly recruited dean asked, after a short interview with the president, "Will I ever see him again?" In most institutions it is the president, upon recommendation of the academic vice president and/or the search committee, who personally appoints the dean to office; the president is invariably involved in recruiting the dean, at least to the extent of interviewing the short list of recommended decanal candidates and either choosing or approving the selection from the list. But the recruitment and appointment process is not by any means the only interaction the dean will have with his or her president. In most institutions, large or small, there are at least three main areas of operational relationships requiring a high degree of cooperation: (a) ceremonial, including commencements, convocations, and other such events; (b) fund-raising activities in private and public sectors; and (c) the dean's efforts to recruit faculty and department chairpersons.

CEREMONIAL ACTIVITIES

Consider first the ceremonial activities in which the dean and the president jointly participate. Obviously the dean must attend, and participate in, every commencement, share the platform even though the president and the guest speaker are the main focus of attention, shake hands, help confer degrees, and meet and greet the public before and after the ceremony. Convocations likewise require the presence of president and dean, and sometimes the dean is the principal speaker. Always in these events, both are depicted as close working colleagues, whether or not that is actually the case. There are also always award ceremonies honoring faculty, students, and public and private figures. It is particularly important that the dean's relationships with the president be free from tension in order that it will be easy for the president to accept the dean's invitation to present awards and honors at college or division ceremonies. Also important is the presence of the president on opening day of an important conference sponsored by the dean's college or academic unit. While many times the dean will have to settle for a professional substitute from the central administration, such as the provost or academic vice president, the dean must, on critically important occasions, be able to deliver the institution's president to open a conference or symposium.

Most institutions have something called an administrative council, which is made up of the president, the vice presidents, all the deans, and sometimes some of the directors. This is different from the president's cabinet or executive staff. In large universities the administrative council seldom meets, because its membership is too large and too diverse to constitute an efficient working body. But in smaller institutions the president may frequently meet with his or her administrative council and some business may actually be conducted at those meetings. In such cases, the dean's relationship with the president is quite important. Meetings with the president and small or large groups of other deans pose both opportunities and hazards. In these types of meetings, the president has the opportunity to compare the deans with each other in terms of their effectiveness in the council. During such occasions it is important for the dean to demonstrate several abilities at once, depending on the issues before the group; the dean should demonstrate leadership, cooperation, ability to play on the same team, tough-mindedness, and generosity. The dean must be an advocate for his or her academic unit, yet be an advocate for the general welfare of the whole institution. During times of great prosperity, dividing up the spoils can be as difficult as accepting, in times of poverty, one's fair share of the misery. All presidents like team players; most presidents admire courage and a proper regard for the welfare of the academic unit entrusted to the dean for protection and nourishment. The appropriate balance of these attributes is the hallmark of a very good dean, and a very good dean is considered a treasure. Thus, the conduct of the dean in council meetings with his or her peers is critical in shaping the relationship between the dean and the president.

Some ceremonial relationships between the dean and the president go beyond what appears to be mere ceremony and become instrumental relationships. There are times in the dean's professional life when the presence of the president is necessary to the dean's plans to effect radical reform or to introduce an innovation of some kind. At one time or another, every dean is going to have to launch a difficult and controversial endeavor. These endeavors can take many forms: the establishment of a new degree program that, while needed, may threaten the status or even the future of old degree programs; the introduction of new standards of performance for faculty or students; the establishment of a new department; or the rare and dangerous act of abolishing an academic department. These are the major types of change that occasionally threaten the equanimity of academic life and the dean's serenity. At such times, it is often important that the initiation of discussion about such matters be left to the dean, with the president in attendance. Generally, the presence of the chief academic officer, such as the academic vice president or provost, is sufficient, but it never hurts to enlist the aid of the president as well. If the new endeavor is highly controversial, the support of the chief academic officer will have been secured in advance, but when the battle is joined, the president is bound to be at least peripherally involved sooner or later, so why not from the start?

FUND-RAISING RELATIONSHIPS

One of the close working relationships a dean can have with the president is in the area of fund-raising. There are many facets to this working relationship. There is need for the president's presence and, sometimes, involvement with the dean in raising funds for one of the dean's projects. There is need for the dean's involvement with the president in raising funds for institutional projects. The president's endorsement and advocacy are needed in federal and private fund-raising projects, such as major contracts, grants, and proposals for a college, division, or other academic unit. And, in the case of public universities and colleges, the president's support is needed in legislative forays to secure funds for new programs, colleges, buildings, and other large-scale projects.

Of course, any large-scale project that raises funds for one of the colleges or divisions in a university has to have the approval of the institution's president before it can be launched. But many times such projects need the active involvement of the president at both the beginning and end, and sometimes in the middle, of the process. Any professional academic fund-raiser will flatly state that an institution's chief fund-raiser is its president; while not usually engaged in identifying prospects or making preliminary contacts with prospects, the president almost invariably has to "close the deal." Thus, the dean cannot raise money for one of the academic components of an institution without the help of the institution's president. And in this way, the dean and the president will be thrown together into a close working relationship in pursuit of gifts or donations. It is during these times, few though they may be, that there is the best chance to educate the president about the work, needs, and aspirations of the dean's college, division, or academic unit.

Just as the dean needs the president to help raise private funds for the college or division, so there are times when the president needs the dean to help in private fund-raising for the institution at large. Generally, deans of professional schools, particularly law, medicine, and business administration, develop excellent relationships with affluent supporters of the institution. A business administration dean of any consequence at all has developed good working relationships with bankers, heads of large and small financial institutions, and other captains of industry. These relationships are important not only to the welfare of the dean's college, school, or division but to the institution at large. Hence, the president will almost always call on the dean for help during a fund-raising project for the institution at large. Usually the president needs the dean's help simply to develop a prospective donor's interest in an institutional priority; sometimes the dean may be called upon by the president to persuade the prospective donor to give to a universitywide project rather than to a project for a single unit: a science building rather than the filling-in of the north end zone of the football stadium; a classroom building rather than an opera house; or, possibly, a wing on the library rather than a wing on the business administration building. In such cases, about all the dean can do is put on the uniform of a team player and hope that the president has a good memory and a long tenure. If the dean can help the president, surely eventually the president can help the dean.

Every once in a while an institution is presented with an opportunity to secure a large grant or contract from a federal agency or a major corporation. Usually, these grants or contracts involve more than one academic department; they may involve many departments, two or more colleges or divisions, or the whole institution. No dean can achieve success in these enterprises unaided. A steering committee is usually formed to secure the grant or contract, with a membership that includes department chairpersons, deans, the academic vice president, and the president. After all the turf battles have been fought and won or lost, after the various levels of departmental and collegiate avarice have been contained and balanced out, the president is called upon to be chief spokesman or advocate. Here again the dean has an excellent opportunity not only to demonstrate sagacity and statesmanship but also to educate the president about the accomplishments, needs, and aspirations of the academic unit containing the departments and programs under the dean's jurisdiction. Quite obviously, such institutional, or at least interdisciplinary, endeavors help to educate the dean about the rest of the institution.

In state-supported or, as some like to define themselves, state-assisted institutions, there occur fairly frequent opportunities, when times are good and the state's general revenue receipts are up, for the institution to make a special request for special funding from its state legislature. Sometimes these requests involve buildings, sometimes special salary increases to meet national competition, sometimes special increases for large-scale equipment purchases. If the dean has developed good relationships with one or more key legislators, the president will often call upon the dean for help. The odds are that deans of professional schools or colleges, such as medicine, law, and business, have already developed these relationships with legislators; even legislators get sick or need legal or financial advice. However, liberal arts deans, engineering deans, indeed, all kinds of deans are also capable of developing excellent relationships with legislators. Any well-run state university or college has a vigorous program dedicated to making certain that state legislators know as much as possible about the institution, and such a program must heavily involve academic deans. Thus, when the president calls upon the dean for help in the legislature, yet another excellent opportunity is presented to educate the president about the dean's part of the institution. In such circumstances, however, the dean must be very cautious and avoid any temptation to cut a deal on the side or try an end run with a legislator. Legislators are politicians, and politicians more than any other group in society like to compromise, make deals, and otherwise encourage special arrangements. That is their nature, and that is the substance of their professional lives. It is a heady experience for a dean to be taken into the confidence of a chairperson of a legislative appropriations committee or a Speaker of the House. The temptation to help the legislator cut a deal is large and sometimes compelling, but the dean, it must be remembered, has to go back to campus and live and work with other deans, the academic vice president, and the president. The dean should never forget which team he or she is playing on; the home team is not in the state legislature.

RECRUITING ACTIVITIES

Most deans like to believe they are charming, persuasive, skillful negotiators. While this is an illusion not limited to deans or, for that matter, to academics in general, it is an illusion that can sometimes be fatal to a dean's effort to recruit a superstar to the college as a major professor or as a department chairperson. The first thing to remember about superstars is that almost without exception they have very large egos. The brilliant, very productive academic scholar is generally characterized by abnormally strong self-confidence, a selfishness that shuts out the world in order to achieve intellectual success, and a belief in his or her own importance. These are not necessarily bad traits and are by no means to be equated with viciousness or malevolence, but they are traits that demand careful analysis when a dean is going about the business of recruiting such a person. The dean needs to remember that important people like to be paid attention to by other important people, and the dean, while an important person, is not as important as the president—or maybe even the academic vice president, although the latter instance is at least arguable. If at all possible, then, the dean should establish an agreement with the president that obligates the president, when possible, to help recruit superstars for the dean's college. Superstars like to be interviewed by presidents; they like to receive letters from presidents urging them to come live and work at the president's institution; and they like telephone calls from the president urging them to take the job the dean has offered them. In addition to helping ensure the success of the recruitment of a superstar, the president's involvement in this process can also help the dean if large additions of funds, equipment, or space are part of the recruitment package. Once again, the dean needs to be very cautious about such matters; it is appropriate for the dean to get the commitment of the president to find the extra dollars or space for the superstar, but that commitment should never be negotiated with the president alone. The academic vice president is the first stop on the way of this perilous journey, and the dean must make absolutely certain that the academic vice president is agreeable to commitments for additional resources. Indeed, the best strategy for the dean in such cases is to get the commitment for resources from the vice president and then for both dean and vice president to get the president committed.

In summary, then, it seems obvious that an academic dean does indeed have many opportunities to work with the president and that the new dean's plaintive question "Will I ever see the president again?" is overdrawn even when applied to the largest of this nation's universities. What is important to remember is that in all of the various ways in which the dean and the president interact, the dean and the dean's group of programs are always on trial as well, for the president will usually tend to judge them by the dean's actions and reactions to the problems, opportunities, and challenges that the dean and the president face together. In many ways, these relationships are the most interesting and exciting part of the dean's job. They are seldom routine or boring.

The Dean and the Chief Academic Officer

The institution's chief academic officer is variously called the provost, the academic vice president, the academic vice chancellor, and, in smaller institutions, the dean of academic affairs or the dean of instruction. For the purpose of discussion in this chapter, the chief academic officer will be referred to as the academic vice president. The relationship between the academic vice president and the dean is much the same as the dean's relationship to one of his or her department chairpersons. Just as the dean relies upon the chairperson to carry out the academic missions of the department, so the academic vice president relies on the dean to carry out the academic mission of the dean's academic unit. Usually two or more chairpersons report to the dean, and two or more deans report to the academic vice president. Just as the dean must balance the needs and aspirations of department chairpersons, the vice president must perform the same balancing act with two or more deans. The larger and more diverse the institution, the greater the pressures on both dean and academic vice president. Most deans, except those responsible for the arts and sciences, are educated in the same subject-matter fields as their department chairpersons. Although an engineering dean may be an electrical engineer whose college or school has departments of civil, mechanical, and chemical engineering, at least dean and chairpersons can all accept each other as engineers. The arts and sciences dean and the academic vice president have one thing in common that other deans do not: both must preside over academic units containing a variety of different and unrelated disciplines about which they have only the most generalized kind of knowledge. This may partially account for the fact that the majority of academic vice presidents in institutions of higher education come from arts and sciences disciplines. They are either better able to cope with their areas of ignorance or they all believe that their own specific disciplines are doorways to all knowledge. One thing is certain, and that is that both the academic vice president and the dean are pushed and pulled by many and various forces and demands. They are occasionally uncertain about the importance of a particular academic discipline or subset thereof and both have to trust and rely on those who report to them. The dean should always remember this and try to engender and nourish the academic vice president's trust. The more trust the academic vice president has in a dean, the simpler and easier life will be for the dean.

BUILDING TRUST AND SETTING GOALS

Trust is relatively easy to establish. In most cases, the dean will have been recruited by the academic vice president, with some help, of course, from the president. True, the primary recruiters of the dean will have been the members of the search committee, but very few deans are ever hired without the endorsement and, indeed, enthusiastic support of the academic vice president. And it is during the courtship ritual of vice president and decanal candidate that the framework of mutual trust should be established. Just as no vice president should promise the decanal candidate program resources that cannot be delivered, so no dean-to-be should promise improvements, breakthroughs, fame, and glory that are impossible to realize. Both persons should commit themselves to try to achieve what is desirable, but the dean should remember that evaluation of job performance comes around once every year, and promises of instant improvement may become embarrassing reminders of failed hopes and stillborn projects. It is also important for the dean to learn as precisely as possible what goals the vice president has in mind for the group of programs under the dean's supervision. Sometimes this is not possible; academic vice presidents sometimes have to be taught what goals are both desirable and achievable. Once some agreement has been reached on the direction or directions an academic unit, college, school, or division will take under the leadership of the new dean, it is vitally important that the dean head the unit in this direction. If, after a period of time, it becomes clear to the dean that the agreement reached on what the unit should become is wrong or unreachable, then the dean and the academic vice president must start over again and plot a new course to follow. In most instances, it will be the dean who plots the course; it will then be up to him or her to convince the academic vice president of the correctness of the new course. Never should the dean change the compass heading without the full knowledge and at least minimal support of the academic vice president.

COMMUNICATION BETWEEN THE DEAN AND CHIEF ACADEMIC OFFICER

How should the dean communicate with the academic vice president? As we noted in chapter 6, there are many different methods available to the dean in communicating with the chairperson of a department and the faculty within it. Some of those can be used in the dean's relationship with the academic vice president; some, such as memoranda, should generally be avoided. In written communication between these two persons, it is more collegial to write letters than to write memoranda. Memoranda are forms of communication most routinely used when more than one person is to receive the same written information. A letter is more personal; it always starts with "Dear"; it always ends with a verbal caress, such as "Sincerely," "Cordially," "Best regards," or "Warm wishes." Letters can be just as businesslike as memoranda, and almost always are more interesting. The dean and the academic vice president are first and foremost colleagues, friends at least in the professional sense, united in a common cause to make the institution and each of its academic units better. Letters are the courteous way to reflect this relationship.

Letters from deans to academic vice presidents should be as brief as possible but should contain clear and unambiguous messages. If a long letter must be written, it should usually follow a personal conference with the academic vice president and should be either a summary of the conference or an elaboration of the points covered during the conference. Long letters, if they must be written, should contain either good news, factual information, or plans for the future. Long letters should not contain bad news; and if at all possible, bad news should never reach the academic vice president in letter form first. The dean should make every attempt to inform the vice president personally or at least by telephone of bad news before submitting it in letter form. No one likes to receive bad news in any form, but the worst form is in a letter read alone in a silent room with no one to talk to, shout at, or commiserate with. The dean should be careful about the volume of correspondence he or she has with the academic vice president; as in every other form of endeavor, there is a golden mean between too much and too little. The academic vice president must be fully informed about the activities of the dean's academic unit, but an information overload can quickly strain the vice president's patience and erode the dean's credibility. Academic vice presidents, like deans, come in all sizes and shapes; some are information freaks and some few really believe that ignorance is bliss. The dean has to restrain the former's appetite and force-feed the latter. Patience and diplomacy are necessary to the successful fulfillment of this task.

There are those in academic life who make a fetish out of the collegial nature of the management of academic programs. They argue that institutions of higher education are not businesses, that vice presidents and deans are colleagues whose word is enough, and that there is already too much paperwork in colleges and universities. Thus, they argue, as much business as possible should be transacted either over the telephone or through personal conference. We have already noted in chapter 6 the unreliability of telephone communication, the vagaries of memory as they relate to unpleasant business transacted through personal or telephonic conversations, and the general chaos that is created when there is no written record of important events. Just as the dean should be wary of department chairpersons who want to transact all business on a "personal basis," so the dean should not allow the academic vice president to conduct business in a like manner. There is, indeed, too much paperwork in academic life now, but most of it is generated by external forces and agencies, at both the state and federal levels. Indeed, in most colleges and universities there is too little paperwork of the kind that records internal transactions, plans, and agreements.

Thus, the dean should not fall for the argument that a colleague's word is good enough. Personal agreements may be conducted in that manner, but business agreements need to be memorialized in writing, especially those between the dean and the academic vice president, who, as we have already noted, has even more forces pushing and pulling at him or her than has an academic dean.

Communication is obviously a two-way street. The dean must keep the academic vice president well informed through letters, telephone calls, and personal conferences. Most of this communication is basically informational in nature and most of it therefore requires no formal response from the academic vice president. Indeed, some of the correspondence can, and should, be lighthearted. When the academic vice president does something intelligent, courageous, or otherwise worthy of congratulations, the dean ought to say so in a note of commendation. Such notes can sometimes be misconstrued as evidence of sycophancy, especially if they are sent too often and in too serious a vein. But a humorous note of congratulations can lighten and brighten a vice president's day and help the relationship between the dean and the vice president.

If the vice president is not particularly communicative, the dean has a problem. There are several ways to deal with unresponsive vice presidents. Some deans bombard them with letters; others try to corner them in a series of personal conferences. Writing lots of letters generally will not solve this kind of problem; the more letters sent, the more uncommunicative the recipient becomes. And this device makes it too easy for a vice president to be unavailable for a series of personal conferences with the dean. The answer to the dilemma is to set up personal conferences with the vice president one at a time over widely spaced intervals and to write a summary of those conferences after each one and send them to the vice president. If the dean's summary is incorrect, response from all but the laziest and dumbest vice president will be swift and forthcoming.

Two of the more important reasons for poor communication from the academic vice president to the dean are that (a) the vice president is relatively ignorant about the discipline or disciplines represented by the dean's college or academic unit, or (b) the vice president dislikes or distrusts the dean. There is a cure for the first malady, although it is slow and painstaking. The dean simply has to devote a great deal of time and energy to educating the vice president. This can be accomplished by inviting the vice president to attend college, division, and/or departmental workshops, by asking the vice president to address college, division, and/or departmental meetings, by going over to the vice president's office to make various presentations about the work of the dean's academic unit, by sending a steady but limited and carefully monitored stream of informational material to the vice president, and by inviting the vice president to as many college, division and/or departmental social events as he or she will attend. Slowly but surely this kind of campaign will pay off, and communication between the vice president and the dean will inevitably improve. If, however, the vice president does not like or trust the dean, the dean has but two choices: go find another job or quietly suffer the studied neglect of the vice president and hope that the vice president soon resigns, retires, or is translated to a presidency in another part of the country.

PRESENTING A BUDGET REQUEST

The most powerful tool of communication between the dean and the vice president is the request budget that must be generated annually or biennially for presentation to the academic vice president. Here all is revealed: the triumphs and failures, the beauty and the warts, the frustrations and the aspirations of the dean and the academic unit. In many large institutions and some smaller ones, this request or planning budget is presented to the academic vice president in the form of a written document and an oral summary. The document must be carefully prepared and the oral summary, if there is to be one, must be thoroughly planned by the dean and whoever else the dean wishes to bring to the presentation. Generally, rhetoric has no place in either the oral summary or in the written document, for while the dean has only one budget to prepare and one presentation to make, the academic vice president has to read several, and in many cases numerous, documents, and listen to a number of oral presentations.

The budget document is the main conveyer of information about the academic unit's needs and aspirations. It should be organized by whatever categories are appropriate to the budgeting style of the institution and its academic vice president, not according to the dean's style. Most academic vice presidents prescribe in advance the format of the annual or biennial budget request document, and so, the dean has no choice to make about the format of the document. The dean should never forget that the oral presentation—if there is one—serves only as a summary of the budget document itself. No oral presentation should be longer than thirty minutes, and consequently the illustrative and supporting detail must be packed into the written budget document itself. The document should emphasize priorities, as described in chapter 4, and the funding priorities should be stated clearly and forthrightly. It is not possible to avoid the issue of priorities, for any good academic vice president will insist that the dean define them in the request budget. It is, of course, possible for a college or academic unit to present several sets of priorities at the same time, each set built on certain funding assumptions: if a 10 percent increase is assured, one set of priorities would be operative; if the assured increase is 5 percent, another set would be the dean's preference; if, alas, there is to be a decrease instead of an increase, still another set of priorities would be recommended by the dean to the academic vice president. The narrative section of the budget document should avoid at all costs recriminations for past penurious treatment as a justification for generous treatment by the academic vice president for the approaching year. It is very hard for a dean to make an academic vice president feel guilty; generally the vice president has too many mouths to feed to be worried about allegations of iniquitous and/or penurious treatment of one particular unit or college. Both the narrative and data sections of the budget document should avoid invidious comparisons of an academic unit's budget with those of other academic units within the institution. It is, however, fair game and good strategy to compare the unit's budget with those of similar units in the state, region, and nation. So long as the comparisons are reasonable, the conclusions to be reached by an analysis of the comparisons can be compelling. Great care, however, must be taken to ensure that the comparable data are really comparable. Finally, the narrative in the budget document should avoid generalized poor-mouthing. Nothing is less conducive to opening the mind of an academic vice president than the opening statement of a budget document that reads something like this: "The college of X, the most poorly funded of all of the nine colleges of this great institution, requests that this year, for the first time in a decade, X be brought to at least minimal funding standards." There are ways to poor-mouth that can, however, have a powerful effect on an academic vice president. For example, the following statement would give sleepless nights to most academic vice presidents: "There are 159 schools of nursing in the United States, and our school of nursing ranks 158th in percentage of general revenue dollars allocated to its equipment, operating expense, and library budgets. With this in mind, the school of nursing this year is requesting a modest increase in its equipment and operating budgets." This is powerful, yet oblique, poor-mouthing; it uses comparable data but comparisons are made with schools or colleges outside the institution; recriminations are avoided and the academic vice president's mind has been opened—wide.

The oral presentation, as noted earlier, is a summary of the budget document. The dean should keep the summary short and simple. The purpose of the summary is to whet, not dull, the academic vice president's curiosity about the programs represented by the dean. As mentioned earlier, a thirty-minute period is the absolute maximum and a fifteen-minute period is probably optimal for the presentation, whatever the size and complexity of the dean's academic unit. The dean should bring along the best speakers among his or her faculty or, if not the best speakers, the most important and impressive department chairpersons and faculty members. The dean should not bring a crowd to the budget oral presentation—three or four persons are plenty for a fifteen- or twenty-minute presentation—but it is important that the dean not do all of the talking. The presentation itself should be as informal as the academic vice president will allow it to be. Four people from the dean's academic unit seated around a round table with the academic vice president and his or her staff will create an optimum environment.

We believe that slides and overhead projectors generally should be avoided; we have found from experience that slides and overhead projectors not only depersonalize the presentation but tend to make the presenters lazy because the presenters do not always think their presentations through; they rely, instead, upon the slides and overhead projectors to remind them what to say next and, in some cases, to do their thinking for them. The dean should pass out short outlines of the presentation and then, talking directly to the academic vice president and his or her staff, make the pitch for the college, school, or division, as the case may be. And, most important of all, the dean must allow time for the academic vice president and the staff to ask questions, make observations, and engage the dean and other presenters in a dialogue about needs and plans. The more involved the academic vice president can become in the dean's budget presentation, the more the vice president will learn and remember about that presentation. The dean must always remember that the object of a budget presentation is to teach the academic vice president, not give a performance.

And what should the budget presentation teach the academic vice president? First and foremost, the dean must make a clear case for the funds requested in the budget request document. But dollar requests themselves reflect, or should reflect, not the mere cost of doing business next year, but why that cost for that business is so important. This means that the budget presentation must deal, however quickly, with the fundamental issues about program development, long-range planning, and the future of the discipline or disciplines under discussion for next year's funding. All of these issues must be powerfully focused on how they affect the intellectual welfare of the students in the dean's college. The whole point of the budget presentation is to improve the education of the students, and this point, while seemingly obvious, needs constant repetition. These are the matters that can make a budget presentation exciting and memorable to its audience.

BRINGING ABOUT CHANGE AND RESOLVING CONFLICT

At least once during a dean's tenure there is going to be a confrontation over initiating a new program or strengthening and/or abolishing an old program. Even though the dean may have been very skillful in preparing for the possible distress and disaffection that may result from the change, he or she may need help. The most immediate and obvious institutional source for such help is the academic vice president, who can provide various kinds of support in the form of political, intellectual, and financial incentives. Sometimes it becomes important for faculty members to understand the strength of the academic vice president's commitment and support for the dean's planned change. A careful analysis by the academic vice president of the intellectual necessity for the change may be all that is necessary to persuade dissidents that the proposed changes are not the end of the world. The analysis will probably be no better than the one prepared by the dean, but the fact that it has been generated by an office and person somewhat removed from the dean's own faculty members gives it more credibility. Pledging financial support often makes the proposed change more palliative; honey catches more flies than vinegar.

If the academic vice president is thoroughly prepared in advance for whatever initiatives, changes, and developments the dean has planned to undertake, it becomes quite difficult for dissident department chairpersons or faculty members to bypass the dean and deal directly with the academic vice president. Nothing can be more debilitating to the authority of the dean than a series of successful end-run plays executed by departmental chairpersons or faculty members. When the academic vice president begins to act for the dean, it is time for the dean to suggest, in as subtle and diplomatic manner as possible, that the academic vice president either take over as full-time dean or stop trying to be a part-time dean. The academic vice president has to be loyal in all phases of the dean's activities, and the dean must always act in such a way as to earn the loyalty and support of the academic vice president. When this has occurred, the academic vice president becomes a powerful force in helping the dean resolve conflict. If it does not occur, the dean should consider finding a position elsewhere.

RECRUITING NEW FACULTY MEMBERS

As noted earlier, important people like to be interviewed by other important people. This means that in recruiting superstars, the dean must use not only the president of the institution but also the academic vice president. Together, the dean and the academic vice president can make a powerful recruiting team. Jointly they can present a certified effort to deliver whatever resources are necessary to convince the superstar to leave a comfortable academic home for a new institution. Superstar academics are generally very wary persons and therefore like reassurance from as many quarters as can be mustered. It is probably not enough for a brilliant microbiologist recruit to hear the chairperson of the Department of Microbiology and the dean promise a new laboratory and a generous budget for equipment. That same message has to be delivered by the institution's chief academic officer and, if possible, by the president. Individuals have a tendency to become advocates for projects in which they are involved. By making the academic vice president a recruiter for a superstar microbiologist, the dean has a good chance of making the academic vice president an advocate for microbiology.

THE ACADEMIC VICE PRESIDENT AS AN ADVISER TO THE DEAN

At most institutions the academic vice president is someone who is thoroughly familiar with the recent history of the institution and is someone who knows all of the deans quite well, generally having had a hand in recruiting many of them. He or she is also the one who will know more than anyone else about the academic budgets for the whole institution. Thus, the academic vice president becomes an invaluable source of information and advice for most deans, for very few of them have the time or opportunity to make an intensive study of their institution's entire academic budget. Indeed, the advice the academic vice president can give is generally far more important than the information on which that advice is based. Therefore, before launching any new major or minor enterprise, the dean should consult with the academic vice president; but conversations about the new enterprise ought to be more than informational. The dean should get as much advice as possible on a variety of subjects, including the feasibility of launching the enterprise, as well as on personnel and fiscal matters. The only caveat we would make is that the dean not seek too much advice too often, or else the vice president becomes the dean. And the dean should always remember that once advice is given, the giver usually expects the advice to be followed.

The Relationship of Deans with Other Deans

Only in the very smallest of institutions is there just one academic dean; in large state universities there may be as many as twenty-five. Each dean will find it necessary to relate in some way with the other deans; and the nature of these relationships, whether cooperative, competitive, or neutral, can be important to the well-being of the institution and its various academic components. Before discussing possible relationships that should or should not be developed, it will be helpful to remember that most institutions have two kinds of deans. The first is a dean of a college, school, or division within an institution who has the responsibility for administering the programs and faculty members of a specific group of disciplines, such as arts and sciences, education, business, or engineering. These deans are not considered part of the central administration of the institution and serve as the president's and academic vice president's line officers in relation to department chairpersons, faculty, and students under their jurisdiction. The second kind of dean is one who has overall institutionwide responsibilities for certain areas, such as the coordination of faculty affairs, student affairs, graduate studies, undergraduate studies, and continuing education. These deans are considered part of the institution's central administration and do not serve as line officers in relation to those faculty members whom they coordinate, but rather as staff officers to their president and vice presidents. Relationships among and between these two types of deans will be discussed in the following paragraphs.

DEANS OF COLLEGES, SCHOOLS, OR DIVISIONS

Let us consider first deans of typical colleges, schools, or divisions within an institution. They have their own budgets to administer, their nonfaculty staff members to hire, tenure and promotion decisions to make, and their own academic programs to maintain. Generally these deans sit together in some sort of committee or council called the Council of Academic Deans, which is usually chaired by the academic vice president or president. In these councils or committees the deans help to formulate educational policy for the institution. Here in these meetings a dean's reputation can be made or broken. Does the dean talk too much? Never say a word? Are the dean's views totally parochial? Is the dean always advancing only the cause of his or her own college, school, or division? Or does the dean exhibit some awareness of larger, institutional issues and concerns? Does the dean grandstand? Is the dean prepared for the council debates and issues on the agenda? Since these council or committee meetings are usually presided over by the academic vice president or, in small institutions, by the president, the quality of the dean's leadership is tested and revealed at each meeting not only to the dean's counterparts but to the dean's superior officers. This impromptu evaluation of the quality of the dean's leadership is confirmed and reconfirmed over a period of several years of such meetings. Everyone can have a bad day; every dean can have a bad council meeting; but the accumulated evidence of two years of monthly meetings pretty well tells the dean's counterparts and the central administrators what kind of dean they have.

We can never repeat too often what we asserted in this book's first chapter: there is never enough money. Consequently, every dean of an academic unit is going to be at least theoretically in competition with colleagues for the annual or biennial allocation of the institution's resources. As noted earlier, unless the institution has developed a system of priorities to guide the decision-making process that allocates resources, competition can become fierce and unrestrained. Such instances are generally rare, since most institutions have some sort of priorities that are well known to deans and faculty members. Land-grant institutions are sure to accord high priority to their agricultural and engineering programs; any institution with a medical school is forced to give it high priority; and other institutions with special missions, such as Georgia Tech or Pratt Institute, will have special priorities. Thus, it is a foolish dean who tries to establish a new set of funding priorities that will overturn a list of historical priorities incorporated in the mission of the institution. Indeed, the more the dean sees himself or herself in competition with other deans for the institution's resources, the less likely that dean is to build a good college, school, or division based on sound intellectual and fiscal premises. Competition, when untrammeled, leads to turf wars, and turf wars lead to bad decisions about the mission and purpose of an academic unit. Unfettered competition leads to unrealistic planning, and unrealistic planning leads to bad fiscal decisions. No dean should give up willingly a competitive edge in the struggle for resources, but no dean should view the institution's resources as open to raiding parties; what is good for the institution is going to be good for school X, but what is good for school X is not always good for the institution.

While competition is one part of a dean's relationship with fellow deans, cooperation is another and greater part. In addition to the general goal that should be held by all deans of making the institution better, many deans cooperate with one another on special projects, particularly in the area of joint degree programs. Typical relationships between academic units are the joint programs offered by business and law in many universities. These kinds of programs give deans an opportunity to work together to improve each others' programs and to bring students together in both units for new or expanded educational experiences. Deans work together in other common projects, such as improving the library, the computer system or systems at the institution, honors programs, and graduate programs. There always exists the opportunity for competition to flourish, even in these cooperative activities; for example, one dean's plan to improve the library might disadvantage another dean's attempt to improve library holdings in his or her area. Generally, however, cooperative efforts result in better understanding among the participating deans and consequently a closer working relationship in all areas.

DEANS AND DIRECTORS WITH INSTITUTIONWIDE
RESPONSIBILITIES

When deans of individual academic units focus attention on concerns related to the use of or participation in institutionwide programs or resources, they encounter another kind of administrator, one who has institutionwide responsibilities. Some of these administrators, usually titled dean or director, are listed as follows: the dean of graduate studies, the dean of undergraduate studies, the dean of continuing education, the dean or director of admissions, the director of the library, and the director of the computer center. As previously mentioned, none occupy line positions with regard to academic department chairpersons or faculty members, and all are considered part of the central administration; they report to it and work for it. Their primary task is to coordinate and supervise specific activities that cross over two or more colleges, schools, or divisions. The persons in charge of these activities, programs, or resources are very important to the deans of the individual academic units. Some of them perform services vital to the life of every academic unit, others act as quality-control officers for parts of the institution's academic enterprise.

As an example of this latter case, consider the dean of graduate studies. Originally, this office was established to control the quality of graduate programs offered in the various colleges and schools of the institution. For a short while in the 1950s and 1960s, the graduate dean in most universities was one of the more powerful and influential officers in the central administration because this office controlled a substantial amount of revenue generated by federal subventions for varying kinds of graduate programs. Such federal programs as the National Defense Education Act, Title IV, brought literally hundreds of thousands of dollars in subvention funds to the graduate dean's office. After the flow of federal aid to these programs was discontinued, the graduate dean's role returned to its original purpose of quality control.

At most universities, the graduate dean presides over an institutional Graduate Council comprised of members generally elected from the graduate faculties of the several academic units. Under the leadership of the graduate dean, the Graduate Council has the responsibility for coordinating graduate studies on a universitywide basis, including (a) developing broad university policies and principles regarding graduate work; (b) establishing and monitoring admission, graduation, and retention standards; (c) maintaining effective liaison with departments offering graduate programs; (d) evaluating existing graduate programs and administrative practices and, if appropriate, recommending revisions, improvements, or abolition; and (e) recommending approval or rejection of new graduate programs proposed by departments in individual academic units of the institution. In addition, the graduate dean, in collaboration with the Graduate Council, is expected to develop systems of inquiry and review to obtain an overview of graduate education and development and to ask for remedial action when necessary.

The deans of the individual academic units or their department chairpersons have their own students, faculty, degree programs, and budget and are responsible for administering them under universitywide policies. The graduate dean has no students, yet has some jurisdiction for them all. The graduate dean has no faculty, yet no faculty member can become a part of the graduate faculty without the graduate dean's approval. The graduate dean has no graduate degree program, yet has some jurisdiction for all of them. The graduate office encompasses the entire university in the purview of its responsibilities. It seldom has any line authority; its authority is limited to quality-control matters. Thus, it is not primarily involved in the development of large departmental or college budgets. The relations between the graduate dean and the deans of individual academic units of the university must be based on mutual trust and respect. At first glance, it might appear that the graduate dean has insufficient power or influence to implement the important responsibilities of his or her office. This is not necessarily the case. The authority to approve and reject proposed new programs, to conduct inquiry and review of each existing graduate program, and to make recommendations to an academic vice president and the Graduate Council are powerful tools that can motivate most department chairpersons and their deans to follow university procedures and maintain universitywide standards. Graduate deans who make full use of this authority and who also have the trust and respect of their academic colleagues and their academic vice president are considered to be influential figures on their respective campuses. Deans of individual academic units must constantly work with the graduate dean to improve the quality of existing programs, to abolish obsolete graduate programs, and to establish new ones. They cannot accomplish these tasks alone, and the graduate dean is a natural ally in these particular endeavors.

The dean of undergraduate studies also acts as a quality-control officer for the institution. This position, a relatively new one in American academic history, exists primarily to make sure that someone is looking out for the welfare of the undergraduate student; consequently, this position is generally found only in fairly large to large graduate research universities. There is sometimes a tendency in such universities to neglect the funding of the undergraduate programs in favor of the graduate programs. The dean of undergraduate studies acts as the institution's conscience in this regard and attempts to facilitate intracollegiate undergraduate advising and transfer activities. Again, this deanship is seldom found in small or medium-sized institutions or in large institutions that have a college of liberal arts and sciences, where almost all freshman and sophomore instruction takes place. If, however, an institution has freshman and sophomore instruction located in several different colleges—for example, a college of humanities, a college of science, and a college of social science—then a dean for undergraduate studies may serve a good purpose.

Deans of undergraduate studies have no students, but like graduate deans, they have some jurisdiction over them all. They have no faculty, yet have some jurisdiction over those faculty assigned duties to their office. While they have no responsibility for degree programs, they are nevertheless vitally concerned with the viability of all of them. And all the while these deans typically have very small budgets. They nevertheless have at least some of the same power and influence to implement the responsibilities of their office as graduate deans do. They have advisory councils, authority to conduct inquiry and review, and the ear of the academic vice president and/or president. Much of their influence is dependent on the extent to which they wish to exercise their authority to conduct inquiry and review and the respect and trust that they are accorded by their academic colleagues and academic vice president. Here then is yet another ally for deans of individual academic units in their various attempts to improve instruction by strengthening current programs, abolishing old ones, and starting new ones.

Many institutions have established divisions or offices of continuing education, which serve many different clients off campus. For some deans of professional colleges and schools, such as medicine, law, pharmacy, nursing, education, social work, and library science, the operation of an office of continuing education is of very great importance. Laws passed by both state and federal governments now require that graduates of these colleges continue their education as long as they practice their professions. This means that the continuing-education dean's office becomes the delivery system for educational services provided by the professional college dean's faculty. The dean of continuing education is usually allocated a budget to buy a faculty member's teaching time from the professional program and to pay travel expenses. It is therefore very important that deans of professional colleges or schools be able to work closely and well with the dean of continuing education.

Other deans or directors who provide services to the individual academic units are the director of the library or libraries; the director of the computing center or centers; and the director or dean of admissions. All of these directors possess special technical skills and knowledge necessary to provide their specialized services, and all receive budgets to carry out the responsibilities of their respective offices. Generally speaking, the deans of individual academic units spend little time directly working with these people. The dean's faculty members may have representation on various policy and advisory committees that work with the library and computer center directors and the director of admissions, but since these officers typically report directly to the academic vice president, the chance for the unit dean to have personal interaction with them is not good. They are usually part of the institution's council or committee of academic deans, and the unit dean works with them in that context. When the faculty of an academic unit believes it is not getting its share of the library book budget or its time on the central computer, if there is one available to all academic units, then its dean has a compelling reason to work with the librarian or the computer director. Generally such occasions are not happy ones. If there is never enough money, there are never going to be enough books or enough computer time. Thus, most of these negotiations end in frustration for all concerned: the dean, the dean's faculty, and the director involved.

Even though some deans and directors with institutionwide responsibilities have small budgets and none have line relationships with department chairpersons and faculty members, their importance should not be underestimated. They have considerable influence on many decisions affecting individual academic units, and it is crucial that they understand fully the needs of faculty members and students. Deans of academic units should make every effort to ensure a good and friendly relationship with these deans and directors and should provide whatever cooperation and assistance are necessary to help them fulfill their responsibilities effectively.

Questions

The following questions are intended to help deans analyze the situations at their respective institutions regarding the ways and extent to which they are involved with their presidents, academic vice presidents, and other deans.

1. a. You probably attend university-sponsored ceremonies over which the president presides. How many ceremonies or similar occasions are sponsored by your college or academic unit for your own faculty and students?
   b. Is your president invited to attend and/or participate?
   c. Do you think that the number of such occasions is just about right?
   d. Would it be an improvement to sponsor more or fewer such occasions where the president is invited to participate?
2. a. To what extent do you work directly with the president on his or her projects?
   b. Your projects?
   c. Would you prefer to work directly with the president on more or fewer projects than at present?
   d. Should you initiate contacts with the president?

3. **a.** Do you call upon your president to help in recruiting certain faculty members for your departments or programs?
   b. Is your president willing to participate?
   c. Should you call on the president more frequently?

4. **a.** Do you believe that your chief academic officer (academic vice president, provost) communicates with you enough?
   b. Does this officer provide you with as much information as you would like to have?
   c. Do you believe that he or she has information that would be useful to you, but that it is being held back from you deliberately? Inadvertently?

5. **a.** Do you believe that you communicate well with your vice president?
   b. Do you provide the vice president with all the information that he or she needs? More than needed? Less than needed?
   c. Do you provide information only when justifying requests or warning the vice president of impending problems?
   d. Do you provide information about good things that are happening to the faculty or students in your college or academic unit in order to let the vice president know how proud you are of certain of their accomplishments?
   e. Should you do more of the latter type of communication than you are currently doing?

6. **a.** Do you have a good track record with the vice president in terms of getting the resources you ask for?
   b. Do you think your track record is better or worse than the track records of the other deans in your institution? If it is better or worse, how do you account for the difference?

7. **a.** Have other deans ever helped you solve one or more of your problems by giving you good advice? Did you ask for the advice?
   b. Have you ever given advice to other deans? Have other deans ever asked you for advice?

    c. Do you feel comfortable socializing with the other deans? How competitive are you with them?

8. a. Are you satisfied with the relationships you have with (1) your president, (2) your chief academic officer (academic vice president, provost), and (3) your fellow deans?

    b. If you are not satisfied, what kinds of relationship would you like and what seems to stand in the way?

10

Frustrations with the Institutional Support Staff

While the dean's energies are almost always focused directly on the academic budget, faculty personnel issues, and program development and enhancement, the daily operation of his or her academic unit is maintained by an almost invisible infrastructure run by the institution's support staff, who maintain control over the nonacademic staff working in personnel, purchasing activities, travel, security, and plant operations and maintenance. The people who perform these jobs, both supervisors and those supervised, are driven by a whole set of imperatives, laws, rules, and regulations that are different from those used by the dean to direct academic activities. Theoretically, at least, the institution's support and academic staffs are united in a common effort to make the institution serve its students better. But quite often there exists a lack of understanding, sometimes even a sense of mistrust, between the academic part of an institution and its nonacademic support staff. Even if no misunderstanding or mistrust exists between the two, there is almost always a sense of frustration that the two sides experience with each other in the daily execution of business. This chapter attempts to examine those frustrations in terms of

218

the dean's interaction with nonacademic personnel staff, purchasing, travel, maintenance, and campus security.

Nonacademic Personnel Staff

In most institutions of higher education in this country, nonacademic personnel employed by the institution are hired, fired, promoted, demoted, rewarded, and punished by a dual system of management that involves the academic employer and a collegewide or universitywide director of personnel services. Sometimes the latter position is entitled director of human resources. The personnel director's office generally establishes the criteria for employment in various nonacademic positions on campus and performs job audits, approves job classifications and reclassifications, and establishes or at least maintains control of salary schedules for all nonacademic positions. In state universities, the authority for the performance of all these activities may be located off campus in some agency in the state capital, thus making the relationship between the dean and the personnel director even more tenuous. In other words, while the dean may certainly hire a secretary, that secretary's salary is established by the personnel director, not the dean; the secretary's job classification (senior secretary, executive secretary, secretary I, II, etc.) is established by the director of personnel. The dean can fire that secretary, but even in this unpleasant act there are often rules of conduct that reach far beyond the boundaries of decorum and common sense. It is therefore vital that the dean understand thoroughly the system of governance of the nonacademic personnel on his or her campus.

Consider some of the difficulties that a dean can encounter with the institution's personnel office. Most such offices process and approve all appointment papers for new or continuing nonacademic positions. This is a process that holds great potential for misunderstanding, mistrust, and even open warfare between the academic and nonacademic parts of the institution. Late processing of appointments means delays in the delivery of the biweekly or monthly paycheck, and unpaid employees are extremely unhappy employees. Personnel directors (or their surrogates in the state capital) formulate and approve job classifications and reclassifications, a critical activity as it relates to keeping faculty, particularly in the sciences and engineering, happy and productive.

Perhaps the most frustrating aspect of the dean's relationship with nonacademic support staff is his or her inability to promote or otherwise reward outstanding people because the rules of the personnel office lack flexibility. Consider the following examples of bureaucratic restraint. The dean has finally managed through luck and/or connivance of the most complicated nature to hire, train, and nurture a truly superior staff assistant. This person's abilities are too good to be true; he or she is so outstanding that it is obvious to all that the dean will be unable to keep that assistant on the job unless higher salaries or promotions in rank are real possibilities. This gem of a person is not demanding, but will surely be recruited away at a higher rank somewhere else in the university unless the dean can offer a fairly stable and consistent schedule of advancement in salary and rank; furthermore, to make matters even more painful, this person does not really want to leave the dean's office, where working conditions are pleasant and challenging. But unless we are considering a truly unusual university or college, the dead hand of bureaucracy will prevent the dean from keeping this staff assistant. If the staff assistant does not supervise at least x number of persons, he or she, according to rules made in some office remote from the college dean's office, simply cannot be promoted from staff assistant to, let us say, administrative assistant or senior staff assistant. Even more galling to the dean is a rule common to most personnel systems whereby the rank level of a secretary assigned to a manager depends on the rank level of that manager. Thus, a dean can have a secretary III, but not a secretary IV, a rank reserved for vice presidents. Generally, there is no solution available to the dean unless circumvention of the whole process is possible by hiring the secretary or staff assistant on a university or college foundation account, but even this ploy is surely to be resisted by the central administration, and this solution, we suggest, is not the best way to use funds from the dean's accounts in the college or university foundation.

Since deans are supposed to spend at least some of their time and energy in solving administrative problems encountered by the faculty, nothing is more frustrating to either the dean or the faculty member than the admission the dean is compelled to make to that distressed faculty member regarding the solution to a particular nonacademic personnel problem: "It is out of my hands." As a painful example, consider the senior faculty member, a highly productive research scholar, who is told by the institution's personnel office that he cannot promote a laboratory technician II to laboratory technician III because—take your pick—(a) the lab tech does not have enough time in grade; (b) the lab tech only supervises two people and must supervise four people before being eligible for promotion; (c) even though the lab tech has enough time in grade to be promoted to rank III, since this lab tech was promoted by waiver from rank I to rank II within a year, a promotion to rank III is not possible for at least eighteen more months; (d) the lab tech does not have a master's degree; or (e) the lab tech has a master's degree, but it is not in the right subspecialty.

The senior research scholar, upon being presented with one or more of these obstacles (or others even less relevant in the judgment of the scholar), naturally presents this problem to his dean for immediate solution, the senior scholar's department chairperson having impaled himself on the barbed wire of the personnel office with no result other than excessive bleeding and a loss of equanimity. The senior scholar will of course compound the problem by announcing to the dean that his whole project is in jeopardy unless this problem can be resolved swiftly; that he will have to return to the federal granting agency over $200,000 in contract funds because he cannot sit around and wait for the personnel office to gain true enlightenment and understanding of the grave nature of the project that the funding agency has asked the senior scholar to undertake; and, finally, that the senior scholar is fed up with the silly personnel rules of the institution, and this latest in a long series of problems is enough to make him think seriously about the offer he still has in his desk from Greatness Tech, an institution that surely understands the importance of bench scientists and their unique needs.

What can the dean do? The rules and regulations have long been in place; battles such as this have been fought over and over. Indeed, some of those rules and regulations have been put in place by the faculty themselves. For example, such rules about a lab tech III having to have a master's degree in a particular subspecialty are generally formulated by impractical faculty insistent upon maintaining "high standards"; yet, ironically, it turns out that the rule has become the object of scorn by someone on the faculty hoist with his own petard. In any but the most mindless personnel system, there is a built-in waiver clause for most salary and job classification issues. Every dean should know thoroughly all the details of these waiver clauses and be prepared to use them with a reasonable degree of frequency. No dean should be embarrassed about invoking clauses in order to make an inflexible system more responsive to the operational needs of his or her academic unit. Of course, anyone can go to the well too often; not every faculty member's research project is completely dependent upon a personnel decision, but deans exist to solve problems, even if it means challenging the systems that rule the daily business of their academic units. And a dean who is unwilling to challenge those systems will be overcome by them.

Purchasing Activities

Most of what we will next observe about university or college purchasing offices will apply primarily to medium-size and large public, tax-supported universities. Privately supported universities are not bound by the vast state bureaucracies that control purchasing activities in all state agencies. It is a rare occurrence to find a state that has completely separate purchasing rules, regulations, and laws for its many different state agencies. Almost always, tax-supported colleges and universities are subject to the same purchasing regulations and laws that govern the state's department of transportation or department of agriculture. Invariably, these regulations and laws frustrate the dean and the faculty members and frequently impede the progress of academic programs, especially the research programs and the instructional programs in such areas as music, art, and theater. Not only are there the standard impedimenta of regular state purchasing regulations and laws (most of which have been written to protect and nourish businesses within the state's boundaries), but in the past decade in many states there has arisen whole new congeries of separate purchasing divisions designed to regulate special items, such as electronic data-processing equipment (not only computers but also software are targets of special concern and supervision). Nothing in state government is so puzzling as the recent spate of newly formed special state purchasing divisions with tax-saving names such as the Institutional Resources Commission and the Electronic Data-processing Council, all designed to regulate the purchase of computers and software. What is puzzling, of course, is that while such equipment once cost millions of dollars per item and thus needed regulation, now the technology (except for huge machines) has become relatively inexpensive. But it can be stated without a great deal of hyperbole that some states now have so many approval agencies involved in the purchase of electronic data-processing equipment that by the time a college or a university secures authority to purchase a computer, that particular machine may well have been superseded by a newer, faster, and sometimes cheaper one. The state barns now have exquisitely configured padlocks on them, but the horses have long since gone.

It must occur to almost every dean at some time or other during the academic year that the institution's purchasing office has no budget of its own, because if it did, it would surely understand how difficult that office's rules and regulations make it to purchase anything. And, indeed, it has no budget of its own; the office exists to spend everyone else's budget in accordance with the institution's and state's purchasing regulations and laws. That such an office must exist is undeniable, and it is axiomatic that the more byzantine the regulations and laws relating to purchasing, the more people must be hired in purchasing to monitor them. In state universities there is a law or regulation for everything that can possibly be bought, but of particular frustration to the dean are the requirements for purchasing publications such as brochures, college catalogs, and other informational material. Requirements regarding printing activities can be so complex that unless an unusual amount of foresight is brought into play, deadlines for distributing the printed material can be missed, sometimes by embarrassing margins. Furthermore, just as the personnel division of an institution matches the rank level of nonacademic positions to the rank of their respective managers, so state purchasing offices often assign specific grades of furniture to the ranks of the persons who will use them. Thus, a department chairperson can have a $200 desk, a dean can have a $350 desk, a vice president can have a $500 desk, and so on. But what does a dean do with a newly recruited eminent scholar from Magnus U. who wants a $1,000 desk? The worst thing for the dean to do is to quote from state purchasing regulations. At Magnus U. they never heard of such silly things as purchasing regulations. The dean has but one course of action in dealing with the request of the new scholar (whose acquisition, while considered a coup throughout the college, has put a discernible dent in the dean's operating budget): go to the institution's foundation and find the money for the desk or, if this source of funding is unavailable, hold a bake sale or a raffle, anything but try to impose alien regulations on the new faculty superstar. Unlike personnel regulations, very few waiver clauses are included in state purchasing regulations; nothing in state government is watched over so carefully as purchases made with the taxpayers' dollars. In privately supported universities, these regulations are generally less structured and waivers generally much easier to obtain.

Vendors present special problems to both deans and those who work in instructional purchasing offices, especially vendors of highly sophisticated and expensive equipment. Many faculty members tend to be careless in their dealings with vendors; the faculty member knows what he or she wants or needs, and there are plenty of vendors loose in the land who are willing to promise to provide the professor with exactly what is wanted, even though the vendor's company cannot, when all is said and done, deliver what has been promised. This state of affairs usually leads to an almost unbelievable series of accusations and counteraccusations. The scapegoat is always the purchasing division: either the purchasing agent misunderstood and misread the faculty member's purchasing request or the purchasing agent understood the request but refused to submit it as transmitted to the vendor. Vendors sometimes make a living from the classic struggle between the faculty and the purchasing division, and it is seldom that the vendor either admits a mistake or fails to pin the blame on the purchasing agent. The fact is that faculty do make mistakes, just as vendors do. Indeed, the odds are that the purchasing agent is usually the least likely of the three parties—agent, vendor, and faculty member—to make mistakes. As we noted in an earlier chapter, the dean is always vulnerable to squeeze plays, and the purchase of equipment is no exception to this general rule. A typical purchasing-related squeeze play can take the following form. Professor Strangelove has enough money from various sources ($100,000) to buy a Super Shell Analyzer, Model 200A. Actually Strangelove really wants a Super Shell Analyzer, Model 400A, but this model costs $125,000. Strangelove orders Model 400A; the purchasing office, distracted in a careless moment or led astray by Strangelove's office, approves the purchase of the more expensive model, having been led to believe that the necessary funds are available. The more expensive model is delivered, and the invoice is presented to Strangelove's department. Then there is hell (and the vendor) to pay. Only a dean with the instincts of Hercule Poirot can sift through the ensuing round of finger pointing to determine what actually happened. And even if the dean-as-detective has the time and patience to discover the truth, what is to be done then? Send Strangelove's Model 400A back to the vendor? Refuse to provide the purchasing office with the extra $25,000? The two options are equally unpalatable, for Strangelove will surely assert that his lifework is thwarted unless he can have the more expensive model. Two lessons can be learned from this story: (a) fallibility is sometimes equally distributed among vendor, faculty member, and purchasing division; (b) the dean must always keep a contingency fund at the ready in order to solve purchasing-related problems.

Travel Allowances

If anything changes more rapidly these days than computer technology, it is the cost of faculty travel and the regulations in both public and private universities and colleges that affect that travel. The latter is a function of the former; the ever-changing costs of airfare in particular drive various bureaucracies into ever more complicated constraints about who may travel, how much travel can be authorized, and for what reasons that travel can be authorized. Since airlines are now unregulated, they hold the upper hand in the dean's struggle to plan a rational budget for the travel expenses of his or her faculty members. State agencies and the central administrations of colleges and universities simply cannot budget with any certitude the expenditure category known as travel. Indeed, things change so rapidly that it is possible for a faculty member to leave campus one week and return the next week to learn that the regulations regarding the just-completed trip have changed and that future travel plans must therefore be modified, almost always in the direction of less travel than originally budgeted for. There is no easy answer to this dilemma, but just as a wise dean keeps a contingency fund to solve purchasing-related problems, so the dean should keep a contingency fund for travel-related problems. The dean should plan and budget for a 15 percent cost overrun for travel expenses for each year's operating budget. Finally, the dean who has accounts in an institution's foundation should not be hesitant to draw on those accounts to provide help. The provision of that kind of help is one of the main reasons for an institution to have a foundation in existence.

Maintenance Staff

When is a dean a landlord and when not? Although institutions have their own individual answers to this question and although in some institutions the dean is not supposed to have any responsibility for lights, climate control, windows, doors, furniture, and the like, while in other institutions the dean may be given a special budget for such concerns, the general answer is that the dean is always the landlord, if not de jure, then surely de facto in the minds of the faculty. No matter that some remotely understood unit on campus generally called Plants and Grounds is supposed to replace light bulbs, paint walls, fix doors and windows—any building the dean works in is his or her building, and anything that goes wrong in that building is first the dean's responsibility. Faculty, even department chairpersons, are usually reluctant to deal with the people in Plants and Grounds, and the dean is usually called upon to negotiate with these folk, generally regarded as the Hessians of the institution. Perhaps it is just as well that faculty members have very little to do with the people in Plants and Grounds, for faculty members are almost always less tolerant of maintenance personnel than are deans. Not much that is either good or constructive can come from encouraging individual faculty members to seek solutions to their problems by dealing directly with Plants and Grounds. The results of such negotiations are likely to be as anarchic and as expensive as encouraging individual faculty to intervene directly in disputes between vendors and the purchasing office. It is generally good policy for the dean to discourage direct contact with maintenance personnel.

If the dean can afford it, there ought to be someone in the dean's office who is specifically charged with the responsibility for all maintenance-related tasks, except those covered by specific maintenance contracts on complex equipment such as gas chromatographs and computers. Light bulbs, door locks, windows, doors, and furniture are all matters that require constant and instant attention, and while in many colleges and universities these matters are the assigned responsibility of the Plants and Grounds people, there are seldom enough of these people to ensure that every burned-out bulb, every broken lock, every malfunctioning door or window is instantly attended to. Someone in the dean's office must be the designated prodder, the official goad of the college, to make sure that proper maintenance and security are provided.

Larger maintenance problems require the dean's personal attention. A leaking roof, the replacement of a malfunctioning climate control system, the renovation of a classroom into a series of offices, the changing of a dry laboratory into a wet laboratory, or the changing of two small classrooms into one large classroom—these are all generally classified as "minor renovations," even though the sums involved to effect these changes are sometimes anything but minor. In addition to the substantial costs that are usually involved in such minor renovation projects, a cost that typically delays the completion of such projects, the dean encounters another obstacle—the real or alleged incompetence of the Plants and Grounds personnel assigned to do the project. In most state universities and colleges a division of Plants and Grounds is assigned the responsibility of performing minor renovation projects. Sometimes the performance of these organizations is both poor and costly. The high cost is a function of the low salaries generally paid to Plants and Grounds personnel. In private enterprise, construction workers command good salaries, and thus the less qualified people are usually the only ones who will work for state agencies such as colleges and universities. Furthermore, since there are few seriously adhered-to deadlines for the completion of minor renovation projects, the workers bring to their jobs very little sense of urgency to complete a project on time. Very few state colleges or universities are able to complete minor renovation jobs on time. How many hundreds of academic deans planned to move into a renovated building at the beginning of an academic year only to move finally when the spring flowers begin to bloom! The dean has very little, if any, control over these matters, and aside from writing anguished letters to the vice president or president, about all he or she can do is to plan to move into, or otherwise use, the renovated building six months after the date of completion originally promised by Plants and Grounds. If the state institution at which the dean is employed allows it, the dean should take every opportunity available to contract with private enterprise. Almost always, in the long run, private enterprise can do the job quicker, better, and cheaper than the institution's Plants and Grounds people.

Security Staff

In matters of campus security (demonstrations both planned and spontaneous, theft, assault, battery, rape, and parking), the dean is not the first person turned to by the faculty. Fortunately for the dean, the campus police, the central administration, or both hold this dubious honor, although often the dean is at least peripherally involved, especially the dean whose students are demonstrating, whose students or faculty are assaulted, whose college property is stolen, or whose faculty member cannot find parking at 10:30 A.M. in the center of the campus. As for demonstrations and student protests, things have changed dramatically since the late sixties and early seventies. These activities are much fewer in number, more formal in character, and generally marked by almost excessive planning on the part of the participants. To be sure, there are still student demonstrations and protests on many campuses, but university and college administrators have learned how to deal with these events just as the students have learned how to conduct them. The anarchy, bitterness, and general incivility now seem absent, for which almost everyone in higher education is thankful. Unless only students from the dean's particular college or academic unit are involved in a particular demonstration, about all a dean is expected to do these days is to remain as far from the scene of action as possible. If only students from the dean's college are involved, then obviously the dean has known from the beginning the cause of the event and, quite probably, the remedy sought by the protesting students. In such cases, the dean must be completely involved in keeping the demonstration within the legal boundaries established by local authority and must be a faithful and constant adviser to the central administration and the campus police. Sometimes the remedies sought by the protesting students can be provided; more often than not, such remedies are impossible to grant. If they could be granted, there would be no need for the protest, or at least much of the excitement and challenge would be absent from the event itself.

Theft is a major problem on most campuses today. Thieves have discovered how vulnerable a university or college campus is, how almost absurdly easy it is to rob a laboratory or library. Thieves also know that the equipment now found on campus is much more valuable than it used to be. As a consequence, the dean must learn to work with the campus police in order to help them prevent his or her college from being overrun with thieves. Historically, academic deans have had very little to do with campus police—or police of any kind, for that matter. But times have changed, and it behooves the dean to foster a close working relationship with campus police. No longer the campus buffoons or the object of undergraduate pranksters, campus police today are well-trained professionals, many of them graduates of the institutions they serve and protect. By making the campus police part of the life of the college, by encouraging them to conduct security workshops for department chairpersons and faculty, the dean can help them protect the college's property, much of which is expensive yet easy to steal. The faculty generally have regarded campus police as an unnecessary and at least semicomic intrusion into the life of the institution, and the campus police, especially the new professionals, have generally regarded the faculty as both arrogant and careless of the institution's property. Both had in the past some justification for their views, but both must now work together, and it is the dean's responsibility to provide the leadership to bring these two groups of people into a condition of mutual respect.

It is sad but true that many campuses are no longer safe from assault, battery, and rape. Few campuses are guarded by high walls and iron gates; they are almost all open communities, open to everyone, including the criminal bent on violence. While the personal safety of the students and faculty is largely the responsibility of the central administration and the campus police, academic deans can and should encourage the campus police to give training sessions to their faculties regarding security precautions that help prevent violence. The dean or his or her surrogate in charge of maintenance should be knowledgeable about conditions that can encourage violence, such as unlighted hallways, building entrances and exits, remote and poorly lighted stairways, poor lock security, and other aspects of the physical plant that make violence a real possibility. The dean cannot make one building a fortress any more than the central administration can make the whole institution a fortress, but by demonstrating proper concern, the dean can teach the faculty to become security-conscious.

We hesitate to introduce the subject of parking, that bane of presidents and provosts and vice presidents, that incredibly emotional issue with the faculty, that topic of both high and low humor. But invariably the dean is regarded by his or her faculty as someone who should be able to convince the shortsighted central administration that parking is a serious matter that can be solved quickly "if only someone will take away the reserved parking spaces assigned to the president and the vice presidents and, of course, the deans." Then, the common wis-

dom dictates, "we should get some real action instead of ex-
cuses about too little money." The fact of the matter is that
presidents, vice presidents, deans, and others with reserved
parking spaces know only too well that giving up reserved parking spaces will not solve the problem. In spite of this knowledge, we know some deans (but no presidents or vice presidents) who have given up their reserved parking spaces, not
in the belief that such self-abnegation will solve the problem,
but simply to escape the heat. The problem really is caused by
a lack of money; when given the choice between a new library
building and a parking garage, the faculty will invariably
choose the new library, all the while wondering why, through
"creative financing," it is not possible to have both. But lack
of funding is not the only cause of the parking crisis that most
campuses experience today, for after all, parking garages can
usually be financed through bonding. The real dilemma is
where to put the parking garage. Most colleges and universities
have campuses whose boundaries are delimited by either law
or economic conditions or both. And as colleges and universities grow, building space becomes precious. Again, given the
choice between sacrificing green space (eating into the lovely
campus mall) or voting against having another parking lot,
most faculty and most administrators unhesitatingly choose to
protect the green space and vote against the parking lot. This
obviously exacerbates the parking problem and increases the
barrage of criticism from faculty and students. We know of no
solution to these problems, for if we did, we would already be
rich and famous. We urge the dean to tread lightly through this
minefield, to take no firm stands, to espouse no single panaceas, to avoid criticism of other panaceas, and to stay as far
away from the topic as possible. There are no cheap and easy
solutions close at hand. But above all else, the dean should not
put the blame on the campus police; they did not invent the
problem and cannot solve it; all they do is enforce the parking
rules and regulations. All one can hope for from the campus
police in this matter is tolerance and occasional mercy.

Acknowledging the Support Staff

When all is said and done, it is important for the dean to remember that while historically there has always been an adver-

sarial relationship between academics, on the one hand, and, on the other, the institution's support staff—its personnel office, its purchasing office, its travel desk, the maintenance personnel, and the campus police—a good dean's obligation is to avoid conflict if at all possible and to make those support systems work for the college. There is enough controversy and struggle in the dean's daily life without creating new problems. Almost always the support staff of any institution wants to help make that institution better; indeed, quite often the support staff is more loyal to the institution than many of its faculty. An institution's support staff, particularly those in public colleges and universities, are generally paid less than their peers in private enterprise. Why, then, do they stay? In most cases (always excepting the lower-level employees in Plants and Grounds), these people have a certain pride in their association with a college or university and work for less just for the privilege of that association. It is their loyalty and pride that the dean must keep uppermost in mind when frustration with some part of the support staff threatens to overwhelm the dean's sense of equanimity and judgment.

How can the dean help to improve the services provided his or her college by the support staff? It is not enough to shrug one's shoulders in the face of disappointment and frustration and say, "Oh well, they are loyal and dedicated people who are doing the best they can." Patience and tolerance are not enough; the dean must seek aggressively to improve those services. The first step on the long road to improvement is to work hard at establishing personal relationships with key persons in each division of the institution's support services. These relationships cannot be ephemeral, for if they are, they will dissolve in the heat of the first crisis. The dean should learn the driving motivations of each of these supervisors and know what pleases them and what frustrates them. In short, the dean should be on a first-name basis with each of these people. Just as important, the key people in the dean's office, the administrative assistant and assistant dean(s), should know who it is in each of these supervisors' offices that really runs the daily operation of those offices. It is said that the chief petty officers really run the American navy; admirals and captains could not function without these chiefs. So it is in many organizations;

there is almost always a chief petty officer who runs things. Thus, if there is understanding and cooperation between the dean's chiefs and the supervisors' chiefs, things will get done. If there is misunderstanding and mistrust between the chiefs, nothing good will ever happen. More specifically, it is necessary that the dean's staff know whom to call, know who is responsible for what in each division. This knowledge saves time, prevents emotional stress, and promotes swift responses to calls for help.

The cliché *faceless bureaucrat* explains a good part of the historical enmity that the faculty has for the institutional support staff. Few department chairpersons and even fewer faculty members, especially in middle-to-large colleges and universities, ever come face-to-face with the institution's director of nonacademic personnel, the purchasing agent, or any of the other heads of divisions that provide support to the academic enterprise. Contact by department chairpersons or faculty is usually limited to dry, almost dusty memoranda or, at best, telephone conversations that are almost always brief and guarded. Hence, the unknown bureaucrat becomes a sinister or coldhearted or ignorant or stupid bureaucrat because he or she is essentially faceless. But when a department chairperson or a member of the faculty can put a face and a personality together with a name and a title, the first step toward understanding and cooperation has been taken. There are, of course, exceptions to this benign view of human nature. Some bureaucrats should always remain faceless, for at this level of abstraction they are more acceptable than in real life, and some faculty members and even some department chairpersons should always be kept hidden from the institution's support personnel. Thus, the dean should actively encourage supervisors and key personnel from all of the institution's support organizations to make presentations and hold workshops for the dean, the dean's staff, department chairpersons, and the leaders among the college faculty. These presentations and workshops will educate both sides and almost always promote better understanding of mutual problems and thus improve daily working relationships.

Once good relationships have been established and maintained, it is important for the dean and his or her staff and all department chairpersons to assume certain responsibilities: (a) Since ignorance of personnel rules is not a legitimate excuse to criticize the personnel division, the dean, the dean's staff, and department chairpersons must know those rules well. The dean should use whatever waiver clauses are available as often as it is justifiable to do so. (b) Department chairpersons should be strongly encouraged to follow through on important purchasing requests; unless an important project is consistently monitored, Murphy's Law has at least an even chance of operating; indeed, passive reliance upon complex bureaucratic systems is what made Murphy's Law famous. (c) Someone in the dean's office must actively monitor the changing rules of the institution's travel desk and keep all key personnel in the college informed of those changes. (d) The dean must always allow for both delays and cost overruns in all maintenance projects, even those undertaken by contract with private enterprise. (e) The dean must make sure that in security matters, the faculty of the college avoids carelessness.

The authors of this book do not believe in either a perfect world or the perfectibility of man, but they believe that if the dean works hard at improving relationships with the support services of the institution and has a good sense of humor, the dean's life, the faculty's lives, the life of the entire college will become at once more serene and more productive.

Questions

1. What problems or frustrations, if any, have you experienced during the past year or two with any of your support agency staff? Which institutional support agencies and what levels of staff member were involved? Were you as dean able to resolve the problem? If so, how?

2. Do you have special strategies that you employ in dealing with support agency staff? What are they?

3. In your opinion, are the problems and frustrations that you have experienced due primarily to official state or institutional regulations or to the staff people who are responsible for carrying out the procedures?

4. If the problems are due to official state regulations or pol-

icies, who has the authority to change them? What procedures are available, if any, to seek relief?

5. If the problems are due only to official institutional policies and procedures, who has the authority to change them? What procedures are available to seek relief?

6. In your opinion, are there justifiable reasons for retaining these policies and regulations as they are?

11

Interaction with the External Public: Alumni, Parents, Trustees, and Legislators

We have discussed all of the major internal relationships that the dean has with other academic and support units within the university. But these relationships, challenging and at times difficult though they may be, do not constitute all of a dean's professional duties and obligations. There is a whole world outside the gates of the campus—a world often referred to by academics as the "real world"—that will test the dean's energies, courage, and intellect just as rigorously as the various constituencies on campus. This world, no more nor less real or unreal than the campus, can be divided into at least four parts: alumni, parents (who may also be alumni), trustees (almost always some of whom are alumni), and legislators (some of whom may be alumni). In most universities and colleges there are special offices, units, or divisions that have been established to deal with these particular segments of the general

236

public. Most institutions have an Office of Alumni Affairs, replete with a director, a staff, and a series of publications. While few, if any, institutions have an office set up for parent relations, generally the institution's Office of Student Affairs is the initial contact point between parents and students. Trustees deal mainly with presidents and provosts. Legislators are apt to deal with anyone who strikes their fancy; they are the most uncontrollable segment of the institution's external constituency, although most universities and colleges try to channel politicians through an office generally referred to as the Office for Governmental Relations. Sometimes this office is part of a unit known as the Office for Public Relations, which generally is concerned with various ways to promote a good image of the university. It is surprising, however, how often an institution's public affairs office is unable to deal with the simplest of academic problems that may attract public notice. The dean cannot rest easy in a belief that since there are people on campus specifically hired to "do public relations," there is no need to worry about public relations. And the Office for Governmental Relations does not, cannot, and will not provide protection from restless or inquisitive or hostile legislators. Indeed, while all of these offices or units that are designed to deal with the public can help the dean interact with it, the dean must conduct his or her own relationships with segments of the public. This chapter, then, will treat those various relationships.

Relating to Alumni

Naturally, the older the institution, the more highly developed will be its Office of Alumni Affairs and its Office of Development. And as a consequence, more of the dean's energy and time will need to be spent with these offices. Privately supported universities like Harvard, Yale, and Princeton must depend upon alumni to provide the funding for a substantial fraction of the institution's endowment. These institutions have developed the care, feeding, and cultivation of alumni to a fine art and have made the deans of their various colleges an integral part of alumni solicitation and development work. Older public institutions of higher learning like the University of

Michigan or the College of William and Mary have also developed extremely effective and sophisticated alumni relations programs. But no matter whether the institution is old or young, part of the dean's responsibility is to conduct an organized alumni relations program. And it may be that developing an alumni relations program in a new institution, public or private, is more difficult than maintaining an ongoing program at an old institution. New institutions have to compete for funds with older, more established institutions, and this means that they must take special care not to lose the interest or the loyalty of their graduates. Thus, a dean at a new institution may find it necessary to work very hard to establish both an alumni relations operation and an institutional development organization.

As good relations are being established with the alumni, the dean should remember that occasionally some alumni can be very demanding, very selfish, and surprisingly ignorant of what goes on in the college from which they graduated. Their most frequent request lies in the area of admissions. They want to make sure their children get admitted to the institution, even when those children are not qualified. Most institutions, both public and private (especially private), try to give some kind of small advantage to children of alumni in the ever more competitive process of admissions selections. But, in an effort either to help a business partner or to impress their clients, or for a variety of other reasons, alumni put pressure on the institution to admit the children of friends or clients. Generally speaking, the dean does not get involved in these maneuvers and, whenever possible, should avoid involvement. Decanal stress is intense enough without increasing it by trying to run an ad hoc admissions operation in the college office. The dean, however, has the option not to get involved, depending upon the case at issue. In other words, if the dean does not want to cash in too many chips with the central admissions office (each unqualified student admitted is a very big chip), he or she can tell the alumnus that in such matters the dean is essentially powerless, that all those decisions are made by the central administration. This, of course, is nonsense, although the general public does not know it. A college dean wishing to do so can have enormous influence on the central admissions office in individual cases.

The decanal decision to intervene has to depend upon the potential of the dean's college for receiving a reward from the alumnus who seeks the waiver of admission standards and upon the extent to which the applicant in question falls below the admission standards of the college or university. Virtually all universities and colleges use waivers of admissions standards, but the serious question is, When is a waiver a favor to an applicant and when is it an outright disservice to the applicant? The old cliché "She's a very good student, but she just doesn't test well" is a cliché because it is true; there are many students who can earn a baccalaureate with a respectable grade point average who simply do not score well on Scholastic Aptitude Tests or American College Tests. But no great favor is done to an engineering applicant who made D's and F's in high school algebra, high school chemistry, and high school physics. It is all a question of judgment based on careful analysis, and that judgment call must come from the dean.

Obviously, the dean cannot cut a deal with the alumnus who is seeking a waiver for an applicant; such an arrangement amounts to criminal behavior. All that can be done is to decide whether or not to seek the waiver based on what is best for the applicant and hope that some day in the future the alumnus will remember the tolerance and generosity of his or her alma mater and of the dean. This sort of decision is almost always difficult; the dean can never give the impression that seats in the college are for sale to potential donors, yet donors are absolutely necessary to the betterment of the college or university. Generally, an answer of no should be given to requests for admissions waivers from alumni, and while responsibility for denial of a waiver can simply be shifted to the central admissions office, especially in the face of an aggressive, importunate alumnus, the dean should take special pains to explain to the alumnus why a waiver is not in the best interests of a particular applicant. Most alumni can understand and accept a reasoned explanation of a denial; very few can accept a simple statement such as "The applicant doesn't have good enough test scores" or "The applicant's grade point average is below the cutoff number."

Alumni are not only an institution's best friends but also its most severe critics. Much of the fuel for their criticism is generated by students currently enrolled in the institution. Often these students are children of alumni, but many times they are children of friends and neighbors of alumni. Students, as we are aware, are quite often prone to exaggeration, and despite enormous efforts of the institution itself, they are in many instances ignorant of what policies and procedures guide the institution in its efforts to educate them. They look at a college or university through very narrowly focused lenses: the courses they are taking, the faculty who is teaching them, and such highly publicized institutional problems as parking, the increase in the cost of tuition that year, and one or two political issues that affect the nation itself. Thus, alumni may get from current student sources a distorted view of course requirements for a degree: why there is a foreign-language requirement, why everyone has to take freshman chemistry, why two courses in calculus are required for admission into the business school. And, despite the best efforts at quality control that a dean can exert, every college has at least one or two faculty who are, in the judgment of the students, not good at classroom teaching. Students make legends out of both good and bad teachers, but usually the alumni hear only about legendarily poor teachers. Finally, of course, students complain about the institution's administration, most often focusing on the central administration rather than college deans. Indeed, rarely does a dean become the target of student complaints, a phenomenon that probably can be explained by the fact that student newspapers (a particularly uninformed source from which most students gather their general knowledge about what is going on) write mostly about the sins and general inadequacies of the central administration; the imbalance exists because there are seldom enough student reporters on any campus newspaper to cover both the central administration and the college deans' offices. This mostly bad information is passed on to alumni, who, in turn, present it in an even more distorted form back to the dean and the president or various vice presidents.

As we have often done before in earlier chapters in this book, we counsel the dean to have patience when confronted by alumni with student-generated complaints. Most of these complaints will be either ill founded or distorted, although some may be factually true. If the dean knows what is going on in his or her college, it is much easier to deal with such complaints. If the dean is ignorant about what is happening in the college, then he or she is much more apt to panic and take action that will later be regretted. Always remember, alumni are generally even more ignorant than students about the true state of affairs in a college or university. The dean must treat seriously every complaint received from an alumnus, must track down all the facts in each case, and must, above all else, provide a written response to alumni complaints, whether those complaints were received orally or in written form. No dean should become impatient with alumni complaints, for each complaint, no matter how trivial or how serious, can provide an opportunity to educate the alumnus making the complaint. Each response presents the dean with a chance to win another friend for the college or university, even if, as usually is the case, an immediate remedy for the complaint is not possible. In carefully responding to the complaint, the dean thus educates the alumnus and can help the alumnus change from critic to advocate. All it takes is patience and hard work.

Criticism sometimes comes from older alumni who have employed the institution's more recent alumni. The general complaint from this quarter is that the more recent graduates of the college or university "don't know anything," or "they can't write," or "they can't make a decent presentation," or "their heads are full of theory and they don't have an ounce of common sense." The authors of this book suspect that this particular brand of criticism is as old as universities themselves and is a product not so much of the pedagogical inadequacies of the institution as it is a product of youth, inexperience, and the impatience of the older generation. It is interesting to note that this form of criticism comes mainly from alumni of the institution's professional colleges, such as business ("They aren't interested in learning about the product they sell"), law ("They don't know how to behave in court"), engineering ("They can't write a decent report"), and journalism ("They don't know how to ask the right questions"). While this book is not the appropriate vehicle in which to conduct yet another version of the classic academic debate about the relative virtues of a general education versus a professional education (some would put the debate more uncharitably: education versus training), it is necessary to assert that most colleges and universities are not interested in preparing their students for specific jobs in specific corporations or industries. Most colleges and universities attempt to do two things at once: to educate their students in a general, liberal arts and sciences sense and to prepare those students to make specific contributions in specific fields of endeavor. This is not an easy task, and it is made more difficult all the time by the insistence of the various professions that the college's curriculum accommodate itself to specific professional imperatives. Add to this insistence the incredible acceleration of technological advances in most professional fields, and the dean of a professional college is faced with a dilemma that not many alumni can easily appreciate. Here the dean must revert to his or her original role, that of educator, and lead the alumni to an understanding of the dual nature of a college education. As we shall see, there are plenty of ways in which the dean can teach the alumni.

Generally, there are far more alumni who act as servants of the university or college than as critics. Most alumni welcome the chance to serve their alma mater, and most of them direct their energies and attention to the specific colleges from which they received their degrees. Some few of them, by virtue of their success in life, serve as inspirational figures to the college or university and come back to give commencement addresses, dedicate buildings (sometimes in their own name), or even come back to join the regular or adjunct faculty. Seldom are their loyalties directed to the institution as a whole, for while they may carry the banner of the institution, wear its colors in their ties, and identify with the general welfare of the institution, they generally make gifts of their wealth and talent to a specific college or academic unit within the institution. These are some of the most important people the deans can cultivate. They are the ones who can fund, help to fund, or find other people and corporations to fund the college's needs, from buildings to professorships to scholarships to equipment and libraries. The dean is always helped in relationships with these individuals by the institution's professional development staff, but usually the dean is the key figure in making the relationship a happy and beneficial one. Sometimes these alumni are controversial; almost always they are strong-willed and even stubborn. The dean has to study them to know their ruling passions, their likes, and their dislikes, and, if at all possible, accommodate to those beliefs. Occasionally it will not be possible to do so without compromising the integrity of the dean or the college or both, but in such rare and difficult circumstances the dean must work closely with the president and the institution's development staff. The needs of the college must be presented to such powerful (and usually wealthy) alumni in a way that the goals of the college become the goals of the alumnus, and thus one flourishes and the other is satisfied. It should be remembered that this task can seldom be accomplished alone; it takes all the talent and skill of the dean, the president, and the development staff.

Alumni, both powerful and not so powerful, can often serve as recruiters. The most obvious area for recruitment activities is the search for good students. Many private institutions have developed highly trained cadres of alumni recruiters who operate in every region of the country to help the institution identify and enroll bright, talented students. But this activity need not be limited to private institutions. Many public universities have developed alumni recruiting activities of their own—activities that are not restricted just to the recruitment of large, swift, and agile young men and women interested in athletic scholarships. Some colleges and universities now have alumni recruiters whose specific task is to identify and enroll National Merit Scholars and other bright and accomplished high school graduates. The dean can help the institution involve alumni in these recruiting efforts, for alumni tend to think first about the colleges from which they received their degrees when they decide what kind of investment of time and energy they will devote to their alma mater. Obviously, the dean is interested in recruiting to his or her college as many bright students as possible, and by encouraging the alumni to help in this activity, two things are accomplished: the college enrolls good students, and alumni who helped bring these students to the college are bound closer to it by learning more about it and investing time and energy in the college through the process.

The dean should also remember that alumni can act as recruiters for the college's faculty and for the institution's administration. Historically, alumni have often been involved in recruiting a president for their institutions, and the older the institution, the more likely it is that alumni will have a major role in this endeavor. Sometimes deans serve on search committees for presidents or provosts or vice presidents, and the better the relationship with the alumni, the greater the influence the dean is likely to have on the selection. If channeled appropriately, this influence cannot help but benefit the dean's college. But these are infrequent events, and the dean is much more likely to have occasion to seek the help of alumni in recruiting faculty members. This is particularly true in professional colleges, such as business, law, and engineering, when an attempt is being made to recruit a highly renowned nonfaculty-type practitioner whose professional contributions make him or her a very desirable addition to the college's faculty. Transitions of this sort—from a professional practice to an academic post—are often difficult for the person to make. There is sometimes need for the help and encouragement of alumni who know and work alongside the person being recruited. Furthermore, a person may be highly successful in a particular profession but be lacking in the temperament necessary for equal success as a faculty member. Sometimes alumni can give excellent advice about that person's temperament and how he or she would function in an academic environment. Thus, the dean has yet another good reason to know as many alumni as possible.

But how can the dean find time to travel through the state, region, or nation to get to know the alumni? There is simply not enough time (or a big enough travel budget) to go out to meet the alumni; they must come to meet the dean. Increasingly, colleges and universities are implementing programs that bring the alumni back to the campus. Colleges within institutions often plan their own special homecoming events in conjunction with the big institutional homecoming event, traditionally scheduled around a football game or some other sports event. Deans should take homecoming seriously and take advantage of the annual institutional celebration to bring as many alumni as possible through the doors of the college. While a football weekend is not an optimum time to get alumni deeply and seriously involved in the life of the college, it is better than nothing. Special college-oriented events should be planned for this time, events designed to please, educate, and, if possible, amaze the alumni. These activities have to be planned in coordination with the major events of homecoming, such as banquets, parades, games, and class reunions, but if the dean takes an active role in helping to plan the major events, he or she can easily plan special, college-related events. At a separate time, a homecoming should be scheduled, if possible, exclusively for alumni of the dean's own college. Again, the major emphasis should be positive, and the accomplishments of the college should be highlighted. But at these special homecomings, sometimes built around the theme of a two- or three-day college course ("Go back to school for a weekend"), a good opportunity is made available to present in detail not only the goals of the college but also its needs and its problems. The alumni should be sent home from one of these events, not discouraged or gloomy, but happy and proud, and if not happy, at least determined to help improve things.

One way to retain the interest and enthusiasm generated during the traditional fall homecoming and/or special, college-related homecomings, is for the dean to invite key alumni to membership on committees that serve the college and its various departments. If the college and its departments do not already have advisory councils (often called visiting committees), the dean should establish them. There should be a collegewide visiting committee and separate departmental visiting committees. At least one alumnus serving on each departmental visiting committee should hold membership on the collegewide committee, and appointed to the collegewide committees should be persons who do not serve or have not served on the departmental committees. Membership on all these committees should be rotating; the period of service should not be brief. A member of a visiting committee ought to serve for at least five years in order to be able to know and understand the unit. In this case, and maybe only in this case, the more committees the better, for this increases the number of advocates that can be recruited for the college, and this expanded membership increases the dean's opportunity to know the largest possible number of alumni.

Now, then, if all these interactions with alumni are energetically and skillfully conducted, if all the complaints are handled properly, if the recruiters are appropriately recruited, if the inspirational figures are guided into productive paths, and if an active core of alumni are put to work to help the college, then the dean can begin to think about soliciting donations—for scholarships, endowed chairs, grants from corporations and foundations, books and equipment, and, yes, even buildings. But, as noted earlier, the solicitation of gifts, or any form of financial support, is a delicate business, and in most cases, help will be needed from the institution's development staff to assure that the benefit from the dean's work will accrue to the dean's college or academic unit. Indeed, in most colleges and universities, no dean is turned loose on the alumni or the general public to solicit gifts from potential donors. The solicitation of funds from the private sector is first and foremost an institutional responsibility, and each dean must fit his or her private giving campaigns into the larger pattern of the institution. If this kind of solicitation is not coordinated and directed by the institution's president, anarchy and failure will be the result. But if the dean's work has been done well, the college and the institution will flourish.

Dealing with Parents

Parents are very important; they produce the college's customers. To be sure, every dean will sooner or later face an irate parent. Just as there is no such thing as the perfect dean, there is no such thing as the perfect college. But for every irate parent there are a thousand happy, or at least satisfied, parents. It is the dean's duty to make certain that this thousand-to-one ratio is maintained during the life of his or her tenure in office. Even at large major universities, parents should not be considered irrelevant irritants that consume the dean's time, time that might be better spent hiring a potential Nobel Prize winner or closing the deal on a million-dollar grant for the chemistry department. Parents are relevant, for if they once turn against the college or university, there will be no need to seek the potential prizewinner or the million-dollar grant. Parents should be taken seriously even before their children enroll in the college or university. Why? Because all the research available on this somewhat esoteric subject indicates that parents are by far the most influential factor in helping the student decide what institution to attend. True, scholarships, institutional prestige, glamorous and successful sports programs, and fraternities and sororities are all factors that help influence the high school graduate to decide where to go to college—but none of these is as important as what the parents think about the institution. Thus, parents can, and do, perhaps unwittingly, become either advocates or adversaries of particular institutions.

What can the dean do about this state of affairs? The easy answer is, not much, so don't worry about it. But this is not true. While the responsibility for promoting a good image of the institution rests largely with the professional staff employed by the central administration and while deans cannot obviously visit the homes of all potential student applicants, they can take some steps to influence some parents. They can help the central administration in its recruiting efforts by writing the best and brightest high school graduates about the advantages of attending the institution. Recent advances in technology, including the laser printer, now make mass mailing look personal, and the dean should take advantage of these innovations and become a recruiter. An occasional speech here and there around the state or region at a service club or a public function is also a way to impress parents and make them think well of the institution.

But more important than promotional material and speeches and letters of exhortation is the reputation of the college and university for how it treats students. There is a large, amazingly effective grapevine out there among the general public that operates to either the advantage or the disadvantage of a college or university concerning how it treats students. Parents of students currently enrolled talk to parents of students yet to be enrolled, and as we all know, bad news travels faster and farther than good news. Thus, the dean's most important work with parents is not done with them at all, but with their children, the students in the college. A great deal about the relationship between deans and students has already been written in chapter 8. Perhaps all that needs to be noted here is that not only must student complaints be taken seriously, but complaints from parents must also be given timely, thoughtful, and, most important of all, accurate responses. Most of these complaints will be without substance or partially, if not wholly, inaccurate. No matter. The complaints have been written with sincerity; parental concern is not a trivial emotion. These complaints cannot be turned over to a secretary to handle; they cannot be filed in a drawer to be answered at a less busy time. They have to be responded to without great delay and without great testiness. To delay is to invite the parent to write to the president, and all that can mean is more work and more explaining than if the complaint has been handled promptly.

Handling complaints promptly and thoughtfully is not, thank goodness, the only way the dean can build a positive image of the college or university in the minds of parents. After all, there are far more happy students than there are sad or frustrated ones. An effort should be made to notify the parents of successful students. While virtually every student is going to tell his or her parents about making the dean's list (usually 3.5 or better) for a particular term, the parents are almost always elated to have that same news confirmed in a congratulatory letter from the dean. A scholarship won, a thesis prize secured, election to a student office—these are all happy occasions not only for the student but for the parents, and usually the parents continue to talk about these triumphs long after the student has forgotten about them. Thus, letters from the dean about these happy events are generally treasured by the parents. Not only should the dean engage in this sort of public relations work, he or she should encourage department chairpersons to help make the parents feel good about the institution. The important thing is that parents must be made to understand that the college or university cares about its students. If an institution has a reputation for caring about its students, its future is golden.

Interacting with the Trustees

After a particularly unsatisfactory conference with the president, the dean may occasionally return to his or her office and muse over the following questions: Who governs the president? Who guards the guardian? The answer, of course, is that the trustees do the governing, and sometimes the decision the dean gets was not really the president's decision, or at least not really the decision the president wanted to make; it was the decision the trustees made. These people who are generally remote from the daily activities of the institution are the policy-makers, and if they do not in actuality make some or all of the institution's policies, they at least ratify and support those that the president has proposed and persuaded them to accept. There are several different terms for the members of this governing body, the two most common of which are *trustees* and *regents*. We will use the term *trustee*, but it is generally interchangeable with the term *regent*. In a perfect world, trustees govern but do not manage. The older the institution, the more apt the trustees are to engage only in governance, but in every institution, young or old, there is always the distinct possibility that one or more trustees will decide to be involved in management decisions. Again, the more trustees there are on the board (some institutions have as many as forty), the less chance there is for them to engage in the practice of managing, but even subsets of large boards have been known to ignore the difference between making policy and implementing it. Seldom, however, does the dean have to worry about whether the institution's trustees are governors or managers; that is a problem that presidents are paid to confront. The important thing for the dean to understand is that everyone has a boss and that the boss of the dean's boss is the board of trustees. The dean who once understands that ineluctable fact of life can also understand why, perhaps only on rare occasions, the president's decision on a particular matter may be absolutely opposite to the president's known philosophy or position on an issue.

As governors, the trustees do more than make or ratify policy; they also act as advocates for the institution and its constituent colleges or divisions. This advocacy usually takes form in fund-raising activities. Indeed, in private universities and colleges the trustees are the institution's chief fund-raisers. They are made trustees because either they can give substantial donations to the institution or they are in positions to influence others to give. In public universities, trustees are seldom expected to engage in fund-raising from the private sector or to give large gifts themselves, although it never hurts a public university or college to have on its board one or more persons of great wealth. Rather, trustees of public universities are chosen to function for their institutions as advocates to the state legislature. Ideally they are expected to defend, nourish, and otherwise protect public universities in the arena of the state legislature. In some states, for some institutions, they are elected by the public on the same partisan basis as other state government elected officials. But most often they are chosen by elected officials, generally the governor of the state. Sometimes they find their way onto boards of trustees because of the political or financial support that they may have given or will in the future give to the elected official who appointed them. In short, trustees are seldom academic people; rarely do they know a great deal about the institutions they are expected to govern, even if they happen to be alumni of that institution. Most trustees of private institutions are alumni and are fiercely loyal to the institutions, although their view of its role and mission may be hopelessly outdated. However, while some trustees of public institutions are often alumni and while their loyalty to that institution may be strong, their loyalties are almost always tempered by political consideration. Some trustees of both private and public boards are there primarily because they are famous; fame is their one and only qualification. And some trustees are put on both private and public boards because of their particular point of view, because of the geographical location of their home and/or business, because of their race or sex or age. In recent years, at some institutions, individuals have been appointed as trustees because they are students. By and large, trustees are successful, energetic, and intelligent people. Sometimes, however, they can be quirky, sometimes capable of highly unpredictable behavior, acting on a dearth of information (they are almost always far too busy to be well informed), yet serving out of a sense of public or private duty.

At most institutions, the most direct way in which trustees affect the dean's life is through the approval of salary structures (this pertains only to private institutions) and the approval of the establishment of academic programs. Only in the smallest of private institutions do the trustees approve salaries by individual line-item action; generally these trustees determine the financial posture of the institution's endowment, together with its projected tuition and incidental revenues, and then they decide what the general salary structures will be for the fiscal year under question. So most deans need not worry about the setting of faculty salaries by trustees; but all deans do need to concern themselves about the fate of their proposed degree programs at the hands of the trustees. And that is why deans must at least occasionally deal with trustees.

A dean's relationship with trustees is a perilous thing. First of all, it is a relationship with the boss of the dean's boss, and thus, except in rare instances, it can never be a very close relationship. Presidents and vice presidents sometimes get very nervous when a dean establishes too close a relationship with one or more trustees. The reason for this nervousness seldom has anything to do with not trusting the dean, but rather a concern for the dean's welfare. Trustees are generally ignorant of academic procedures and value systems. They are often highly impressionable people, quick to judge, and, while not slow to forgive, easily bewildered when they encounter differing opinions and ideas about the institutional policies and procedures. Thus, the dean works in a minefield when interacting with them. A careless dean can vigorously advocate with one or a small group of trustees a position of advantage for his or her college only to find that other trustees cannot, or will not, accept that position. A lone zealous trustee with a particular idée fixe may persuade a dean to a particular point of view about the college or institution as a whole, and then the dean, pumped up by this newly found trustee friend, may find that the reason the trustee is a loner is that none of the rest of the board puts any credence in that trustee's views or judgment. Sometimes the dean may be tempted to cut a deal with one or more trustees, a deal that has no great support in the central administration. The deal may go through or it may not, but what is certain is that the trustees come to campus only six or eight times a year, while the president and the vice president come to work every day. In other words, the potential always exists that the dean, in dealing with the trustees, can get trapped, compromised, and whipsawed. It is best for the dean to keep most trustees at arm's length most of the time. Machia-velli's advice is appropriate here: "Put not your trust in princes."

There are times, however, when the dean must interact with trustees. Trustees generally are the final authority for the ap-proval of any new degree program the institution wishes to establish, and this means that the president and the academic vice president need the dean's help in making the case for whatever new degree program is proposed in the dean's col-lege or division. If the new program is at the baccalaureate level, the dean and the vice president, along with the presi-dent, generally make the proposal first in writing and then orally to the trustees. Usually it is the dean who writes the pro-posal and carries the main force of the argument before the board. If the proposed new degree program is at the graduate level, generally the institution's proposing team is made up of the president, the academic vice president, the graduate dean or vice president for research, and the college dean. But since it almost always is the dean who initiates the original proposal, he or she must be a major participant in the negotiations with the trustees. Thus, the dean must know the trustees, at least those who are responsible for program approval activities, and obviously the better the dean knows them, the easier the job will be in successfully presenting a proposal. This interaction works both ways; the more the trustees know about the col-lege, the more likely they are to be sympathetic to its aspira-tions and plans for developing new programs. The dean there-fore has to involve the trustees in the work of the college and make them aware of its role and mission, its strengths and weaknesses, its needs, and the demands that are made of it from the rest of the university, its major constituents in the professions, and its alumni. Sometimes a trustee is best in-volved by being placed on one of the college's visiting commit-tees; sometimes the best way is to simply recruit the trustee to be an advocate for the college, a fairly easy task if the trustee is an alumnus. But always these interactions should be done with the full knowledge and support of the central administra-tion. The optimum set of circumstances for the dean in these endeavors is to be encouraged, even directed, by the central administration to establish good working relationships with one or more trustees and make them advocates. Then such things as program approvals and fund-raising projects for the college by the trustees become easier and generally pleasant challenges for the dean.

Working with the Legislature

In public universities, the state legislature is yet another layer of bosses beyond the institution's board of trustees. These people are in some ways the most important group of all power figures that the dean may ever have to work with. State legislatures normally provide anywhere from 70 percent to 90 percent of an institution's annual operating budget, depending upon the size and maturity of the state university or college. Large, comprehensive research-oriented universities sometimes derive as much as 30 percent of their annual operating budgets from sources other than state appropriations; smaller universities and colleges without significant research programs must depend almost exclusively on annual state appropriations. The percentage of state contributions to the institution's operating budget also varies in accordance with the institution's endowment and private giving programs, for in recent years many state-supported institutions have developed substantial endowments. Indeed, some state universities make a point of describing themselves as "tax-assisted" rather than "tax-supported" institutions. Nevertheless, all public colleges and universities are heavily dependent upon the annual appropriations from state government. (Some state institutions get a biennial appropriation, but biennial budgeting is largely a fiction because biennial appropriations are made only to be changed annually.) Most state universities are so tightly budgeted that a swing of 3 percent in an annual appropriation can mean the difference between a good and a bad year. No wonder, then, that deans, vice presidents, and presidents pay very close attention to all legislative activities and work very hard to mount successful legislative programs each year.

Not only do state legislatures control at least 70 percent of a public institution's annual budget, but they also pass laws annually that affect the very life of the institution—sometimes, unfortunately, right down to a level of micromanagement that can include teacher-student ratios in certain kinds of freshman and sophomore classes. In addition to setting general salary structures for the faculty and support staff, state legislatures pass laws that establish personnel policies (fringe benefits, job classifications, hiring policies for nonacademic staff, retirement plans, travel and moving expenses, to name a few). State legislatures are generally the final approval authority for the establishment of large programs in universities, such as new law schools, medical schools, and engineering schools. Sometimes, particularly in rapidly developing states, the state legislature usurps the function of the board of trustees and tells the board where a new law school or medical school will be established. (Although the university that is the recipient of a legislatively mandated new school, such as law, medicine, or engineering, will publicly deny having had anything to do with such legislative action, seldom do legislatures decide capriciously and independently that the state needs such new schools located at particular universities; almost always a great deal of political activity on the part of the receiving institution has gone on behind the scenes.) Legislatures also finally will determine whether or not a state may establish a new college or university, will determine its location (always a fascinating study in power politics), and sometimes will even determine the name of the new institution.

What does the dean have to do with all these far-reaching decisions? How does the dean figure in these large and powerful fields of force? The answer is, generally, very little. But it is absolutely necessary that the dean understand clearly how these forces work in order to make the best plans possible in such a volatile environment. A dean in a public university always operates in a state of desperate contingency, and the plans for his or her college are often hostage to such things as the price of a barrel of oil or a change in political party control of the state legislature and/or the governor's office. This is not to say that the dean must run and hide while the gods war with one another; it is not to say that the dean cannot plan rationally for the future of the college. Very few state universities have ever been shut down by a state legislature, and while in recent years in various parts of the country state universities have seen their budgets cut drastically for short periods of time, inevitably the state university as an institution has not only endured but prevailed. (Indeed, it is the private college or university that is most at risk in today's society.) But the more the dean knows about the workings of the state legislature, the better he or she will be able to determine the difference between a teapot tempest and a tornado.

It is important to remember that in most state legislatures only a few of the legislators are seriously interested in the education process itself. The nuts and bolts of personnel policies, program approvals, audit reviews, and the academic successes and failures of colleges and universities either mystify or bore the large majority of legislators. But those who are interested in, and knowledgeable about, the academic process must be carefully cultivated, further educated, and fully heeded. Generally, these are the people who become chairpersons of committees and subcommittees on higher education, and the work of these and appropriation committees usually determines the annual fate of the university and the dean's college or division. Whenever possible, the dean, with the full knowledge and approval of the president, should try to bring these key legislators to the campus to teach them as much as possible about the college, its faculty, and its students. Deans, however, should follow the general rule of staying away from legislative sessions and should strenuously avoid, unless commanded or asked, appearing before subcommittees and committees of the legislature. The games played during legislative sessions are serious and complex; political agendas are almost incomprehensible to the tyro, and the chances for disaster are fairly large when one appears before a subcommittee or committee, unless one is thoroughly coached beforehand.

Although only a few legislators try to understand how a university works, virtually all legislators are deeply interested in funding them. The major task facing each session of the legislature is to fund appropriately all of the state's agencies. In virtually every state, education is one of the two or three major consumers of the tax-levied dollar. Typically, education consumes about 30 percent of the state's annual budget and is thus a very highly visible part of each annual appropriations act. And curiously, or perhaps sadly, education, especially higher education, is the most vulnerable part of a state's budget. Universities and colleges are not highly visible engines of economic development; they appear to produce nothing tangible. They are extremely costly enterprises, and their cost always soars upward. ("Why do they always need more books?") They are populated by people who (in the view of some taxpayers) from time to time cause trouble of a particularly uncomfortable kind in that they are constantly posing moral and ideological dilemmas for legislators and the general public to solve. These academic employees do not, to the lay public, appear to work hard. ("How can a professor work an eight-hour day and yet teach only twelve hours a week?") All these misconceptions come into play when budget-setting time arrives during the session. That is why no dean can treat lightly any request or complaint made by a state legislator. And that is why the central administration and the college deans must work so hard, not just during the legislative session but all year long, to educate legislators.

While it is to the great benefit of the state universities and colleges that there are always in every state legislature at least a small number of legislators who are seriously interested in, and concerned with, the institutions' welfare, sometimes these people can be a mixed blessing. A deeply concerned legislator may also be an activist, reform-minded legislator who wants to help improve the university but only on personal terms. For example, this sort of person may be both an admirer and a critic of the university, admiring its undergraduate programs but critical of "all the resources that are siphoned off the undergraduate program to support research." Thus, unless checked, this legislator may decide to introduce a bill to earmark appropriated funds for undergraduate teaching and constrain the percentage of such funds that can be used to support research activities. It generally takes all the persuasive powers that both the central administration and the dean possess to make the legislator understand that teaching and research cannot be divorced from one another, that each feeds off the other, and that to constrain one is to constrain both. Reform-minded legislators who are supporters of education almost invariably are prone to become involved in micromanagement, and seldom, if ever, do these people know enough to be able to understand the operation of the law of unintended consequences. They simply believe that if something is wrong, a law can be passed to correct it. (This tendency of reformist legislators is not limited, by the way, to those interested in higher education.) This is why presentations to such people must be carefully thought out; this is why deans and others in a university or college need to think twice before presenting reformist legislators with horror stories about the impoverishment of this or that aspect of the institution.

As noted earlier, life is never simple in politics; seldom is anything what it appears to be. Deans should always remember that legislators have their own constraints, and no matter how devoted they may appear to be to the cause of higher education, their first devotion is to the people who elected them, a concept that should not surprise anyone who believes in the theory of democracy. Deans sometimes misunderstand this truism, especially if they are dealing with a legislator who is an alumnus, and most especially if this particular legislator-alumnus represents a district some distance from the district in which the dean's college is located. This legislator may pledge unwavering loyalty to a program that will benefit the dean's college or university, but if that program somehow becomes hostage to another, totally unrelated issue in the legislator's home district, the chances of the university's program becoming reality are slim or none. Furthermore, all states have more than one state-supported institution of higher education. This leads inevitably to political as well as academic rivalries, and quite often it becomes necessary for universities to logroll or trade off in order for each competitor for the state dollar to achieve any measure of success in securing funding. Deans should constantly bear this fact in mind in their interactions with their colleagues in other state-supported institutions in the state. In the political process, the universities and colleges that join together to seek funding from the legislature fare far better than those who engage in give-no-quarter, take-no-prisoners conflicts. While compromise in political competition may mean fewer dollars to each of the competitors, fewer dollars are better than none at all. One particular state university may refuse to compromise and may win one battle during one legislative session, but there is always another session next

year, and most state legislatures have a substantial turnover
every few years. As politicians are fond of saying, "It's a round
world, and what goes around, comes around."

Perhaps the most dangerous game that politicians sometimes play with universities is the let's-use-the-state-univer-
sity-as-a-football-at-election-time gambit. Presidents, vice presidents, and deans, especially deans of professional colleges
that are subject to state licensure laws, should seldom take
sides in elections to the state legislature. Only if the integrity
of the college or university is impugned by electioneering legislators should representatives of the university come out and
fight, and even then, it is wise to leave most of the defense to
the university's board of trustees, for that is one of their main
functions—to protect the institution from irresponsible politicians. But if in the unhappy event that the trustees are unwilling or unable to defend the university during an election campaign, then the spokesperson for the university has to be the
president. Deans, unless they are ready to retire, ought not to
get involved in these parlous events. When politicians attempt
to use universities as issues in their campaigns, they usually
use them in a positive way: "If you elect me, I will make sure
that our state universities will be second to none in this great
nation." Now, that is a battle cry to warm the cockles of every
academic heart, but no one should be fooled by it into actively
joining the campaign against the opponent of the speaker of
those golden words. It is appropriate to encourage those laud-
able sentiments, but foolhardy to believe that they will either
come to pass or that the speaker's opponent is evil. The opponent may have a surer grasp of the potential of the state's general revenue receipts and may also happen to know that, for
instance, unless state taxes are raised by 14 percent, the state's
universities are not likely to achieve sudden eminence. Most
academics tend to overlook the fact that to the general public,
taxes are a graver issue than improving the quality of higher
education. This is the great disadvantage for the dean who
works in a public university; such an institution can never be
sure what next year's appropriation will bring. However, a
dean working in a public university knows that thanks to the
taxpayer, there will always be another appropriation next year.

Deans in some private institutions are not always blessed with such reassurance.

Questions

These questions are designed to help deans review their own ongoing relationships with the various segments of the public.

1. How much of your professional time is spent in dealing with complaints from alumni?

2. Do you have, or are you in the process of developing, an organized group of alumni from among graduates of your programs? How well is the group functioning? Have one or more of your alumni assisted in recruiting students or obtaining financial gifts or grants for the programs?

3. Do many parents make complaints directly to the dean's office? What is the general nature of their most frequent complaints? What percentage of your time is spent in dealing with them? In your experience, have any of the complainers ever converted to being advocates? In what ways have parents directly helped your programs?

4. What direct experiences have you had with members of your board of trustees? Have your interactions with them been at the request of the president or vice president or at the direct request of the board or one of its members? Have you ever requested to appear before the board? Was permission granted or denied? What presentation did you want to make to the board? Have any of your interactions with the board benefited your programs? Which programs were they and how was the interaction initiated? How did it get on the agenda? Did any of your presentations receive neutral or negative responses from the board? What were the circumstances?

5. How closely do you keep track of legislative activity during legislative sessions? How well do you keep updated on new or continuing laws that may affect your institution or programs? Have you ever helped the president or

vice president provide information about your program to one or more legislators individually or in committee? Under what circumstances? Did you ever make a presentation by yourself? Under what circumstances? Do you think the presentation—either yours alone or the one made together with the president or vice president— made a difference?

12

How Am I Doing and Where Do I Go from Here?

This book was written with the central idea of treating in some detail all of the possible challenges and problems that the dean might face during his or her tenure, a task that demanded consideration of all of the various kinds of people with whom the dean might interact in the course of making the college better for its students and faculty. Thus, it has turned out to be a lengthy book, and we are perhaps like the person who, when asked what time it was, responded with a manual on how to build a watch. Deans are not watchmakers, but the time they keep is certainly more than a mere counting of minutes and hours. They have complex jobs and are called upon to solve intricate problems, and the best attribute they can bring to the job is patience. Perhaps, then, they deserve a manual as detailed and lengthy as this one.

But, when all is said and done, and when all of the advice in this book is either heeded or in some cases appropriately ignored, inside the mind of a conscientious dean there will always hover the question "How am I doing?" The answer lies outside this book and in the minds of the dean's constituents, the central administration, the chairpersons, the faculty, the students, the support staff, and all those outside the university or college who in one way or another affect the fortunes of the dean's college or division. It is to these people that the dean must go—not, of course, with the blunt question "How am I doing?" but with a much subtler approach, the main ingredient of which is careful listening. Good listening is the key not only to survival but to success. A dean who cannot listen cannot survive. While this maxim sounds simple, it is not, for there are many different ways to listen—and as many ways to fail to listen.

Sources of Evaluation

The easiest way for the dean to find out if he or she is doing a good job or a poor job is to listen to the academic vice president, president, or whoever conducts annual evaluations. (As noted earlier, any dean who is not evaluated annually by a supervisor should insist upon instituting the practice of annual evaluations.) In most cases, it is the provost or academic vice president who evaluates the dean. A courageous vice president can be extraordinarily helpful, and if the vice president is frank and open, yet generous, the dean can gain solid information concerning his or her job performance. Unfortunately, however, there is not a surplus of academic vice presidents who are frank and open, yet generous. A few, curiously enough, are almost totally nondirective and avoid the imperative voice at all costs. Deans should not even try to make sense out of an evaluation given by a nondirective vice president. But most vice presidents, while not always candid, will attempt to give useful advice and criticism during the course of an evaluation. The advice or criticism may be obliquely presented, but it is there. This is where the dean must become a good listener, listening carefully for the casual observation, the throwaway remark that reveals what the evaluator really thinks about some aspect of the dean's job performance. The vice president might say, "Well, Frank, I see that you missed the last two of the president's retreats. Of course, you've been very busy with that national office you hold in the American Association of Electrical Engineers, or whatever the name of that organization is." A dean who is a poor listener will hear only the phrase "very busy with that national office" and come to the erroneous conclusion that the vice president thinks it great that the dean holds a national office. A good listener will hear the phrases "missed the last two of the president's retreats" and "whatever the name of that organization is" and come to at least two conclusions: (a) it is not a good idea to miss the president's retreats, and (b) the vice president is not overly impressed by the organization in which the dean holds a national office. These conclusions may lead the dean to listen even closer for any hint that the vice president believes that dean to be neglecting college business for off-campus activities. It is possible, of course, to listen too hard, to be too clever at exegesis and thus become at least slightly paranoid. The important thing, however, is to avoid becoming a selective listener; the dean must listen to all of the evaluator's sentence, not just the dependent clause that carries the good news. Sometimes, the vice president may choose not to have an evaluation conference but instead to write an evaluation letter. As noted earlier, the best practice is to do both. Generally, nondirective vice presidents and shy or weak vice presidents write letters instead of holding evaluation conferences. In such cases, the dean must become a good reader instead of a good listener, and usually such an evaluator will offer more clues in a letter than in conversation, which most of the time is clueless.

If deans find it sometimes difficult to get a useful evaluation from their supervisors, it is often even more difficult to get a sense of their job performance from those whom they supervise, the department chairpersons. Just as most deans are reluctant to be totally candid about the job performances of their vice presidents, so the chairpersons are not often willing to be open with their deans. It does little good for the dean to say to the chairperson, "How am I doing?" This almost always results in a clumsy and awkward sequence that leaves both parties wondering about the other's sense of proportion.

But chairpersons provide plenty of clues to the dean who simply stops and thinks about what has gone on in the past year. If a dean has a college or division with ten department chairpersons and one, or possibly two, of them have performed badly during the past year, that bad performance is probably not the fault of the dean, although the dean should never feel absolved from that kind of blame simply on the basis of statistical odds. The poor performance of one out of ten chairpersons may in fact be the dean's fault. If, however, four or five of the ten chairpersons have performed badly during the year, it is time for the dean to do some soul-searching. Has the dean given good directions openly and clearly? Has the dean spent time during the year advising those chairpersons who performed badly? Here it may be useful to review some of the lessons presented in chapter 6. In many cases, a chairperson's poor performance may be due to the unwillingness or inability of the dean to share relevant thoughts and ideas with the chairperson.

A very good source of information about the nature of the dean's job performance is the faculty. They are usually even less willing than department chairpersons to state their criticisms directly to the dean—although some senior faculty, full professors with long service, are afraid of no one and no thing; they are cardinals of the church and listen even to the pope with impatience. If a group of faculty meet with the dean to request that they be appointed as a goals committee or a committee on strategic planning for the college, the dean should immediately recognize that his or her leadership is being questioned. The message here to the dean is that the college is floundering, is rudderless, and the dean has no vision of the future or, worse yet, a vision not only clouded and dim, but wrongheaded. The dean should look back over the year and make a rough estimate of how many faculty have come into the office to give (not *offer*, but *give*) advice about various aspects of the college. Has the dean been inundated with such faculty visits? If so, something is awry, for although no dean is ever safe from the visits of one or two senior professors who believe that part of their job description is to give the dean monthly advice or from the occasional idealistic new assistant professor who comes to tell the dean how well the college was run back when he or she got a Ph.D., wave after wave of faculty giving the dean advice can only mean one thing—the faculty members do not believe the dean knows how to be a dean. In such cases, it may be time for the dean to take the diagnostic test designed for chairpersons (see chapter 6) and apply it personally.

Perhaps the most ambiguous source of information for the dean to use in self-evaluation is the dean's staff of assistant and/or associate deans. Sometimes the advice from these quarters can be excellent; sometimes it is worthless. A very great deal depends upon what kind of people the dean selected to be the assistant and/or associate deans of the college. If the dean appointed genial, competent yes-men or -women, the evaluation they give about the dean's performance is probably going to be worse than useless; it is likely to be misleading. If, however, the dean has appointed strong, independent-minded people as assistant and/or associate deans, the evaluation may turn out to be very useful. No matter how strong and independent-minded these people may be, it must be remembered that they are the dean's closest associates, persons with whom the dean has shared triumphs and failures, and the words they use in their evaluations will be tempered by these associations. In order for this kind of conference to be successful, the dean must take pains to let these colleagues know and believe that their criticism is truly welcome. Here, perhaps more than anywhere else, the dean must listen acutely for the kind of insight that shows how things are going. It is sometimes useful, especially if the relationship between the dean and the assistant or associate dean is close, to make the dean's evaluation of the assistant or associate dean the occasion for the assistant or associate to evaluate the dean. A sharing of insights into each other's job performance may turn out to be a time of truth.

What, then, is the ultimate purpose of the dean's self-evaluation? First, this process helps to avoid surprises. The most devastating kind of surprise is to learn, after believing that one is doing well, that one's job performance is regarded by most of one's colleagues as poor. Yet, no matter how hard the dean works and no matter how scrupulously the dean heeds the advice this book offers, if the dean is not a good listener, he or she can be terribly surprised. But more important than the avoidance of surprise is the necessity for the dean to know how well he or she is doing in order to assure that the college is continuously getting better. If deans are not helping to make their colleges or divisions better, then they must either improve their performance or find something else in life to do.

Planning for the Future

After having spent about six years in the deanship, most incumbents begin to think, particularly at self-evaluation time, about what else life might hold in store for them. Six years of hard work, long hours, and a reasonable amount of success normally make a dean begin to think either about greater challenges or about a return to a quieter life. At this writing, the national average length of time for a dean's tenure is about six years. In that length of time, the dean will have recruited at least 25 percent of the college's faculty; either the college's budget will have been improved or it will be apparent that it will be a long, long time before it will be improved; and the new programs the dean wanted to put into place are indeed in place and functioning or their establishment as viable programs is imminent. In other words, in six years the dean can tell what kind of progress has been made under his or her leadership. If the dean's goals are being realized, he or she can begin not only to enjoy these successes but also to look forward to both more success and a possible change in venue. And if all is not so bright and promising, then the dean will want to look for a change.

Thus, there will arise the question of how long one should stay in the deanship. The answer will, of course, depend upon the circumstances. For some, initial success and the prospects of added success are simple encouragements to stay in the job and continue to work for the improvement of the college. For others in the same or similar circumstances, six successful years in a job means it is time to move on to other jobs. And for those who have not experienced at least minimal success, six years is clearly a time to wheel and confront the future.

There are, of course, internal and external pressures on the dean who has begun to contemplate seriously his or her future. Of more importance are the internal pressures. How does the dean view each morning? Does he or she wish to get to the office ready, perhaps even eager, to deal with the problems that are inevitably brought in with each high tide of the mail delivery? Or does the dean creep like a schoolboy to work, already weary of what he or she knows will be waiting in the in-box? If the dean begins to exhibit any of the following behavior patterns, then the internal pressure is building at a rate such that the dean should ready himself or herself for a graceful departure from the job:

1. *Procrastination:* If the dean puts off decisions, drags them from one quarter or semester into the next, the college is not being well served; not to be fancy about it, but procrastination can often be a reflection of an unconscious desire on the part of the dean to let the next person who becomes dean make the decision.

2. *An overwhelming sense of déjà vu:* All or almost all the problems facing the dean seem to have a certain sameness, a repetitive quality, a quality that makes the dean ask, "Haven't I dealt with this same problem at least five times already?"

3. *A slowly growing suspicion that the dean not only knows all the answers to the questions that are directed to him or her but that the dean knows in advance what the questions will be.*

4. *A growing impatience with the children on the faculty.* As noted earlier, every college has a few—perhaps no more than one or two—people who, although brilliant perhaps in their fields of specialty, are correctly classified as being in a state of arrested emotional development. These are the people any dean sees over and over; these are the people whose major need—"pay attention to me; I am very special"—must be fulfilled at least once a term for as long as they remain on the faculty.

At any rate, these four states of mind, these four attitudes toward work are strong, infallible warnings that the dean should not ignore.

If there are few signs of internal pressure on the dean to begin thinking about changing jobs, there may be external pressures that the dean ought to recognize. If the provost (or academic vice president) tells the dean it is time to leave, then it is time to leave. It might be tempting under certain special conditions for a dean to believe that he or she can prevent the provost or academic vice president from forcing the dean out of office. Very rarely can such battles be won; the circumstances must be such that the provost is so unpopular or so mistrusted that the dean can rally either the president or the faculty or both to defend the dean, and the provost leaves instead of the dean. But this can only happen in a very badly managed college or university, and there are not many such institutions around. If the faculty wants the dean to leave, then it is time to leave. The only way the dean can improve his or her college is to lead the faculty into making improvements, and if the faculty will not follow the dean's leadership, then nothing can be done and it is time to hang it up. It does not matter much if the dean has the support of the provost; while this may be reassuring, it does not constitute an advantage that can be turned into an operational reality that will allow the dean to keep trying to improve the college.

If helping to hire an outstanding faculty for the college, finding ways to increase the college's budget, and putting into place new and exciting programs give the dean a sense of pride (not to mention a quiet sense of euphoria), then he or she is psychologically ready to consider seriously a larger job in academic management. The dean should indicate to the provost and the president his or her belief that a greater challenge will bring an even greater sense of accomplishment and then begin to pass the word quietly on the dean's private network that he or she is ready for a bigger job. Clearly, the dean's president and provost must be the first to know, because they are normally the people in the best position to help. Furthermore, common sense and simple courtesy demand that they be told first. Nothing could be more awkward for the dean than for the president or provost to learn from other sources that the dean is restless and has put his or her biographical resume on the streets. The dean will need good references from the president and the provost, and it is important for the dean to learn very early in the game how good these references are likely to be. Once the dean has made up his or her mind to seek another job, he or she must act fast. In these circumstances, the worst thing to do is nothing, to sit passively waiting for lightning to strike. No matter how discreetly the dean may conduct the search for another job, word will get out. There is no such thing as a closely held confidence in academic life. Once the word is out that ''the dean is looking around,'' his or her effectiveness is generally cut in half, so the break should be made as quickly and as cleanly as possible.

If, however, the signals, internal, external, or both, are bad, then the dean must leave, and the only question remaining is how and when to leave. Once the dean's mind is made up, the sooner he or she can leave, the better. Once the dean has announced that he or she is leaving the job, little can be done to forward the business of the college; everything tends to settle into a holding pattern during the wait for the new leadership to arrive. Therefore, the dean should quickly inform the provost and the department chairmen of his or her decision to leave the job, and the search for a replacement should begin as soon as possible. While it may occur to the dean that the best thing to do is to step aside immediately and persuade the provost to appoint an acting dean, generally this is not a good idea. Unless the dean has lost absolutely all the trust and respect of his or her faculty or of his or her provost, the dean should remain in place until the new dean is appointed. An acting dean, even if very good, seldom has a good chance, as noted earlier, to be appointed as permanent dean. Thus, for example, if the outgoing dean has an excellent associate whom he or she believes would be outstanding in the job, generally the worst thing that could happen to the associate dean would be an appointment as acting dean. No, it is far better for the excellent associate dean to be a legitimate internal candidate for the deanship than to be frustrated by working in the role as acting dean.

The outgoing dean should stay on and expend all of his or her energy in making the transition between outgoing and incoming deans as productive and as useful as possible. In most cases, the outgoing dean has amassed a large store of information and insight about the operation of the college, its strengths and weaknesses, its potential for growth and improvement. This extremely valuable experience is best shared during the transitional period, and the outgoing dean owes it to the college and the university to make that transition a productive period and thus to help the incoming dean as much as possible.

Where does the successful outgoing dean go? How the dean conducted himself or herself during the tenure of the deanship can often tell a great deal about the dean's next step in life. If, despite the advice of the authors, the dean insisted on trying to teach a class or continue to conduct research, and if these activities were not related to public relations concerns but were, rather, what the dean really wanted to do, then the chances are good that the outgoing dean would be very happy to become once again a full-time faculty member. If, on the other hand, the dean forsook all teaching and research activities, started frequenting meetings of national Washington-based associations such as the National Association of State Universities and Land-Grant Colleges (NASULGC), the American Council on Education (ACE), and the American Association of State Colleges and Universities (AASCU), and even started reading books like this one, then the chances are good that the dean is not only not ready to give up academic administration but is ready to become an academic vice president or provost or even a president.

The fact that a deanship can become a routine job after six to ten years does not mean that academic administration itself becomes of necessity routine after ten years (it usually takes at least fifteen years of academic administration at the decanal level and above to absolutely exhaust the last vestiges of patience and goodwill of the incumbent). There are larger and more varied challenges in such jobs as the academic vice presidency and the presidency. For the dean who has done a good job and who has enjoyed his or her experience while doing that job, the chances of continuing in academic administration at a higher level are excellent. In fact, given those conditions, appointment to higher levels is almost inevitable if the dean is in the sciences, humanities, social sciences, or engineering.

Sometimes, though not often, the four decanal afflictions mentioned earlier (procrastination, a sense of déjà vu, a sense of omniscience, and impatience) relate not to the function of the job but to its environment. In other words, it is entirely possible for a dean to become disinterested in his or her incumbent position but to be vitally interested, even charged up, about a deanship in another university. There is nothing wrong with this; moving from a deanship in a small, relatively obscure school to a large, nationally visible school is a normal progression, and many persons in academic life have held deanships at more than one institution. A change of environment can completely rejuvenate an academic administrator, and almost always that change contributes substantially to making the person more productive and more effective in his or her new job. Every once in a very great while a person will leave a decanal position in a small college to become a department chairman at a much larger university. Almost invariably the university that is the recipient of such a move profits enormously because the erstwhile dean brings with him or her a wealth of experience that cannot be replicated by persons who have served only as department chairmen.

If, however, the dean chooses not to continue in academic administration, what options are open to him or her? At least five are readily apparent: a job with one of the many national (or regional subsets of) professional organizations; a job with a local, regional, or national foundation; a job with a government agency; a job in one of the many facets of consulting; or, most obviously and most likely, a return to the faculty in order to teach and conduct research. Each of these options has its own particular advantage, and each is entirely appropriate for the dean to consider.

American higher education is almost overwhelmed by the professional associations that it has spawned. Every discipline in the academic organization of higher education is represented by a professional association; indeed, many disciplines are represented by as many as four such associations. (Think, for example, of the organizations representing the general discipline of psychology.) Alongside this bewildering array of organizations are the associations for administrative activities (for example, the Council of Graduate Schools and the National Association of College and University Business Officers). And astride all these are the large national institutional associations, such as those mentioned above. These organizations are important to the intellectual, political, and financial life of the disciplines and institutions they represent. Most of them do very important work for their constituencies. Most of them need academics who have spent major portions of their lives on campuses to help shape the policies and procedures of those organizations. Too often the staff members of the professional associations lack the experience of having lived and worked on a university or college campus for a significant period of time. Former college deans and former professors can make invaluable contributions to the work of these associations while leading a varied and challenging life.

As numerous as the professional academic associations are, they cannot begin to approach the number of foundations in America that are able to support various activities in higher education. There are all kinds of foundations—in scope, international, national, regional, and local—that are actively involved in making grants of various kinds to institutions of higher education. While not all of them gave to higher education, in 1988 there were 146 foundations that each had assets of over $100 million. Clearly, foundations constitute major targets of opportunity for fund-raising activities conducted by colleges and universities. The more than 25,000 foundations registered in 1988 in the United States gave away a total of $2,216,647,033. This is a lot of money in anyone's league, and universities and colleges were quite active in seeking their share of support from that $2 billion pool.

Almost all foundations that do business with colleges and universities are in the need of knowledgeable, seasoned academic officers who can guide them in making sound decisions about giving away their money. This process is a difficult and challenging one; for example, in 1988 the Ford Foundation received seventeen thousand proposals and approved for funding nineteen hundred, an acceptance rate of 11.1 percent. Foundation work is important, challenging, and requires both great analytical skill and solid knowledge of the academic process and the academic value system. Former deans can bring these attributes to foundation work and thus make significant contributions to the general improvement of higher education in the nation.

A few former deans accept positions in federal or state government agencies, where their executive skills and experience in the leadership of a profession may be important. For example, a former dean of agriculture is sometimes called upon to serve the U.S. Department of Agriculture or a former dean of education may be asked to assume full-time directorship of a specific project in a state department of education. The stature and experience of former deans as academics may be especially valuable to agencies that provide grants and/or contracts to colleges and universities for training and research programs. Agencies such as the U.S. Department of Education, the National Science Foundation, and the National Institutes of Health often employ former university administrators to assist in selecting institutional programs to be funded and to monitor the programs after they have been initiated. Government jobs often are not career commitments but involve a special short-term assignment.

Then there is consulting. For those who like the life of a nomad, consulting can be fulfilling, even occasionally exciting. The former dean who wants to be a consultant has two choices: he or she can sign on with an established consulting firm or can print up some business cards, hang out a shingle, and go into business for himself or herself. The safer of the two options is to become a member of an already established firm that specializes in academic consulting. In this way, the former dean can be guaranteed work, but there are not many such firms in the nation (less than a hundred). And their profit margins, even among the most successful, are not large. Former deans have much to offer such firms, but only rarely does the former dean find a "perfect fit" with the consulting firm who has hired him or her. As a consequence, working for such a firm is just as likely to be dreary as it is to be exciting. If the former dean wants to establish his or her own consulting business, it is well to remember that the success rate for such individual ventures is very low; something like one of every twenty such starts generates enough work and a high enough margin of profit to make the activity worthwhile. The act of consulting, however, is appealing to most faculty and deans, for consulting is a form of teaching. When done right, consulting is teaching at its highest professional level, and its rewards, while not always munificent, are of the same satisfying kind as those experienced in the classroom.

But the best option available to the dean who wants to give up administration is obviously teaching and research. After all, before the dean was a dean, he or she was a faculty member, with, in all likelihood, the rank of professor. It is possible for someone who has been in administration from six to ten years to return to the classroom and to the library or laboratory and flourish. It is not easy to do, but neither is it impossible. Often those in administration who have returned to the faculty have not much difficulty in returning to practicing the art of teaching. True, the returning dean must catch up on the subject matter and find new approaches to old subject matter. He or she usually has a whole new array of instructional technology to master. But teaching is fun; it is hard work, but it is inspiring work. The great difficulty comes, not in reentering the classroom, but in taking up research again in either the library or the laboratory. Writing that first proposal for a new grant or contract is a tremendous challenge to the ex-dean. There is so much to learn and so much to relearn. New ideas that once came quickly (but did not always bear fruit, even if they were exciting) now come more slowly and with greater effort. However, the rewards for success are not only more satisfying but sweeter. To return to the demanding self-discipline of research after years away from it and to experience triumph in that discipline is truly significant. And what could be more natural for the ex-dean than to return to the work that he or she prepared for during all those years in graduate school?

The authors have one final warning and one final note of hope for those deans who are returning to the faculty. The reborn faculty member must get himself or herself ready for no staff, no secretary, no perks (reserved parking place, private bathroom, great seats at cultural and athletic events), and a sharply reduced social life. Perhaps the greatest loss is the secretary, while the greatest gain is fewer ritual appearances and performances. If the outgoing dean has been lucky, the secretary will have become a silent partner who has made a complex life simple. This loss is almost incalculable because suddenly the indicia of the clerical aspects of academic life come swarming in on the reborn faculty member. And parking! A dean does not really need a reserved parking place, because deans generally come to work earlier than their faculties, but ironically, when the dean gives up that perk, the need for a reserved place becomes acute. While most former deans welcome the greatly reduced social life, sometimes their spouses do not: the silence after all the retirement parties and receptions can be deafening. Overriding all these minor inconveniences is the fact that the first day of the newborn faculty member's new status is his or her own personal Independence Day.

However, deans who enjoy academic administration and are good at it generally do not return to the faculty. If they have carefully examined their motivations to move into academic administration, if they have come to know themselves and their own strengths and weaknesses, they do not become disenchanted with administration. On the contrary, many of them not only flourish as deans but move on to bigger jobs in colleges and universities and lead happy and productive (although hectic) lives. It is only with the kind of strong and wise leadership provided by these types of people that colleges and universities, those most fragile and complex of all social organizations in America, will flourish.

Bibliography

ABBOTT, FRANK C., ed. *Faculty-Administration Relationships*. Washington, D.C.: American Council on Education, 1958.

ABRAMSON, LESLIE W., and MOSS, GEORGE W. "Law School Deans: A Self-Portrait." *Journal of Legal Education* 29, no. 1 (1977), 6–30.

ADAMS, BERNARD S. "The Essential Reconciliation—Academic Tradition and Societal Service." *North Central Association Quarterly* 46, no. 4 (Spring 1972), 385–89.

ADAMS, HAZARD. "Chairmanly Politics: Form and Content." *ADE Bulletin* 55 (November 1977), 21–25.

ADAMS, HAZARD. *The Academic Tribes*, 2nd ed. Champaign: University of Illinois Press, 1988. (ERIC Document Reproduction Service No. ED 297 632)

AMERICAN ASSOCIATION OF COLLEGES OF NURSING. *The Dean as Administrator: Roles, Functions and Attributes. A Compilation of Presentations from the Executive Development Series I: "Have You Ever Thought of Being a Dean?" (1980–1981)*, Vol. 1. Washington, D.C.: AACN, 1981. (ERIC Document Reproduction Service No. ED 210 954)

AMERICAN ASSOCIATION OF COLLEGES OF NURSING. *The Dean as Scholar: Clinical Competence, Teaching, Research and Publication. A Compilation of Presentations from the Executive Development Series I: "Have You Ever Thought of Being a Dean?" (1980–1981)*, Vol. 2. Washington, D.C.: AACN, 1981. (ERIC Document Reproduction Service No. ED 210 955)

AMERICAN ASSOCIATION OF COLLEGES OF NURSING. *The Dean as Colleague: Dean, Student, Faculty, Administrative Relationship. A Compilation of Presentations from the Executive Development Series I: "Have*

You Ever Thought of Being a Dean?'' (1980–1981), Vol. 3. Washington, D.C.: AACN, 1981. (ERIC Document Reproduction Service No. ED 210 956)

AMERICAN ASSOCIATION OF COLLEGES OF NURSING. *The Dean as Person: Rights and Responsibilities. A Compilation of Presentations from the Executive Development Series I: "Have You Ever Thought of Being a Dean?'' (1980–1981)*, Vol. 4. Washington, D.C.: AACN, 1981. (ERIC Document Reproduction Service No. ED 210 957)

AMERICAN ASSOCIATION OF COLLEGES OF NURSING. *A Monograph Sequel: Have You Ever Thought of Being a Dean?* Washington, D.C.: AACN, 1983. (ERIC Document Reproduction Service No. ED 228 968)

ANDERSON, G. LESTER. *The Evaluation of Academic Administrators: Principles, Processes, and Outcomes.* University Park: Pennsylvania State University, Center for the Study of Higher Education, 1975. (ERIC Document Reproduction Service No. ED 129 198)

ANDERSON, WILLIAM M. "Characteristics, Preparation, and Attitudes of Selected Public Junior-Community College Deans of Instruction." Ph.D. diss. Southern Illinois University at Carbondale, 1973. (ERIC Document Reproduction Service No. ED 100 421)

ANDES, JOHN, ed. *New Academic Deans.* Proceedings of an Institute for New Appointed Academic Deans, Gainesville, Fla., August 1968. (ERIC Document Reproduction Service No. ED 070 426)

ANELLO, MICHAEL, ET AL. *Goals for a Changing University.* Papers presented at the Conference in Higher Education, The Colonnade, Boston, June 1975. (ERIC Document Reproduction Service No. ED 131 775)

ANNARELLI, JAMES J. *Academic Freedom and Higher Education.* New York: Greenwood Press, 1987.

ANTHONY, JOHN H. "Moving Up the Administrative Ladder." Paper presented at the Conference of the National Council on Community Service and Continuing Education, Toronto, Canada.

ARENDS, RICHARD I., ET AL. "The Educational Dean: An Examination of Behaviors Associated with Special Projects." Paper presented at the Annual Meeting of the American Association of Colleges for Teacher Education, Detroit, February 19, 1981. (ERIC Document Reproduction Service No. ED 199 217)

ARENDS, RICHARD I., ET AL. "The Educational Dean: An Examination of Behaviors Associated with Special Projects." *Journal of Teacher Education* 32, no. 5 (September-October 1981), 14–20.

ARGYRIS, CHRIS, and SCHON, DONALD A. *Theory in Practice: Increasing Professional Effectiveness.* San Francisco: Jossey-Bass, 1974.

ARTER, MARGARET H. "Career Advancement from Institutional Research to Academic Management Utilizing Institutional Research." Paper presented at the 21st Annual Forum of the Association for Institutional Research, Minneapolis, May 17–20, 1981. (ERIC Document Reproduction Service No. ED 205 119)

ASTIN, ALEXANDER W. *Maximizing Leadership Effectiveness: Impact of Administrative Style on Faculty and Students.* San Francisco: Jossey-Bass, 1983.

ASTIN, ALEXANDER W., and SCHERREI, RITA ANNE. *Maximizing Leadership Effectiveness.* San Francisco: Jossey-Bass, 1980.

AUSTIN, ANN E. *The Work Experience of University and College Administrators.* Washington, D.C.: American Association of University Administrators, 1984. (ERIC Document Reproduction Service No. ED 259 690)

AYERS, ARCHIE R., and HOLLIS, ERNEST V. "Differentiating the Function of Administrative Officers in Colleges and Universities." *Higher Education,* 20, no. 4 (1963), 3–6, 19.

BACHMAN, JERALD G. "Faculty Satisfaction and the Dean's Influence: An Organizational Study of Twelve Liberal Arts Colleges." *Journal of Applied Psychology* 52, no. 1 (February 1968), 55–61.

BALDERSTON, F. E. *Managing Today's University.* San Francisco: Jossey-Bass, 1974.

BALDRIDGE, J. VICTOR. *Academic Governance.* Berkeley, Calif.: McCutchan 1971.

BALDRIDGE, J. VICTOR. *Power and Conflict in the University: Research in the Sociology of Complex Organizations.* New York: Wiley, 1971.

BALDRIDGE, J. VICTOR, and DEAL, TERRANCE E. *Managing Change in Educational Organizations.* Berkeley, Calif.: McCutchan 1979.

BALDRIDGE, J. VICTOR, ET AL. *Policy Making and Effective Leadership.* San Francisco: Jossey-Bass, 1978.

BALDWIN, ROGER G., and BLACKBURN, ROBERT T., eds. *College Faculty: Versatile Human Resources in a Period of Restraint.* San Francisco: Jossey-Bass, 1983.

BARKER, SANDRA L. "The Influence of Academic Deans on Colleagues and Superiors." Paper presented at the Conference on Postsecondary Education sponsored by the Association for the Study of Higher Education and the American Educational Research Association Division J, San Francisco, October 28–30, 1984. (ERIC Document Reproduction Service No. ED 251 055)

BARZUN, JACQUES M. "Deans Within Deans." *Atlantic Monthly,* February 1945, 76–81.

BARZUN, JACQUES M. *The American University*. New York: Harper and Row, 1968.

BASIL, DOUGLAS CONSTANTINE. *Women in Management*. New York: Dunellen, 1972.

BAUER, RONALD C. *Cases in College Administration*. New York: Bureau of Publications, Teachers College, Columbia University, 1955.

BAUM, EDWARD. "Evaluating the Evaluation Process for Academic Administrators." *College and University* 58, no. 2 (Winter 1983), 182–93.

BAXTER, JAMES P. "Some Functions of the Academic Dean." *Association of American Colleges Bulletin* 42 (May 1956), 245–53.

BENNIS, WARREN G. "Leadership Theory and Administrative Behavior: The Power of Authority." *Administrative Science Quarterly* 4 (1959), 259–301.

BENNIS, WARREN G. "The University Leader." *Saturday Review*, December 9, 1972, 42–50.

BERRY, MARGARET C., ed. *Women in Higher Education Administration: A Book of Readings*. Washington, D.C.: National Association for Women Deans, Administrators, and Counselors, 1979. (ERIC Document Reproduction Service No. ED 191 342)

BESS, JAMES L. "Faculty Perspectives on Administrator Effectiveness." Parts of this paper were presented at the Annual Meeting of the American Educational Research Association, Montreal, April 11–15, 1983. (ERIC Document Reproduction Service No. ED 232 538)

BLACKWELL, THOMAS EDWARD. *College and University Administration*. New York: Center for Applied Research in Education, 1966.

BLAKE, ROBERT R.; MOUTON, J. S.; and WILLIAMS, M. S. *The Academic Administrator Grid*. San Francisco: Jossey-Bass, 1981.

BLANCHARD, B. EVERARD. *Educational Leadership in Teacher Education*. Illinois, 1979. (ERIC Document Reproduction Service No. ED 185 036)

BLAU, PETER M. *The Organization of Academic Work*. New York: John Wiley, 1973.

BLAU, PETER M., and SCOTT, W. R. *Formal Organizations*. San Francisco: Chandler, 1962.

BLUMBERG, ARTHUR. "Beyond Something Called the Deanship: A Story About a Memorable Academic Leader." *Teachers College Record* (1988), 85–98.

BOGUE, E. GRADY. *The Enemies of Leadership: Lessons for Leaders in Edu-*

cation. Bloomington, Ind.: Phi Delta Kappa Educational Foundation, 1985.

BOGUE, E. GRADY, and SAUNDERS, ROBERT L. *The Educational Manager: Artist and Practitioner*. Worthington, Ohio: Charles A. Jones, 1976.

BOWKER, LEE H. *The Academic Dean*. Washington, D.C.: American Association of University Administrators, 1981. (ERIC Document Reproduction Service No. ED 216 652)

BOWKER, LEE H. "The College Dean: A Case of Misconception about the Importance of Teaching." *Liberal Education* 67, no. 4 (Winter 1981), 319–26.

BOWKER, LEE H. "The Academic Dean: A Descriptive Study." *Teaching Sociology* 9, no. 3 (April 1982), 257–71.

BOWKER, LEE H., and LYNCH, DAVID M. "The Operational Importance of Social Science and Graduate Deans." *Teaching Sociology* 12, no. 1 (October 1984), 47–70.

BOWKER, LEE H., and LYNCH, DAVID M. "Strategies Deans and Vice-Presidents Can Use to Enhance Teaching in Their Institutions." Paper presented at the National Conference of the American Association for Higher Education, Chicago, March 17–20, 1985. (ERIC Document Reproduction Service No. ED 256 224)

BOWKER, LEE H., and LYNCH, DAVID M. "What Every Department Chair Should Know about the Dean: Findings from Four National Surveys." Paper presented at the 69th Annual Meeting of the American Educational Research Association, Chicago March 31–April 4, 1985. (ERIC Document Reproduction Service No. ED 255 113)

BOWKER, LEE H., ET AL. *The Administration of the Liberal Arts in American Colleges and Universities*. Indiana: Indiana University of Pennsylvania Graduate School, 1985. (ERIC Document Reproduction Service No. ED 256 221)

BOYER, RONALD K., and CROCKET, C. "Organizational Development in Higher Education." *Journal of Higher Education* 44 (1973), 339–425.

BOYLAN, HUNTER R. "Approaching Accountability: Some Steps Along the Way." *NASPA Journal* 10, no. 4 (April 1973), 322–27.

BRANN, JAMES, and EMMET, THOMAS A., eds. *The Academic Department or Division Chairman: A Complex Role*. Detroit: Balamp, 1972.

BRAWER, FLORENCE B., and PURDY, LESLIE. "Faculty Evaluation Workshop for Community College Deans of Instruction." Report of a workshop coordinated by the ERIC Clearinghouse for Junior Colleges and held at the University of California, Los Angeles, June

27–28, 1972. (ERIC Document Reproduction Service No. ED 065 119)

BRUBACHER, JOHN S., and WILLIS, RUDY. *Higher Education in Transition*, 3rd ed. New York: Harper and Row, 1976.

BUCHEN, IRVING H. "The Swinging Monk." *Intellect* 102, no. 2358 (Summer 1974), 497–500.

BUCKLEY, WILLIAM F. *God and Man at Yale*. Chicago: Regnery, 1986.

BURNS, GERALD P., ed. *Administrators in Higher Education*. New York: Harper and Row, 1962.

BURNS, JAMES MACGREGOR. *Leadership*. New York: Harper and Row, 1978.

CAMPBELL, ROALD F., and GREGG RUSSELL T., eds. *Administrative Behavior in Education*. New York: Harper and Row, 1957.

CAPEN, SAMUEL P. *The Management of Universities*. Buffalo, N.Y.: Foster and Stewart, 1953.

CARNEGIE COMMISSION ON HIGHER EDUCATION. *Governance of Higher Education: Six Priority Problems*. New York: McGraw-Hill, 1973.

CARSON, JOSEPH O'HARA. "An Analysis of the Leader Behavior of Junior College Deans As Viewed by Student Leaders." (Ph.D. diss., Florida State University, 1962).

CARSON, JOSEPH O'HARA, and SCHULTZ, RAYMOND E. *A Comparative Analysis of the Junior College Dean's Leadership Behavior*, 1964. (ERIC Document Reproduction Service No. ED 012 175)

CARTER, CHARLES M. "Are Small Liberal Arts Colleges Selling Out Their Liberal Arts?" *College and University* 62, no. 1 (1986), 55–65.

CATTELL, J. MCKEEN. *University Control*. New York: Science Press, 1913.

CHICKERING, ARTHUR W. *The Modern American College*. San Francisco: Jossey-Bass, 1981.

CHRONISTER, JAY L. "Implementing Management by Objectives." *Community College Review* 2, no. 1 (Spring 1974), 61–69.

CLARKE, MARIANNE, ET AL. *The Role of Science and Technology in Economic Competitiveness: Final Report*. Washington, D.C.: National Governors' Association Center for Policy Research and Analysis, 1987. (ERIC Document Reproduction Service No. ED 293 696)

CLEMENS, BRYAN T., and AKERS, S. J. "The Dean in Transition: On Making Commitments and Becoming a Facilitator." *NASPA Journal* 10, no. 3 (January 1973), 218–23.

CLEVELAND, HARLAN. "The Dean's Dilemma: Leadership." *Public Administration Review* 20 (1960), 22–27.

CLEVELAND, HARLAN. *The Education of Administrators for Higher Education*. Urbana: University of Illinois, 1977. (ERIC Document Reproduction Service No. ED 163 829)

CLEVER, GEORGE. "The Native American Dean: Two Shirts in Conflict." *NASPA Journal* 21, no. 2 (Fall 1983), 60–63.

COATES, RICHARD H., ET AL. *The College or University Dean*. Waco, Tex.: Baylor University Press, 1955.

COHEN, ARTHUR M., ed. *Toward a Professional Faculty: New Directions for Community Colleges, No. 1*. San Francisco: Jossey-Bass, 1973.

COHEN, MICHAEL D., and MARCH, JAMES G. *Leadership and Ambiguity: The American College President*. New York: McGraw-Hill, 1974.

CONANT, MIRIAM B. "The Academic Dean as a Subversive Bureaucrat." *Educational Record* 48, no. 3 (Summer 1967), 276–84.

CORSON, JOHN J. *Governance of Colleges and Universities*. New York: McGraw-Hill, 1960.

COWAN, GERRI A. *The Relationship Between the Values and Attitudes of Department Heads of Administration and Educational Leadership Toward Selected Educational Innovations in the Southeastern United States*. Alabama, 1984. (ERIC Document Reproduction Service No. ED 249 829)

CRAWFORD, ANNA LEE. "Skills Perceived to Lead to Success in Higher Education Administration." Paper presented at the Annual Meeting of the American Educational Research Association, Montreal, April 11–15, 1983. (ERIC Document Reproduction Service No. ED 232 519)

CYPHERT, FREDERICK R., and ZIMPHER, NANCY LUSK. "The Education Deanship: Who Is the Dean?" Paper presented at the annual conference of the American Educational Research Association, San Francisco, April 19–23, 1976. (ERIC Document Reproduction Service No. ED 126 020)

CYPHERT, FREDERICK R., and ZIMPHER, NANCY LUSK. "Inservice Education Needs of Education Deans." *Viewpoints in Teaching and Learning* 5, no. 4 (October 1978), 90–103.

DEARING, G. BRUCE. "The Relation of the Dean to the Faculty." *Journal of General Education* 15 (October 1963), 191–201.

DEFERRARI, ROY, J., ed. *Functions of the Dean of Studies in Higher Education*. Washington, D.C.: Catholic University of American Press, 1957.

DEJNOZKA, EDWARD L. "The Dean of Education: A Study of Selected Role Norms." *Journal of Teacher Education* 29, no. 5 (September-October 1978), 81–84.

DEMERATH, NICHOLAS J.; STEPHENS, RICHARD W.; and TAYLOR, R. ROBB. *Power, Presidents, and Professors.* New York: Basic Books, 1967.

DENEMARK, GEORGE. "Coping with Declining Resources in Teacher Education: What Deans Can Do." *Journal of Teacher Education* 34, no. 3 (May-June 1983), 36–42.

DIBDEN, ARTHUR J., ed. *The Academic Deanship in American Colleges and Universities.* Carbondale: Southern Illinois University Press, 1968.

The Dimensions of the Dean's Tasks: Proceedings of the Conference for Newly Appointed Junior College Deans (1st Appalachian State College, Boone, North Carolina, August 6–10, 1962). Tallahassee: Florida State University; and Gainesville: University of Florida. (ERIC Document Reproduction Service No. ED 016 463)

DOBBINS, CHARLES G., and STAUFFER, THOMAS M. "Academic Administrators—Born or Made?" *Educational Record* 53 (1972), 293–99.

DOLAN, R. EDMUND, and MITTLER, MARY L. "The Cluster Dean; Innovation in Administration." *New Directions for Community Colleges* 4, no. 1 (Spring 1976), 25–37.

DRESSEL, PAUL L. *Handbook of Academic Evaluation.* San Francisco: Jossey-Bass, 1976.

DRESSEL, PAUL L.; JOHNSON, F. C.; and MARCUS, P. M. *The Confidence Crisis: An Analysis of University Departments.* San Francisco: Jossey-Bass, 1970.

DRUCKER, PETER F. *The Effective Executive.* New York: Harper and Row, 1967.

EBGERT, ROBERT L. "I Wouldn't Have Missed It for Anything." *Journal of Teacher Education* 35, no. 2 (March-April 1984), 43–50.

EBLE, KENNETH E. *The Art of Administration.* San Francisco: Jossey-Bass, 1979.

EDELMAN, M. *The Symbolic Uses of Politics.* Urbana: University of Illinois Press, 1964.

EHRLE, ELWOOD B., and EARLEY, JANE F. "The Effect of Collective Bargaining on Department Chairpersons and Deans." *Educational Record* 57, no. 3 (1977), 149–54.

EHRLE, ELWOOD B., and BENNETT, JOHN B. *Managing the Academic Enterprise: Case Studies for Deans and Provosts.* New York: Macmillan, 1988.

ELIOT, CHARLES WILLIAM. *The University Administrator.* Cambridge, Mass.: Riverside Press, 1908.

EUWEMA, BEN. "The Care and Feeding of Deans." *College and University* 39 (Spring 1964), 257–63.

EWING, DAVID W., ed. *Long-Range Planning for Management.* New York: Harper and Row, 1972.

FAIRBANKS, DOUGLAS C. "Concordance of Expectations Toward the (Humanistic) Leader Role of the Dean of an Emerging School or College of Education: Viewed by Deans and Faculty Members in the State of Michigan" (Ph.D. diss., Michigan State University, 1971; *Dissertation Abstracts International,* 3050-A [1971]).

FARQUHAR, ROBIN H. "Two Years in the Life of a Dean." Paper presented at an Ontario Institute for Studies in Education—University Council for Educational Administration Career Development Seminar, Toronto, November 6, 1978. (ERIC Document Reproduction Service No. ED 203 796)

FELTNER, BILL D., and GOODSELL, DAVID R. "The Academic Dean and Conflict Management." *Journal of Higher Education* 43, no. 9 (December 1972), 692–701.

FENICHEL, ALLAN H. *The American Corporation: Justice, Freedom, and the University.* New York: Black Rose, 1987.

FINNEGAN, DARRELL F. X. *The Function of the American Dean in American Catholic Higher Education.* Washington, D.C.: Catholic University of America, 1951.

FISHER, CHARLES F. *The Use and Effectiveness of the Case-Study Method in the Inservice Training of College and University Administrators.* Washington, D.C.: American Council on Education, 1972. (ERIC Document Reproduction Service No. ED 078 734)

FISHER, JAMES L. *Power of the Presidency.* New York: Macmillan, and American Council on Education, 1984.

FREEMAN, GLORIA E. "A Profile of Top-Level Women Administrators in Higher Education in Washington, D.C." Study conducted as dissertation requirements for Ed.D. degree. (ERIC Document Reproduction Service No. ED 144 472)

GAINES, FRANCIS. *Presidents and Deans: A Changing Academic Scene.* 1987. (ERIC Document Reproduction Service No. ED 285 474)

GANT, J. L. "Effective Schools, Colleges, and Departments of Education: The Dean Is the Key." President's address presented at the Annual Meeting of the American Association of Colleges for Teacher Education, Detroit, February 22–25, 1983. (ERIC Document Reproduction Service No. ED 230 549)

GARIUS, FRITZIE EMMA. "Differential Interest Patterns of a Selected

Group of College and University Administrators." (Ph.D. diss., University of Michigan, 1963).

GARNIER, BERNARD. "Deans in Canadian Universities: A Managerial Perspective." *Canadian Journal of Higher Education* 12, no. 2 (1982), 1–16.

GERRY, FRANK C. "Reflections on Faculty Unionization: Academic Implications." *Liberal Education* 64, no. 2 (May 1978), 171–81.

GIBB, CECIL ASTIN, ed. *Leadership: Selected Readings*. New York: Penguin, 1969.

GIDEONSE, HENDRIK D. "Politics and Personhood and Why Deans Need Strong Constitutions for Both." Paper presented at the Annual Meeting of the American Educational Research Association, San Francisco, April 19–23, 1976. (ERIC Document Reproduction Service No. ED 123 773)

GILOSETH, BRUCE L. "Research and the Busy Dean: Utilizing His Resources." *NASPA Journal* 9, no. 1 (April 1971), 228–32.

GIROUX, YVES M. "Training University Administrators at the Université Laval." *International Journal of Institutional Management in Higher Education* 8, no. 1 (March 1984), 33–39.

GOERSS, KATHERINE VAN WESSEM. *Women Administrators in Education: A Review of Research, 1960–1976*. Washington, D.C.: National Association for Women Deans, Administrators, and Counselors, 1977.

GOLDBERG, ARTHUR. "Reflections of a Two-Year-College Dean." *NASPA Journal* 11, no. 1 (July 1973), 39–42.

GOODNER, J. "A Check List for Top Administrators." *College Management* 9, no. 5 (1974), 24–28.

GOULD, JOHN WESLEY. *The Academic Deanship*. New York: Teachers College Press, 1964.

GRIFFITHS, DANIEL E., and McCARTY, DONALD J., eds. *The Dilemma of the Deanship*. Danville, Ill.: Interstate Printers and Publishers, 1980.

GROSS, EDWARD, and GRAMBSCH PAUL V. *University Goals and Academic Power*. Washington, D.C.: American Council on Education, 1968.

HAAS, LEONARD. "The Academic Dean in American Teachers Colleges." *Educational Administration and Supervisor* 42 (March 1956), 134–40 (from a Ph.D. of the same title, University of Minnesota, 1954).

HAMMONS, JAMES O., ed. *Role of the Academic Dean in Implementing Accountability: Anatomy of a Conference for Deans of Instruction in*

Two-Year Colleges. Durham, N.C.: National Lab. for Higher Education, April 28, 1972. (ERIC Document Reproduction Service No. ED 075 014)

HAMMONS, JAMES O., ed. "Changing Instructional Strategies. New Directions for Community Colleges, Number 17." *New Directions for Community Colleges* 5, no. 1 (Spring 1977) San Francisco: Jossey-Bass.

HANZELI, VICTOR E. "The Educational Leadership of the Academic Dean." *Journal of Higher Education* 37 (November 1966), 421–28.

HARDWICK, CLYDE T., and LANDUYT, BERNARD F. *Administrative Strategy*. New York: Simmons-Boardman, 1961.

HARLAN, CLEVELAND. "The Dean's Dilemma: Leadership of Equals." *Public Administration Review* 20, no. 1 (Winter 1960), 22–27.

HART, SYLVIA E. "The Dean Is Seated at Her Desk." *Nursing Outlook* 25, no. 11 (November 1977), 708–12.

HAWKES, HERBERT E. *Through a Dean's Open Door*. New York: McGraw-Hill, 1945.

HEEREMANN, BARRY, ed. *Changing Managerial Perspectives: New Directions for Community Colleges, No. 13*. San Francisco: Jossey-Bass, 1976.

HENDERSON, ALGO D. "The Dean Is Busy." *North Central Association Quarterly* 32 (October 1957), 179–85.

HENDERSON, ALGO D. "Finding and Training Academic Administrators." *Public Administration Review* 20, no. 1 (Winter 1960), 17–22.

HERSEY, PAUL. *The Situational Leader*. New York: Warner, 1984.

HODGKINSON, HAROLD L. "Adult Development: Implications for Faculty and Administrators." *Educational Record* 55, no. 4 (February 1974), 263–74.

HODGKINSON, HAROLD L., and MEETH, L. RICHARD, eds. *Power and Authority*. San Francisco: Jossey-Bass, 1971.

HOGGES, RALPH. *The Administrator and Politics: Strategies for Success*. Florida, 1979. (ERIC Document Reproduction Service No. ED 178 013)

HORN, FRANCIS H. "The Dean and the President." *Liberal Education* 50 (December 1964), 463–75.

HYNES, WILLIAM J. "Strategies for Faculty Development." *New Directions for Higher Education. No. 47*, 12, no. 3 (September 1984), 31–38.

INGLIS, SIDNEY A. "Profile: Characteristics of Ryan Era, Dean of Education." *California Journal of Teacher Education* 4, no. 3 (October 1977), 106–28.

INGRAHAM, MARK H., and KING, FRANCIS P. *The Mirror of Brass: The Compensation and Working Conditions of College and University Administrators.* Madison: University of Wisconsin Press, 1968.

JOHNSON, BETTY M., and GEORGE, SHIRLEY A. "The Decision-Making Structure and the Dean." *Administrator's Update.* (ERIC Document Reproduction Service No. ED 263 496)

JOUGHIN, LOUIS. "The Faculty and the Dean." *Liberal Education* 49 (December 1963), 502–12.

KALUZYNSKI, THOMAS A. "The Academic Personnel Responsibility— How Much of It Do We Want?" *Journal of the College and University Personnel Association* 34, no. 2 (Summer 1983), 46–50.

KAPEL, DAVID E., and DEJNOZK, EDWARD L. "The Education Deanship: A Further Analysis." *Research in Higher Education* 10, no. 2 (1979), 99–112.

KAPLAN, WILLIAM. *The Law of Higher Education.* San Francisco: Jossey-Bass, 1985.

KAPLOWITZ, RICHARD A. *Selecting Academic Administrators: The Search Committee.* Washington, D.C.: American Council on Education, 1973.

KAUFFMAN, J. E. "The New College President: Expectations and Realities." *Educational Record* 58 (1977), 146–68.

KEANE, G. F. "Strengthening College Administration." *Management Control* 17 (1979), 56–61.

KELLER, GEORGE. *Academic Strategy: The Management Revolution in American Higher Education.* Baltimore, Md.: Johns Hopkins University, 1983.

KELLEY, EDWARD P., and RODRIGUEZ, ROBERT L. "Observations on Collective Bargaining: Implications for Academic Management." *Liberal Education* 43, no. 1 (March 1977), 102–17.

KEMERER, FRANK R. "The Role of Deans, Department Chairs, and Faculty in Enrollment Management." *College Board Review* 134 (Winter 1985), 4–8, 28–29.

KIMMONS, WILLIE JAMES. *Black Administrators in Public Community Colleges: Self-Perceived Role and Status.* New York: Carlton, 1977.

KLINGENSTEIN, KENNETH. "Academic Support Systems: A Networked Approach." *Cause/Effect* 7, no. 5 (September 1984), 14–19.

KNOWLES, ASA S., ed. *Handbook of College and University Administration—Academic.* New York: McGraw-Hill, 1970.

KOCH, HARLAN C. "And So You Are a Dean!" *North Central Association Quarterly* 36 (March 1964), 49–58.

KOFF, ROBERT H. "Dean Power: Or, On Providing Good Reasons Why Someone Should Not Do Something." Paper presented at the American Educational Research Association Meeting, San Francisco, April 1976. (ERIC Document Reproduction Service No. ED 139 802)

KONRAD, ABRAM G. "Deans in Canadian Higher Education." *Canadian Journal of Higher Education* 10, no. 2 (1980), 53–72.

KUNKEL, RICHARD C. "Toward Applied Leadership Development: Gamblings of a Rookie Dean." *Journal of Teacher Education* 31, no. 1 (January–February 1980), 30–34.

LAFFEY, JAMES, ET AL., eds. *Educational Decision Makers in Temporary Systems.* Proceedings of the Educational Decision Makers Conference, Chicago, October 1977, and St. Louis, May 1978. (ERIC Document Reproduction Service No. ED 206 588)

LAHTI, ROBERT E. *Innovative College Management: Implementing Proven Organizational Practice.* San Francisco: Jossey-Bass, 1973.

LARSEN, MAX D., and WADLOW, JOAN K. "Affirmative Action: A Dean's Role." *Journal of Educational Equity and Leadership* 2, no. 4 (Summer 1982), 274–81.

LARSON, JON, ET AL. "Higher Education Planning Perspectives: An Historical Overview, the Administrators' Perspectives, and the View from Two-Year Colleges." *CUPA Journal* 39, no. 2 (1988), 1–14.

LATTA, E. MICHAEL, and HARTUNG, A. BRUCE. "The Junior College Dean: The Man and the Position." *Junior College Journal* 41, no. 1 (August–September 1970), 19–22.

LAWRENCE, JOYCE V., ET AL. *A Study of the Graduate Deanship: Does Gender Make a Difference? Report of the Committee on Women, 1983–84.* Washington, D.C.: Council of Graduate Schools in the U.S., 1984. (ERIC Document Reproduction Service No. ED 253 176)

LAZEROW, HERBERT I., and WINTERS, JOHN M. "In Quest of a Dean." *Journal of Legal Education* 26, no. 1 (1974), 59–86.

LEWIS, DARRELL R., and DAHL, TOR. "Time Management in Higher Education Administration: A Case Study." *Higher Education* 4, no. 1 (February 1976), 49–66.

LINNELL, JOHN. "The Academic Dean As Enabler." *Liberal Education* 60, no. 3 (October 1974), 368–76.

LOHEYDE, KATHERINE JONES. "Faculty Development: What about Administrators?" *Improving College and University Teaching* 30, no. 3 (Summer 1982), 101–4.

LOUIS, KAREN S., ET AL. "University Policies and Ethical Issues in

Graduate Research and Education: Results of a Survey of Graduate School Deans." ASHE 1988 Annual Meeting Paper. (ERIC Document Reproduction Service No. ED 303 100)

LUNSFORD, TERRY F. *The Official Perspective in Academe: University Administrators' Views on Authority*. Berkeley: University of California, Center for Research and Development in Higher Education, 1970. (ERIC Document Reproduction Service No. ED 040 694)

LUTZ, FRANK W. "The Deanship: Search and Screening Process." *Educational Record* 60, no. 3 (Summer 1979), 261–71.

LUTZ, FRANK W. *The Governance Implications of Deanship Selection: And Other Selected Thoughts on the Process*. University Park: Pennsylvania State University, Center for the Study of Higher Education, 1979. (ERIC Document Reproduction Service No. ED 174 135)

LYLE, EDWIN L. "Should the Dean Teach?" *Liberal Education* 49 (October 1963), 379–83.

LYNCH, DAVID M., and BOWKER, LEE H. *Graduate Deans and Graduate Education: A National Study*. Indiana: Indiana University of Pennsylvania, Institute for Advanced Research, 1984. (ERIC Document Reproduction Service No. ED 247 872)

LYNCH, DAVID M., ET AL. "Chief Liberal Arts Academic Officers: The Limits of Power and Authority." *Studies in Higher Education* 12, no. 1 (1987), 39–50.

MCCARTY, DONALD J., and REYES, PEDRO. "Models of Institutional Governance: Academic Deans' Decision-Making Patterns as Evidenced by Chairpersons." Paper presented at the Annual Meeting of the Association for the Study of Higher Education, Chicago, March 15–17, 1985. (ERIC Document Reproduction Service No. ED 259 641)

MCCARTY, DONALD, and REYES, PEDRO. "Organizational Models of Governance: Academic Deans' Decision-Making Styles." *Journal of Teacher Education* 38, no. 5 (1987), 2–8.

MCFERRON, J. RICHARD, ET AL. "Assessing and Supporting Quality in the Liberal Arts: The Role of the Chief Liberal Arts Academic Officer." *Journal of Education Administration* 26, no. 2 (1988), 393–407.

MCGANNON, J. BARRY. *Relationship of the Departmental Chairman to the Academic Dean*. St. Louis: Saint Louis University, 1968. (ERIC Document Reproduction Service No. ED 026 963)

MCGANNON, J. BARRY. "The Academic Dean: Dimension of Leadership." *Liberal Education* 59, no. 3 (October 1973), 277–91.

MCGRATH, EARL J. "The Office of the Academic Dean," in *The Admin-*

istration of Higher Institutions under Changing Conditions, edited by Norman Burns. Chicago: University of Chicago, 1947.

MACHIAVELLI, NICCOLO. *The Prince.* New York: Mentor, 1952.

MCVEY, FRANK L., and HUGHES, RAYMOND M. *Problems of College and University Administration.* Ames: Iowa State College Press, 1952.

MARK, SANDRA FAY. "Leadership in Higher Education: Success Attributions and Self-Perceptions of College Administrators." Paper presented at the Annual Meeting of the Association for the Study of Higher Education, Chicago, March 14–16, 1984. (ERIC Document Reproduction Service No. ED 245 607)

MARSHALL, M. "How to Be a Dean." *American Association of University Professors Bulletin* 42 (December 1956), 636–43.

MARTIN, JOSEF. *To Rise Above Principle: The Memoirs of an Unreconstructed Dean.* Champaign: University of Illinois, 1988. (ERIC Document Reproduction Service No. ED 295 548)

MATTFIELD, JACQUELYN A. "Many Are Called, But Few Are Chosen." Paper presented at the 55th Annual Meeting of the American Council on Education, October 6, 1972. (ERIC Document Reproduction Service No. ED 071 549)

MAYHEW, LEWIS B. "Shared Responsibility of the President and the Dean," *North Central Association Quarterly* 32, no. 2 (October 1957), 186–92.

MILLER, RICHARD I. "The Academic Dean." *Intellect* 102, no. 2354 (January 1974), 231–34.

MILLETT, JOHN DAVID. *Decision Making and Administration in Higher Education.* Kent, Ohio: Kent State University Press, 1968.

MILNER, CLYDE A. *The Dean of the Small College.* Boston: Christopher Publishing House, 1936.

MONAHAN, WILLIAM G. *Status Identities in Academic Education Units: A Q-Factor Analytic Exploration.* West Virginia, 1979. (ERIC Document Reproduction Service No. ED 185 941)

MOOMAW, W. EDMUND. "Participatory Leadership Strategy." *New Directions for Higher Education,* No. 47 12, no. 3 (September 1984), 19–30.

MOORE, KATHRYN M. *The Top-Line: A Report on Presidents' Provosts', and Deans' Careers. Leaders in Transition: A National Study of Higher Education Administrators.* Washington, D.C.: American Council on Education, 1983. (ERIC Document Reproduction Service No. ED 231 301)

MOORE, KATHRYN M. *Women and Minorities. Leaders in Transition: A National Study of Higher Education Administrators.* Washington,

D.C.: American Council on Education, 1984. (ERIC Document Reproduction Service No. ED 225 459)

MOORE, KATHRYN M., ET AL. "The Structure of Presidents' and Deans' Careers." *Journal of Higher Education* 54, no. 5 (September-October 1983), 500–15.

MORRIS, VAN CLEVE. *Deaning: Middle Management in Academe.* Champaign: University of Illinois Press, 1981.

NEUMANN, LILY, and NEUMANN, YORAM. "Faculty Perceptions of Deans' and Department Chairpersons' Management Functions." *Higher Education* 12, no. 2 (April 1983), 205–14.

NICHOLS, R. F. "The Ambiguous Position of the Graduate School Dean." *Journal of Higher Education* 30, no. 3 (March 1959), 123–27.

OLSWANG, STEVEN G., and COHEN, WILLIAM D. "The Identified Need and Means for the Inhouse Training of Higher Education Administrators." Paper presented at the Annual Meeting of the Association for the Study of Higher Education, Washington, D.C., April 1979. (ERIC Document Reproduction Service No. ED 174 178)

OPPELT, JOHN. "Sustaining Faculty Leadership." *New Directions for Higher Education.* No. 47 12, no. 3 (September 1984), 39–42.

Papers on Efficiency in the Management of Higher Education. Berkeley, Calif.: Carnegie Commission on Higher Education, 1972.

PARTRIDGE, PATRICK V. "A Workshop for New Deans of Instruction with Little Background in the Junior College: An Analysis." 1968. (ERIC Document Reproduction Service No. ED 031 218)

PERKINS, JAMES ALFRED. *The University as an Organization.* New York: McGraw-Hill, 1973.

PERLMAN, D. "New Tools and Techniques in a University Administration." *Educational Record* 55 (1974), 34–42.

PETER, LAURENCE J., and HULL, R. *The Peter Principle.* New York: Morrow, 1976.

PHILLIPS, ELLIS LAURIMORE, JR. *A New Approach to Academic Administration.* New York: Teachers College, Columbia University, 1969.

PHILLIPS, ROBERT L. "Selecting the Academic Dean." *Educational Record* 50, no. 1 (Winter 1969), 66–70.

PINE, GERALD. *Deans as Teachers in the Field.* Portsmouth, N.H.: New England Teacher Corps Network, 1980. (ERIC Document Reproduction Service No. ED 186 415)

POLCZYNSKI, JAMES J., and THOMPSON, A. GRAY. "Determinants of Successful Management by Objectives Implementation Efforts Within Higher Education." *International Journal of Institutional Management in Higher Education* 4, no. 3 (November 1980), 255–70.

Policy on the Selection of Administrative Personnel. Redding, Calif.: Shasta College, 1971. (ERIC Document Reproduction Service No. ED 057 777)

PORRECO, ROCCO ERNEST. "The Position of the Graduate Dean in Times of Austerity." Address presented at the 10th Annual Meeting of the Council of Graduate Schools in the United States, Miami Beach, Florida, December 3, 1970. (ERIC Document Reproduction Service No. ED 047 623)

PORTER, JOHN D. "Classroom Utilization: Pacing Departments on a Scheduling Diet." (ERIC Document Reproduction Service No. ED 280 390)

POSKOZIM, PAUL S. "New Administrators—A Statistical Look at Movement Within the Ranks, 1982–1983." *Change* 16, no. 7 (October 1984), 55–59.

POWERS, DAVID R. *Making Participatory Management Work.* San Francisco: Jossey-Bass, 1983.

POWERS, MICHAEL J. "A Management Information System for Academic Administrators." *AEDS Journal* 11, no. 4 (Summer 1978), 97–106.

PRICE, WILLIAM C. "Effective Management in Higher Education." *College and University* 53, no. 1 (February 1977), 33–41.

RADLEY, VIRGINIA L. "The Humanist Dean and Management Systems." *Liberal Education* 60, no. 2 (May 1974), 228–35.

RASMUSSEN, GLEN R. "Evaluating the Academic Dean." *New Directions for Higher Education* 6, no. 2 (1978), 23–40.

REDMAN, GEORGINE M., and ANDREW, LOYD D. "Deans of Nursing: Pathways to the Deanship." Paper presented at the AERA Annual Meeting, New Orleans, 1988. (ERIC Document Reproduction Service No. ED 299 864)

REHNKE, MARY ANN. "Strategies for the Challenge Facing Women in Higher Education Administration." Paper presented at the Annual Meeting of the National Association of Women Deans, Administrators, and Counselors, Cincinnati, April 12, 1980. (ERIC Document Reproduction Service No. ED 184 396)

RICHMAN, BARRY M., and FARMER, RICHARD N. *Leadership, Goals, and Power in Higher Education: A Contingency and Open-Systems Approach to Effective Management.* San Francisco: Jossey-Bass, 1974.

RILEY, GARY LEE. "Patterns of Decision, Control and Evaluation in Academic Organizations" (Ph.D. diss., Stanford University, 1973; *Dissertation Abstracts International,* 148-A [1973]).

ROADEN, ARLISS L. "The College Deanship: A New Middle Manage-

294 BIBLIOGRAPHY

ment in Higher Education." *Theory Into Practice* 9, no. 4 (October 1970), 272–76.

ROBIN, K. V. "Dean of Instruction: A Critical Look." Paper presented at Association of Canadian Community Colleges Conference, November 1974. (ERIC Document Reproduction Service No. ED 099 021)

RODMAN, JOHN A., and DINGERSON, MICHAEL R. "University Hiring Practices for Academic Administrators." *Journal of the College and University Personnel Association* 37, no. 2 (1986), 24–30.

ROSEMAN, GARY HARLAN. "The Role and Background of Graduate Deans in American Colleges and Universities" (Ph.D. diss., University of Mississippi, 1972; *Dissertation Abstracts International,* 3328-A and 3329-A [1973]).

ROUCHE, JOHN E., and BAKER, GEORGE, III. "The Community College President as Transformational Leader: A National Study." *Community, Technical and Junior College Journal* 38, no. 5 (1988), 48–52.

RUSSELL, JOHN H., and AYERS, ARCHIE R. *Case Studies in the Liberal Arts College: Academic Administration.* Washington, D.C.: U.S. Government Printing Office, 1964. (ERIC Document Reproduction Service No. ED 057 718)

RYAN, JOHN W. *Portrait of the Graduate Deanship.* Washington, D.C.: Council of Graduate Schools in the U.S., 1976. (ERIC Document Reproduction Service No. ED 125 487)

SAGARIA, MARY ANN. "Deans' Managerial Skills: What They Need and What They Bring to a Job." *Journal of the College and University Personnel Association* 37, no. 2 (1986), 1–7.

SAGARIA, MARY ANN. "Administrative Mobility and Gender: Patterns and Processes in Higher Education. *Journal of Higher Education* 59, no. 3 (1988), 306–26.

SALMEN, STANLEY. *Duties of Administrators in Higher Education.* New York: Macmillan, 1971.

SANDEEN, ARTHUR. "Research: An Essential for Survival." *NASPA Journal* 9, no. 1 (April 1971), 222–27.

SAVILLE, ANTHONY. *Competencies: Middle Management Roles in Higher Education.* 1975. (ERIC Document Reproduction Service No. ED 126 030)

SAVILLE, ANTHONY. "Interpreting Middle Management Roles in Higher Education." *College Student Journal* 12, no. 4 (Winter 1978), 387–92.

SBARATTA, PHILIP. "Academic Deans: Keeping the Heart Pumping."

Community and Junior College Journal 54, no. 3 (November 1983), 21–22, 27.

SCHNEIDER, ELIZABETH ANNE. "A Study of the Differences in the Expectations and Perceptions of Presidents, Deans, and Department Chairmen of the Functions of the Academic Dean in Private Liberal Arts Colleges in the North Central Association" (Ph.D. diss., Southern Illinois University, 1970; *Dissertation Abstracts International*, 5153-A and 5154-A [1971]).

SCHROEDER, GLENN BURNETT. *Leadership Behavior of Department Chairmen in Selected State Institutions of Higher Education.* Philadelphia: Temple University, 1969. (ERIC Document Reproduction Service No. ED 037 153)

SCHUH, JOHN H. "The Decision-Making Process in the Liberal Arts College of Large Universities." *College and University* 50, no. 2 (Winter 1975), 177–82.

SCOTT, ROBERT A. "Middle-Level Collegiate Administration in a Period of Retrenchment." *College and University* 53, no. 1 (February 1977), 42–56.

SCOTT, ROBERT A. "The Development of Competence: Staff Needs and Training Goals in American Higher Education." Paper presented at the 4th International Conference on Higher Education, University of Lancaster, August 29–September 1978. (ERIC Document Reproduction Service No. ED 157 428)

SCOTT, ROBERT A. *Uncertain Loyalists: A Brief Look at Role Conflicts among Collegiate Middle-Managers.* 1978. (ERIC Document Reproduction Service No. ED 156 105)

SCOTT, ROBERT A. "The 'Amateur Dean' in a Complex University: An Essay on Role Ambiguity." *Liberal Education* 65, no. 4 (Winter 1979), 445–52.

SELDIN, PETER. *Evaluating and Developing Administrative Performance: A Practical Guide for Academic Leaders.* San Francisco: Jossey-Bass, 1988.

SERGIOVANNI, THOMAS J., and CORBALLY, JOHN E. *Leadership and Organizational Culture.* Chicago: University of Illinois, 1988.

SHAWL, WILLIAM F. *The Role of the Academic Dean.* Los Angeles: University of California at Los Angeles, ERIC Clearinghouse for Junior College Information, 1974. (ERIC Document Reproduction Service No. ED 092 210)

SIVAGE, CAROLE R., ET AL. "Operationalizing Advocacy: An Analysis of Dean's Roles as Project Directors of Dean's Grants." Paper presented at the Annual Meeting of the American Educational Research Association, Los Angeles, April 14, 1981. (ERIC Document Reproduction Service No. ED 206 587)

SIVAGE, CAROLE R., ET AL. *Politics, Power, and Personality: The Roles of Deans in Dean's Grant Projects.* Minneapolis: University of Minnesota, National Support Systems Project, 1982.

SKIPPER, CHARLES E. "Four Indicators of Administrative Effectiveness." Paper presented at the Annual Meeting of the American Educational Research Association, New York, March 22, 1982. (ERIC Document Reproduction Service No. ED 216 634)

SKIPPER, CHARLES E., and HOFMANN, RICHARD J. "Indicators of Administrative Effectiveness." Paper presented at the Annual Meeting of the American Educational Research Association, San Francisco, April 1979. (ERIC Document Reproduction Service No. ED 172 638)

SLIMMER, VIRGINIA M. "Advancement Factors of Women in Administration: Patterns and Perspectives." Paper presented at the 68th Annual Meeting of the American Educational Research Association, New Orleans, April 23–27, 1984. (ERIC Document Reproduction Service No. ED 247 836)

SMITH, A. "Staff Development Goals and Practice in U.S. Community Colleges." *Community/Junior College Research Quarterly* 55, no. 3 (April-June 1981), 209–25.

SPITZBERG, IRVING J., JR. *Changing Universities: The Politics of Innovation in a Large Multiuniversity.* Occasional Paper No. 8. Buffalo: State University of New York, Buffalo, Department of Higher Education, 1981. (ERIC Document Reproduction Service No. ED 201 242)

STALCUP, ROBERT J., and WILSON, JERRY L. "Inservice Programs for Administrators: Problems and Prospects." *Catalyst for Change* 11, no. 2 (Spring 1982), 19–22.

STALCUP, ROBERT J., and WILSON, JERRY L. "Preparing College Administrators: Fact and Fancy." Paper presented at the 35th Annual Meeting of the National Conference of Professors of Educational Administration, Seattle, August 16–21, 1981. (ERIC Document Reproduction Service No. ED 210 827)

STAUFFER, THOMAS M. "Selecting Academic Administrators." *Educational Record* 57, no. 3 (1977), 170–75.

STEIN, RONALD H., ET AL. *Professional Ethics in University Administration.* San Francisco, Jossey-Bass, 1981.

STEINER, STUART. "The Dean's Participation: Necessity or Lunacy?" *New Directions for Community Colleges* 3, no. 3 (Autumn 1975), 51–58.

STEINKRAUSS, PHILIP J. *New Dean, Old Problems, and $8,000: A Report on Faculty Development.* Joliet, Ill.: Vice President for Academic Affairs, College of St. Francis, 1978. (ERIC Document Reproduction Service No. ED 158 669)

SUMMER CONFERENCE OF ACADEMIC DEANS. *Yearbooks.* Stillwater: Oklahoma State University, 1941, 1948–57, 1957–63.

THOMAS, ALICE. "The Roles of Assessment in the Private Institutions in Minnesota." (ERIC Document Reproduction Service No. ED 283 459)

THOMPSON, ROBERT PERCY. "A Study of the Characteristics, Role, and Functions of Academic Deans of Two-Year Colleges" (Ph.D. diss. University of Nebraska, 1971; *Dissertation Abstracts International,* 2447-A [1971]).

THORSEN, BYRON WAYNE. "Authority Expectations for the Academic Deanship in Local-Cosmopolitan Colleges: A Q-Analysis" (Ph.D. diss., University of Iowa, 1970; *Dissertation Abstracts International,* 4499-A [1971]).

Today's Academic Leaders: A National Study of Administrators in Community and Junior Colleges. University Park: Pennsylvania State University, Center for the Study of Higher Education. 1984. (ERIC Document Reproduction Service No. ED 258 668)

TODD, CARL ELBERT. "The Perceived Functions of the Junior College Academic Dean in the Improvement of Instruction" (Ph.D. diss., University of Alabama, 1965).

TRIEZENBERG, DONALD. "The Target Ratio Model for Planning and Budgeting. Effective Use of Resources: SCUP 11 in Retrospect." *Planning for Higher Education* 5, no. 6 (December 1976), 1–5.

TROYER, HOWARD. "The Faith of a Dean." *Liberal Education* 50 (March 1964), 49–58.

TUCKER, ALLAN. "Decentralized Graduate Administration with Centralized Accountability." *College and University* (Winter 1965), 132–39.

TUCKER, ALLAN. "Continuing Education and the Battle of the Deans." *NUEA Spectator* 24, no. 2 (1968), 4–6.

TUCKER, ALLAN. "Beginning of the End for Graduate Deans?" *College and University Business* 46, no. 5 (1969), 43–44.

TUCKER, ALLAN. *Chairing the Academic Department: Leadership among Peers,* 2nd ed. New York: Macmillan, 1984.

TUCKER, ALLAN, and MAUTZ, ROBERT B. "Presidential Evaluation: An Academic Circus." *Educational Record* 60, no. 3 (1979), 253–60.

TUCKER, ALLAN, and MAUTZ, ROBERT B. "Belling the Academic Cat." *Educational Record* 61, no. 4 (1980), 38–42.

TUCKER, ALLAN, and MAUTZ, ROBERT B. "Academic Freedom, Tenure, and Incompetence." *Educational Record* 63, no. 2 (1982), 22–25.

TUCKER, ALLAN, and MAUTZ, ROBERT B. "Solving the Teacher Education Problem: A University-Wide Obligation." *Educational Record* 65, no. 2 (1984), 34–37.

Twenty-second Annual Rank-Order Distribution of Administrative Salaries Paid 1988–1989. Fayetteville: Arkansas University, 1988. (ERIC Document Reproduction Service No. ED 305 004)

WALKER, DONALD E. *The Effective Administrator.* San Francisco: Jossey-Bass, 1979.

WARD, MERLE SCOTT. *Philosophies of Administration Current in the Deanship of the Liberal Arts College.* New York: Columbia University, 1934.

WEISENSEE, MARY G. *Factors Perceived to Hinder or Facilitate Long-Range Planning in Professional Education.* Minnesota, 1979. (ERIC Document Reproduction Service No. ED 181 829)

WHITMORE, JON, and TRENT, JUDITH S. "Ideal Interactive Roles of Chairs and Deans." *Association for Communication Administration Bulletin* 52 (April 1985), 29–32.

WILLIAMS, E. K. "A Man for All Seasons," *Liberal Education* 51, no. 3 (October 1965), 396–403.

WILLIAMS, ROBERT L. *The Administration of Academic Affairs in Higher Education.* Ann Arbor: University of Michigan Press, 1965.

WILLIAMS, RONALD A. "A State Perspective: Reconciling Institutional Autonomy and Statewide Planning." Paper presented at the League for Innovation in the Community College Conference, Charlotte, N.C. (ERIC Document Reproduction Service No. ED 298 793)

WINANDY, DONALD H. *The Academic Deanship—An Annotated Bibliography.* (ERIC Document Reproduction Service No. ED 013 657)

WISNIEWSKI, RICHARD. "The Dean of Education and the Looking-Glass Self." Paper presented at the Annual Meeting of the Society of Professors of Education, Chicago, March 1977. (ERIC Document Reproduction Service No. ED 162 443)

WOLVERTON, ROBERT E. "The Chief Academic Officer: Argus on the Campus." *New Directions for Higher Education,* No. 47 12, no. 3 (September 1984), 7–17.

WYGAL, BENJAMIN R., and OWEN, HAROLD JAMES, JR. "Governing a

Multicampus District." *New Directions for Community Colleges* 3, no. 2 (Summer 1975), 27–36.

YOUNG, ROBERT B., and GAMMELL, WILLIAM J. "The Deaning of a President." *Journal of College Student Personnel* 23, no. 5 (September 1982), 429–33.

ZIRKEL, PERRY A. "Faculty Bargaining and Campus Governance: Rhetoric vs. Research." (ERIC Document Reproduction Service No. ED 267 727)

ZOFFER, H. J. "A College Administrator Looks at Collective Bargaining." *Journal of the College and University Personnel Association* 26, no. 3 (July-August 1975), 33–40.

Index